W9-AZM-940

YOU and YOUR CHILD'S PROBLEMS

BY Grace H. Ketterman, M.D.

Teenage Rebellion (with Truman E. Dollar)
How to Teach Your Child About Sex
*The Complete Book of Baby and Child Care for Christian
Parents* (with Herbert L. Ketterman, M.D.)
You and Your Child's Problems

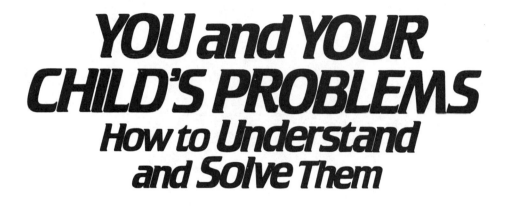

YOU and YOUR CHILD'S PROBLEMS
How to Understand and Solve Them

Grace H. Ketterman M.D.

Fleming H. Revell Company
Old Tappan, New Jersey

Library of Congress Cataloging in Publication Data

Ketterman, Grace H.
  You and your child's problems.

  Includes index.
  1. Child rearing.   2. Parent and child.   3. Child
psychology.   4. Parenting.   I. Title.
HQ769.K43   1983   649'.1   83-3222
ISBN 0-8007-1355-9

TO
my parents,
who loved and
helped me through
my problems of
growing up

Contents

Preface

Recent statistics indicate that one out of 1.8 marriages is ending in divorce. One out of ten girls in their teens will bear a child out of wedlock, and up to 90 percent of high-school young people will be sexually active before they finish school. Some schools estimate that 70 to 80 percent of their students are regularly abusing drugs or alcohol. Child abuse is more extensive and severe than anyone can tabulate because only the most extreme cases are reported. The abuse of parents by their children is increasing and spouse abuse is so frequent that most larger cities have shelters to protect the abused persons. Young people continue to run away from home, and often this is due to sexual or other physical abuse by their parents or stepparents. Runaways support themselves through stealing, prostitution, or other crimes, and few successful attempts have been made to rehabilitate uncounted thousands of them. This formidable list does not include crimes of an even more serious type.

Less than sixty years ago, a great many people died each year of tuberculosis, smallpox, yellow fever, diphtheria, poliomyelitis, whooping cough, and pneumonia. There is now not a single case of smallpox in the entire world, according to public health reports. Yellow fever, diphtheria, and polio are almost nonexistent, and many younger physicians have never seen a case of measles.

The virtual eradication of these dreaded physical diseases, usually fatal, has been due to preventive medicine. The discovery of vaccines and other immunizing agents has stopped the spread and, in a few cases, even the existence of these illnesses. Antibiotics, furthermore, have proved highly curative of many more once fatal diseases.

This book is intended to help caring families find an inoculation that will help prevent the heartache of emotional illnesses in their children. It describes the most common, basic causes of such problems: the need to understand healthy principles of training and discipline; how to live with serious physical and psychological handicaps; how to communicate clearly and lovingly; and how to develop positive attitudes.

Tools for understanding your children are offered. Their basic emotional needs, how they think, the development of their social interactions, and their fundamental spiritual nature are described.

Recognizing the signs and symptoms of serious childhood problems is not an easy task for most parents. Describing common behavioral disorders as well as emotional, physical, psychological, and social problems will help parents define these problems as well as understand them. Best of all, simple, workable steps to alleviate these painful troubles are outlined.

I have provided sources for help that are available in most communities and have offered guidelines for knowing when such help should be used.

Above all else, I have tried to remind parents of the hope that is always present for them. Through understanding comes forgiving. By forgiveness, love and peace are restored, and when love exists, joy and laughter can express the exuberance in life that is emotional health.

Introduction: Preparing to Help Your Child

Whether you are a novice as a parent or a veteran who has already made all the mistakes in the book, plus a few of your very own, what you want the most is to be a good mother or father. And the evidence of that success, obviously, lies in the sort of child you rear. If your child is successful in his or her schoolwork and social life, and if he is emotionally and psychologically balanced, you are likely to pat yourself on the back and feel proud.

On the other hand, if your child is doing far less to achieve success in sports or grades than his potential allows, or if he is moody or depressed, you are likely to believe you are a total failure. You may feel like kicking yourself, giving up, and letting your child become the "bum" you fear he is.

Let me warn you to save both the pats and the kicks. Even the most successful child often has underlying weaknesses, and the most troubled children I have seen have a great many assets to call upon.

To evaluate your child's problems, and find ways to solve them, demands courage and information. Helping a troubled child—and his even more troubled parents—requires preparation.

Here you will find basic information that will help you evaluate your habit patterns as parents. You may use this information to prevent mistakes or to begin the strategies of change

that will correct those errors, and thus begin the healing of the
hurts in your troubled child.

THE INFLUENCE OF YOUR OWN PARENTS

No matter what our age or educational background may be,
all of us bring into our parenting the good habits we learned
from our parents as well as the poor ones. In times of stress,
we intuitively fall into those old, half-forgotten patterns. Depending on what those patterns were, they may or may not
work.

To explain that, let me share an experience from my own life.
My mother was a warm, loving person, but she often disciplined
us with lectures that were highly emotional and ended with my
feeling both guilty and resentful. Because I loved my mother,
and most of all because of the helplessness of childhood, I had
no escape from those painful times. After each such session,
however, I would go to my room and vow that if I ever had children of my own, I would never yell at them.

Years later, with those memories tucked away and almost
forgotten, I did indeed have three lovely children. And true to
my childhood vows, I never yelled at them. (Well, *almost*
never!) But when our oldest child reached early adolescence,
she became a bit rebellious and sometimes rude. One day as we
were walking together, chatting more as friends than as mother
and daughter, she said, "Mother, you know, I think you don't
yell at me enough!"

What great wisdom our children often display, if only we are
listening for it! She was absolutely right! In avoiding my
mother's emotional lectures, I had unknowingly been too quiet,
and my children were missing some of the reprimands they in
fact needed.

To be effective parents, you need to get accurate information
about parenting skills. The way your parents raised you may
have been superb and worked wonderfully for you. If so, glean
from their wisdom and ways all of the best, and apply it. But be
aware of the need to adapt and modify methods enough to fit
your unique child in today's troubled world.

If your parents, like mine, were imperfect, however, avoid my
mistakes. Do not go to the opposite extreme and make another

set of blunders. Sift through their mistakes and find their good intentions. By seeing their loving motivation, you may forgive their poor methods and find a warmer, loving relationship with them. But most importantly, you may find the middle-of-the-road approach that will avoid those troublesome extremes with your children.

TALK IT OVER WITH YOUR SPOUSE

Once each of you parents has sorted through your childhood experiences and found out the helpful and damaging things your parents did, sit down and talk over these discoveries. In each other's memories you will often be able to point out strengths and weaknesses in your own parenting habits. All of us have "blind spots"—things we do, unconscious of why we do them, or even that, in fact, we *are* doing them! Finding these through the eyes of a loved and trusted spouse can help open our eyes to enjoy the good we do or to correct the errors we make. Do be certain, however, that you stay constructive and loving during this process. It's remarkably easy to fall into attacking and defending processes rather than exploring and correcting mistakes or reinforcing positives.

There are many advantages to the sharing of parenting by fathers and mothers. One of the great benefits is that of learning from each other good methods of child rearing. As you talk with each other about your parents and your childhood, you may be surprised how certain approaches of your parents to problems appeal to your spouse. You may well have taken them for granted. Take such ideas, decide together how you can apply them to your children, and help each other test them out and practice them.

THE MEDIA'S CONFUSING APPROACHES

It is confusing to hear and read about the many approaches to child rearing in today's world. Almost every month there are new articles in magazines and on television that disagree emphatically with last month's approach. Parents are often tempted into a complicated game of psychological hopscotch, or they may give up reading and listening, falling despairingly into their old but familiar blunders.

Please avoid both of these mistakes! Read and listen all you wish, but talk over the ideas you pick up. Think about their long- and short-range effects on your child. Discuss your own personalities and see if a particular suggestion really suits you. You will have poor success with a method of training your child that simply goes against your own temperament.

Out of all of your information, as out of all your childhood experiences, the two of you may collect a few gems—insights and ideas that will increase your success and your joy in parenting.

BE WILLING TO COMMUNICATE

I hope you are becoming acutely aware that this business of being good parents demands excellent communication between you! This will be discussed in detail in chapter 2, but you do need to understand now that your information about parenting must include communicating with your children. Had I not been willing to listen to my rather sassy daughter, I would have missed her vital awareness of the need for more strict discipline. And had I not responded with the awareness of why I had been too gentle, it would have been much harder to change.

Remarkably early in their lives children have an amazingly clear and simple wisdom. Listen to them and respond constructively, and you will avoid and correct many mistakes.

AVOID LABELING

In preparing for parenthood, or evaluating and correcting your parenting skills, you need to watch for a few common pitfalls. First, carefully avoid putting one another in a certain "pigeonhole" or labeling each other. Because your husband acts a little like his stern, unemotional father, it need not follow that he is, in fact, the spitting image of him. Your accusations about such a possibility may push him into the very mold you fear. And accusing your wife of being exactly like her domineering, controlling mother may have the identical effect.

Seeing in your children personality traits or physical likenesses of a relative may endear them to you. If, however, those similarities have a painful association with problem relatives, you may unconsciously label your child as being like them—with disastrous results. Children, even more than adults, quickly learn to fit the label describing them, so you may create or exaggerate a problem by your very fears.

I call this process transferring identities, and the answer to it lies in understanding and insight through discussion. Your awareness of such a possibility will enable you to identify this often unconscious process in yourself or in your spouse. Be kind and honest enough to share this priceless insight with your spouse. In discussing the idea, you will be surprised how easy it becomes to discover your child as unique and individual. Even if he or she resembles someone else in certain ways, he is not, in fact, that other person. So let your anxiety be laid to rest. Help your child become that special person he was meant to be!

PARENTING ALONE

Now all of this sharing, discovering, and discussing sounds great—but what about you single parents? There are so many of you heroically struggling alone through the vicissitudes of parenting. Here are some suggestions for you special parents.

First of all, *give yourselves permission to need and ask for help.* It's common, in my experience, for single parents to try extra hard to manage alone, in order to avoid burdening friends or relatives (and sometimes to prove to themselves they can make it alone). Most single parents can, in fact, make it alone, but they wear out in the process, and deprive themselves as well as their children of some very enriching supports.

So think about all of the needs you have and all the caring people you know. You will probably find that for each need, there is a special person who would like to help you. Without overburdening anyone, therefore, you may call on one person to be a sounding board to discuss ideas with you. Another will be glad to advise you on troublesome issues or share his or her own discoveries and answers with you. Another may enjoy giving some time and role modeling to your children.

Next, single parents especially *need to communicate clearly with their children.* Not only will this help you understand that child himself but it may give you remarkable insight about another child as well. Be careful to avoid setting up one child as a parent figure for the others, or even a tattler, but do listen to each of them and observe them at work or play. They will tell you a great deal.

Finally, as a single parent, you will find that *writing down your feelings, concerns, and ideas* will help almost as much as discussing them. Though it is laborious and time-consuming, the very process of writing will clarify the issues. In reading what you have written, you may think of many of your own solutions. Getting your anxieties out of the treadmill of your thoughts and into visible form, makes them less ominous and more possible to resolve.

Whether you are married or single, have a child who seems successful or one who is beset with problems, there are some facts you need to know as parents. In the following chapters, we will look together at the basic causes of trouble in children, and their remedies.

Part I

The Root Causes of Childhood Problems

1
Training and Discipline Problems

AVOID EXTREMES

Each child and the circumstances surrounding him or her requires special handling. Expecting too much or too little, being too strict or too lenient, starting too soon or too late—all create their own sets of problems for child and parents.

Too Strict

Larry's parents were unbending in their strict demands of him. Television did not exist in their home, but every hour of the day was structured with some supervised work or activity. He was allowed very little time to play or to sit and watch the clouds change shape. When the children at school discussed television, he sat by silently, unable to enter into their reflections. When his classmates giggled over funny happenings, he looked on with envy because he rarely experienced free laughter in his serious family. Larry was a social misfit because of his parents' extreme strictness.

These parents wanted Larry to study hard, be successful in school, and be creatively productive. Certainly they loved him and wanted only the best for him. They simply went too far in their demands.

Too Lenient

Susan, on the other hand, was showered with so-called advantages. She had, at the age of nine, her own stereo and television in her room. Her slightest wish was satisfied in her parents' loving desire to make her happy. They failed to realize, however, that material gifts, far from making a child happy, can make her feel guilty. When children are not required to contribute to the family's good, when they have too few responsibilities and too many privileges, and when they are too undisciplined, they feel useless and—nearly always—guilty. It is healthy for children to earn their privileges and most of their material wishes.

In working with many public-school children over a period of five years, I have been impressed with the parallel between home responsibilities and school achievement. In a high percentage of cases, children who had difficulty keeping up their schoolwork and who made poor grades carried almost no responsibilities at home. Their parents expected little of them and tended to do for them grudgingly the jobs they left undone. These parents mistakenly believed that doing nearly everything for their children would make them grateful and they, in turn, would try to please their parents. This is a well-intended but mistaken belief.

THE BEST MOTIVATORS

Children are best motivated by three basic factors:

1. *Respect for the authority and consistency of the parents (and later, teachers).*
2. *Personal pride in their own proven ability to accomplish worthwhile tasks independently.*
3. *Mutual love shared with parents and family, which involves pride and rejoicing in one another's successes, and support and encouragement in failures.*

The Overachievers

On the other end of the spectrum from the low achievers are those who strive too hard for success. In an all-out effort to satisfy their parents' high expectations, these children work beyond their true ability. While overachievers do experience success, they often do so at a tragic cost. I know children who have falsified their grades or who have actually run away to avoid their parents' displeasure over grades that did not measure up. Sooner or later, the overachiever lays upon himself the duty of driving himself to the limit and beyond. This results in a variety of emotional and often physical symptoms of the stress such a driven state involves.

Parents, you need to observe your children carefully for their individual potential in all areas. Check out your impressions from time to time with friends and especially with teachers. Help your children discover and develop their strengths to the maximum but not beyond. Help them overcome or accept their weaknesses. *But above all, cherish them for who they are.* It is out of your love and acceptance—unconditional—that your child will accept himself. This is the cornerstone of self-confidence, and confidence is the strength of your child's true success in life.

IMPORTANCE OF BEING CONSISTENT

In working with troubled children and their families over a period of twenty-five years, I have learned much. One of the most valuable lessons is that of the necessity of being *consistent* in the training of children.

Recently I shared my ideas about consistency with a group of parents, and I must have overemphasized the point. An anxious-looking mother stood up during the discussion time and said, "But Doctor Grace, I've tried so hard, and I just can't be perfect! How can I be consistent?" I've learned that her interpretation is shared by many—that to be consistent means being perfect. That is far from true and I was grateful to give up my own heroic efforts to be perfect.

Being consistent simply means that, in a given set of similar circumstances, you react reasonably the same most of the time. If you scold and punish your child one day when she spills her milk, do so every day—unless you find a better way to deal with spilled milk. You can imagine a child's tension if she finds you scolding one day but patiently and quietly mopping it up the next day. She may, in fact, need to spill milk regularly to test out your reaction.

Needed: Self-Control

Developing the habit of consistency is hard and requires great self-control. I am not a morning person. I can happily work late at night, but I would rather, if the truth were known, not open my eyes until at least midmorning. Our children, however, arrived with the audacity of being hungry and even happy to greet the morning at 6:00 A.M.! Hard as I tried, I could not always summon the willpower to smile at them as I changed diapers and fixed breakfast. Heroically, though, sometimes I was even pleasant. As they grew older, they often went off to school and I to work in a pretty sour mood.

Realizing this grim setting was of my own doing, I knew I was the one who must change. I mustered all of my willpower and set out to be pleasant every morning. I went to each child's bed and woke him or her with a kiss or a tickle. I hinted at a surprise for breakfast, and let them know I loved them—even in the morning. Once they recovered from their shock, they loved the new routine. Breakfast became fun, and we all faced our day with the confidence of consistent love, rather than the gloom of uncertainty. The secret in this example for you parents, by the way, is this: you will feel so great about your better parenting, it will be well worth all of your efforts!

Consistency Between Parents

About the time you conquer your personal inconsistencies, you may discover another hurdle. That is the difference between you as mother and father in your disciplines. Each parent comes from a unique family, different from the other's. From that background each of you brings specific expectations and methods into your parenting.

When one of you is lenient and the other strict, your children will promptly decide which is the easier mark. The natural desire to have their way will cause them to manipulate one of you against the other. Before you know it, they will have you parents arguing over them, and they will be off having a great time.

They will, however, almost certainly feel guilty and even afraid of the rift they have created between you.

The answer to this form of inconsistency is simple to find but hard to apply! Obviously you parents must sit down together and formulate a set of policies that will serve as a guide for your children's responsibilities and privileges. Discuss this thoroughly, reach definite agreement, and write down your final plan. It is best when you can include your children in such a discussion, because their ideas and input will help them to cooperate more willingly. Children of even three or four who talk fairly well can be surprisingly involved in such planning.

NEXT—THE FOLLOW-THROUGH

The hard part of this family agreement is the enforcing of it. Even with the best of intentions, children will resist and test out these rules. So it is inevitably up to you parents to firmly and gently insist on compliance. Be careful to stick together in your feelings and attitudes as well as in your words. Children are extremely sensitive and have an uncanny way of knowing when you are about to give in or are really in disagreement over a particular issue.

It is so much easier to give up the struggle with a peevish, nagging child than to consistently follow through in your training and discipline. But to allow him to break the rules even occasionally will give him a destructive sense of power that will cause serious trouble for both you and him later on. Furthermore, giving in to your child reluctantly, or with anger, puts him in a double bind. He may have his way—at the cost of losing your approval and love. It takes an unusually mature and wise child to choose your approval over his own desires, so he is caught between guilt and disappointment.

Don't Rescue Your Child

One of the common mistakes parents make in the area of consistent discipline is based on a sense of pity for a child. Whether it is one's own severity or that of the spouse, it is tempting to feel that perhaps the child has suffered entirely too much. And when, just at the crucial point of nailing down a much-needed lesson, the parent relents, the impact of an important lesson may be lost.

Let me explain this important point by an example which I have used before. When our son was young, he was a practiced daydreamer. He invented all sorts of devices in those dreams, but forgot about feeding the pets or cleaning up his room. In spite of my firm commitment to avoid yelling at my children, I did scold and lecture this child at times. He was small for his age and being the youngest in his grade as well, he had some tough times in those days.

One evening, I was exceptionally short of patience, and he was even more irresponsible than usual. Not only did I scold and lecture him but I also sent him to his room without dessert. I was really angry with the little fellow. After we both quieted, I began to think about my childhood. How frightened and sad I had felt when my mother scolded me! How little and defenseless my son was! Hadn't I been too harsh with him? Did I indeed expect too much of him? And what if I took away his priceless imagination? I felt more and more sorry for him and increasingly guilt-ridden over my tough discipline.

Unable to stand my own bad feelings any longer, I went to the kitchen, cut a sizable piece of chocolate cake, poured a glass of milk, and took them upstairs where he was lying, remorseful, on his bed. He was far wiser than I, because he said with amazement in his voice, "Mom! You just spoiled the whole thing!" How right he was! There are times, to be sure, when we may be unfair and too angry. Then an apology is in order. But more often than not, you may trust your "tough love" and avoid rescuing your child from the very discipline that may finally get the important point across.

Though I have never played golf, my friends who do play tell me an important rule of that game. It is "Follow through!" When a club hits that golf ball, it is tempting to a novice to stop the swing. But much of the valuable energy it takes to make the ball fly toward its target is lost in that stopping. A much better game, at least on the long shots, will be possible if one swings that club on around in a complete circle.

The same principle applies to baseball. A home run may depend not just on good aim but on the powerful follow-through of the batter's swing as well.

These are clear, visual examples of the follow-through you need in disciplining and training your children. You may be nicely balanced in your expectations and timing; you may be reasonably consistent most of the time in setting limits and promising consequences; but if you fail to actually follow through with those rewards and punishments, you will be allowing a situation to grow that will produce trouble—for you and your child.

IMPORTANCE OF NOT BEING TOO PATIENT!

For several months, I counseled a family of two children, a mother, and father. The children were intelligent and attractive, and the parents were genuinely loving and concerned about some serious school problems these children were both experiencing.

Both parents had been subject to very strict rules when they were children. They remembered harsh punishments and sometimes beatings when they disobeyed even the least bit. They knew more fear and resentment than trust and happiness in their early lives, and naturally they wanted their children to have warmer memories than they had.

When Jill, their third-grade daughter, refused to finish her arithmetic paper, the parents spoke to her about it, and she promised to do it the next day. But the next day, Jill "forgot" about it. Her parents were planning to take the children skating on Friday evening, so they promised Jill she could go skating only if she did her arithmetic assignment. Daily they reminded her, and daily Jill promised but failed to actually complete the task.

Friday came and the mother and father knew they needed to stay with their commitment—no work, no skating. They even went so far as to remind Jill of their earlier threat. Now Jill really loved to skate and she had looked forward all week to that special Friday-night treat. When she heard the possibility that she might not get to go, she wailed and finally threw a tantrum. Both Mother and Dad recalled their own sad times as children, and Jill's anger echoed the rage of their parents. They

simply were not strong enough, and they gave in to Jill's en-
treaties. She went skating, did not need to fulfill her responsibilities, and learned that throwing a fit had great benefits.

Millie was tired of raising children. Her first three had turned
out well—and she was congratulating herself on that success
when the youngest, a girl, hit the "terrible teens." She was
stubborn and often felt lonely after her older brother went off
to college. Shirley isolated herself with her music and dreamed
of the time she, too, would go off to college. Those dreams failed
to finish her geometry, and the music lulled her to sleep rather
than motivating her to study history.

Both Millie and her husband reminded Shirley of her duties.
Occasionally, the mother allowed Shirley's jobs around the
house to go untended, waiting for her to follow through with her
responsibilities, but ultimately, Millie could not tolerate the
messes, and often she would relent and do those tasks herself.

Shirley became more and more depressed. She felt vaguely
guilty for the extra work she dumped on her mother and the
worry she caused her dad by failing in school. She began to give
in to a sense of helplessness and at times she was furious with
the adults who let her get by with such bad habits. When they
did special favors for her to try to bring her out of her moodiness, she could not even express appreciation because she felt
so unworthy.

At long last, the three of them worked out a plan to teach
Shirley how capable she was and how caring the parents were.
They wrote out a weekly routine so no one could forget. Millie
used all of her willpower to avoid rescuing her daughter and
Dad backed her up by refusing any privileges until the duties
were done. In spite of Shirley's anger and pleading, they held
firm. Bit by bit, she began to assume her responsibilities at
home. Her parents quietly thanked her and held firm with their
expectations. As time went by, Shirley realized that peace of
mind and the satisfaction of her achievements were actually
worth the efforts. It was more fun to see a clean room and hear
Dad's pride in her than to lie around listening to albums.

The significant value of following through is the double result
it involves. As Shirley's parents followed through, so did
she. And when she began to follow through, her schoolwork improved, her self-esteem grew, and her family relationships became a joy.

SUMMARY

Being too strict and harsh in parental expectations and punishments will cause either angry rebellion or depression and discouragement. Both involve a serious threat to the value of healthy self-esteem. A child who is willful and energetic is likely to rebel, while a child who is more quiet and compliant will try hard to please but eventually will give up for lack of approval.

The nature and background of the parents will influence their manner of parenting and determine the child's response as well as the development of his personality. The parent who may be too strict can be loving enough to avoid serious harm to the child; but a very angry, basically disapproving parent is quite likely to become estranged from his child, causing discouragement—or fear.

Inconsistency causes confusion in the developing child. It sets the stage for a child's need to misbehave in order to test out the limits and see where they are—or are not. Such a child is likely to become neurotic later on—with the nervous habits this involves. If he is strong willed, he may cover up his tender feelings with layers of indifference or anger. Such a child may develop a disorder of his character and can be so hardened that it becomes extremely difficult, if not impossible, to reach the tender part of him. A child who is the subject of seriously inconsistent parenting will at best have severe problems in developing self-control since he will learn to "parent" himself as his mother and father parented him—inconsistently.

Failure to follow through in training a child is a sure way of allowing him to explore only part of his true potential. His achievements, both in quality and in number, will be proportionate to the parental requirements of responsibility. The clearer parents are about their expectations, and the more regularly they follow up, the more likely it is that the child will find his best and measure up to it.

Above all else, good, successful training and discipline never damage a child's priceless sense of self-worth but enhance it. Damage may be done through anger and disapproval, through neglect or indifference, or through pampering and overprotecting; the end result is still the same—a child who feels, behaves, and achieves far below his best potential because he comes to believe he is less than he actually is.

Each child is born with her or his own maximum capability for living. Your ultimate goal as parents must be to help your children realize that potential. Whether that maximum is smaller or larger is not so important. What does count is your willingness to explore with your individual, unique child what his own best is, develop that, and be proud of it! Self-esteem is first seen and understood through the mirror of parental esteem.

2
Communication Problems

In almost all areas of life, success or failure may be influenced, if not determined, by the quality of the communication that takes place. In no part of life, however, is this more true than in the family. You may know ever so well what you intend to say to your child, but if he fails to understand what you are saying, you may as well forget it. That is not communication. This is my best definition of good communication: *it is the sending out to someone of an idea, feeling, or need in such a way that what the other person understands is reasonably identical to what you intended to say.* It is remarkably difficult to make such an event happen. Let's take a look at some of the interferences to good communication.

BARRIER OF LANGUAGE

Lou Ann was expecting her third child and the oldest, a charming girl of four, had been especially excited about the new baby-to-be. During the course of the pregnancy, it happened that the family traded in their old car for a shiny new one. Despite the excitement of the new car, Susie became quiet and sad. Both parents tried in vain to get her to explain her unusual moodiness. One day, when they had almost given up their efforts, Susie asked softly, "Mommy, do we really have to trade in Kevin when we get our new baby?" Lou Ann's relief made her reassurance most convincing, and she explained that we only "trade in" old cars or equipment, never people! Susie was her happy self again.

Almost all children under the age of eight (or even ten), think

31

in such concrete, realistic terms. Their lives reflect simple directness, and they lack the ability to translate exact words into symbolic meanings. If a child like Susie had a doll whose arm was broken, she would see all broken arms as being severed from the body. Therefore, a report of a friend's broken arm might frighten her severely; or if she saw that friend's arm still attached, even though encased in a cast, she might not believe that arm had been broken.

Even among older children or adults, the same word may have very different meanings. In fact, the dictionary is full of words that actually have very opposite definitions. The word *critical* is a fine example. As a child I understood that word with dread, because my mother would examine my job of dusting the chairs with a *critical* eye. All too often, I had to do them over! As an adult, however, I hold that word in high esteem, because it now means that my own *critical* eye (or another's) can correct mistakes and avoid offending or hurting people.

It is extremely important, therefore, that you learn to check out what your child (or anyone with whom you communicate) actually heard you say. And that is as simple as asking, "Sally, what did you hear me say?" Or simply, "Please repeat what I have just said!" Not only does this verify that she heard you accurately but also that she heard you at all. And that is important, because what you say to your child should be important—because you love her.

BARRIER OF INSENSITIVITY

More often than not, in families, it is more than words and ideas that are transmitted in communication. It is also feelings and needs.

When our children were young, I learned to explain to them my state of mind and body at the end of a long, trying day. I would say to them something like this: "Children, I want you to know that I've worked very hard today, helping people who have big problems. I'm tired and may be impatient and grouchy if you fuss at me or each other. So I want you to be kind and helpful, and we'll all have a happier evening."

I was trying to give them clear information that related to my needs and feelings, as well as something they could do to help me—and themselves. After her first full day in the first grade, my youngest daughter leaned her tired head in one little hand at dinner and said, "Mommy, please be nice to me—I've had a hard day!" What a gift that was! She had learned how to express her needs and feelings in a way even a busy mother could not miss!

There are many times, however, when such understanding and caring are missing. Often I have sat with families who were aching for love and understanding, but they did not know how to ask, and acted out those needs in disguised ways. Mary had an intense desire to be a good mother, but to her that meant everything had to be done exactly her way. Her rigid inflexibility frustrated her son and thwarted the development of his own initiative.

One day Steve, the son, was talking with her in my office. He was earnestly explaining what he would like to do to change their unhappy life-style. As I looked at her, I realized that Mary had not heard Steve's words and had missed the earnestness of his feelings. She was intent, instead, on her next statement about why he should do things her way.

Good communication demands that we be sufficiently in control of our own feelings so that we can truly *listen* to the other person.

Insensitivity to another's feelings can block the most important levels of communication. Working in an institution serving severely troubled young people has taught me a great deal. One teenage girl would come to my office daily with loud complaints about the food, school, the staff, and life in general. It seemed that none of my answers or corrective measures helped. One day I asked, "Diane, is it really the food that bothers you? I think something else is troubling you!" Out came her tears along with a long, sad story of the neglect and abuse of her past. Learning to listen with my heart and not just my ears was an invaluable lesson.

Trying to help a child by belittling his problems is another common mistake of adults. Janie came home from school one day, sobbing. Her best friend had refused to talk to her and had deliberately chosen to play with another girl who did not like Janie. Her mother had lived through enough similar experiences to know they were usually temporary. By next week, Janie's friend would weary of the other child and return to her long friendship. Being of a rather impatient nature, however, her mother said, "Janie, you're just making a mountain out of a molehill. Now dry those tears and help me fix dinner."

Janie dried her tears, but she began to learn to keep her troubles to herself. Her sadness was increasingly covered over with anger at Mother's seeming lack of understanding. Her mother even had the information that could have helped her teach Janie a basic positive bit of wisdom. Had Mother gently taken Janie in her arms, dried her tears, and *listened*—what a different result there may have been!

Certainly, a crying child must not be pampered and the crying thereby encouraged! But Mother could have said, after comforting Janie briefly, "Janie, when I was a little girl, a friend snubbed me once, and I have never forgotten that. But do you know what happened? In just a few days, she found out her new friend gossiped about her and she came back to being friends with me again. Now what do you think you can do to win back your friend?" In these few words Janie could find understanding, hope, and guidance in taking action to correct the problem.

Perhaps you are a parent who grew up without such comfort from your own family. You will find it difficult to know how to react to the troubles of your child in a compassionate manner. We do tend to pattern after our own parents' methods, and when they did not satisfy your needs, you will find it hard to do any better.

Reacting With Compassion

Here are some suggestions for you, if this is your situation:

1. *Use your imagination.* Put yourself in the place of your child and think about what you would need or want if you felt troubled as he or she does. Try out ideas that come to you.

2. *Remember!* Situations that cause troubles are unique to each child, but they are also remarkably similar. The chances are that you went through experiences quite similar in principle to your child's. What did you need at those times? As you recall this, even though you may feel awkward at first, offer it to your child.

3. *Go to playgrounds or parks and observe other families.* You will see at least a few other parents responding posi-

tively to the troubles of their children. Learn from them and adapt their ways to your own personality and situation.

UNDERSTAND YOURSELF

Not only is communication impaired through being insensitive to another's tender feelings but also from failing to get in touch with your own. You may have had parents like Janie's, who taught you too quickly to dry your tears and hide your emotions, rather than solving the problems underneath them. To communicate well, you need to back up and rework that unconscious belief and change that habit.

As I was beginning that very process, I was leading a group-therapy session one day. One of the members was weeping about a frustrating event in her life. She often wept in the group and found people who were willing to comfort her. I had observed how charmingly she received the comfort, but she was not really growing or mastering the art of problem solving for herself.

On this special day, therefore, I became aware of feeling like Jill's mother. I wanted to go to her, dry her tears, and comfort her in her grief. Instead of doing so, I quietly described how I felt and asked her if she needed to stay a little girl in order to be "mothered" or if she was ready to work out some of her own solutions. She was startled and frankly admitted that she loved the babying but really wanted to grow. And she did.

PUT FEELINGS INTO WORDS

Such an idea will work even more effectively in your own family. You know each one and his special habits of weakness as well as potential strength. Your own feelings will often be an accurate clue that will guide you in helping your child. Your feelings may be worry, anger, sadness, or joy, depending on the situation. Just practice recognizing and putting them into words.

There is, by the way, another benefit to this habit. Putting any feeling into accurately descriptive words demands exercising your mind. And the more your mind takes charge of your feelings in a healthy, expressive way, the more effective a person you will be. Your mind needs to control your emotions rather than allowing feelings to dominate your life.

Failure to recognize one's deeper feelings and their ever-accompanying needs can result in disaster! Jim was getting into serious difficulty in his social life and his studies. His father was gone much of the time, leaving his wife lonely and his young son with the too-adult job of comforting and helping her. Jim desperately needed firm limits to be established and consistently enforced. When he did not find these boundaries, he wildly attempted increasingly mischievous and even wrong behaviors in his need to get someone to set them.

Jim's mother told him repeatedly to do his schoolwork, feed his dog, and help her care for the yard. When he didn't want to, however, she simply could not bring herself to follow through. To discipline Jim in any way would have prompted some anger from him. Mother needed Jim's constant love so much that she unconsciously refused to risk that loss, even for a short time, by properly punishing him. When she finally recognized that her loneliness was really for her husband, she was set free to be Jim's parent instead of making him a substitute spouse.

LEAVE YOUR PAST BEHIND

Finally, to communicate honestly and openly, you need to be free from your past. Much more than we realize, in fact without knowing it at all, we take into our own selves the conflicts and misunderstandings we once had with our own parents—and we live these out with our children, as I did by refusing to reprimand my daughter to avoid the extreme scoldings of my mother.

One day I realized that I needed to make peace with my mother, even though she had died many years before. All alone, and very quietly, one day I sat down with my memories and feelings. I imagined Mother sitting in her old rocking chair and told her all the sad, frightened, frustrated feelings I had known with her during my childhood. I explained how I yearned for her understanding and confidence in me, and how I resented her unbending rigidity. Privately, I wept, I raged, and I explained.

Then I moved to the chair where I had placed her in my imagination. I tried to feel as Mother felt and think as she did. Thanks to our struggles, I found that surprisingly possible. And I answered all the words and feelings I had just expressed as I felt sure she would have done, had we ever had such a real conversation. To my amazement, I discovered a brand-new realization that my mother loved me very much. The methods she sometimes used were not so good, but the motives that prompted them were flawless. As I recalled the losses and griefs of her own childhood, I finally understood the woman my mother was. By understanding her love, I could easily forgive her mistakes. Remarkably, I was free of the sadness over our life struggles and her death. I am now free to profit from her good traits and to avoid those errors.

You may not feel comfortable with such an imaginary scene! Then try writing out a dialogue or some letters. Perhaps your parents are alive and could actually talk with you about those painful events and feelings. I have known several adult friends to do this with their elderly parents with amazingly loving results. You are unique and must find your own way, but do finish the old, uncompleted business with your parents if you want to be truly free to be good parents yourselves.

READ BODY LANGUAGE

Second only to the awareness and use of my own emotions in communicating has been my schooling in body language. By now it has become second nature to me, and I do it intuitively. But in the beginning, as in all new learning, it was laborious.

More often than not, people feel one way, but they try to talk another, and their gestures, tone of voice, posture, and facial expression say yet another thing. In my experience, it is these latter signs that point to the most reliable levels in communication. To confuse matters further, the body's signs may be mixed, just as the person's feelings are often confused. But this, too, can help you to clarify just what is being said.

In counseling a father, I frequently saw him with one hand outstretched as if appealing for help. The other hand, however, was so tightly clenched into a fist that the knuckles were white. When I asked him to look at his own hands, his face broke into a smile of awareness. He was feeling helpless and needy on one hand, but on the other, he was furious at the predicament he and his family were in. Seeing this so clearly helped us to make some decisions and plans that set them free.

Feeling helpless is common, and almost universally people find this intolerable. The helplessness may be denied by words and thoughts, but it is easily seen in tears, a droopy mouth, or sagging shoulders. The eyes are, in my experience, the most reliable sign of inner feelings. William Blake, the poet who described the eyes as "the window of the soul," was quite right. Careful self-training can help people control the lines of the face, the posture, and the gestures of their hands. But only the most practiced people can hide the expression of their eyes.

Practice reading and checking out body language with your children. It will help you and them to explore the total scope of understanding and loving communication. Do your child's eyes look frightened? Ask him what he fears. Be prepared, though, for his denial. He may be so busy trying to be brave that he will not even admit the fear.

Dangers of Knowing Body Language

Once you get really adept at this new skill, you need to be aware of certain dangers. First, you may get caught in an argument about your observations and the other person's admitted feelings. Such an argument can only be a lost cause. By their very nature, unconscious feelings can't be recognized by their owner, even though you, the observer, may be exactly right. In that event, your best tactic will be, "David, you are a brave boy, but your eyes do look scared when you talk about Jim's trying to pick a fight. I want you to know it's a healthy fear you may feel. We'll ask Daddy to teach you how to defend yourself if you ever have to." This reflects courage in the face of danger, honesty regarding the fear, and your permission to feel that without losing respect. You have also helped turn the boy's thoughts toward some solutions.

The other danger is this: it is quite tempting to turn your skill into an unfair advantage. To know something about another person that he does not know himself can give you power over him. You must choose. Will you use this lovingly, constructively, to help him? Or will you use it to gain power over him and manipulate him? Remember, in choosing, that what you practice with your children is the very technique they will learn to use with you!

Above all, then, be in harmony with yourself. Be so attuned to your feelings, so honest about them, and so wise in their expression, that you set the best of all examples—a mature person who is so honest he can be trusted, so constructive he can be loved, and so human he can be patterned after!

INFLUENCE OF ATTITUDES

A Positive Influence

My grandmother was a quietly powerful influence in my life. She lived with us until she died (much as she seemed to have lived—quietly, peacefully, in her sleep). Life had not been easy for her. Against the advice of her family and friends, she left a comfortable home and secure life-style in Pennsylvania. In the mid-1890s, train travel was far from comfortable, but she packed all of her belongings in a trunk and valise and traveled to Kansas alone. Concerned family members had warned her that only prairie grass and wild Indians awaited her.

But Hannah knew better. She knew Jacob awaited her and that love, adventure, and the call of God's exciting plan would be there for her. And so they were. She and Jacob were married, settled into a small farm home and, between planting and harvesting, he traveled as a pioneer evangelist, sharing the joy he knew as God's man.

After the birth of four children and the death of one, Jacob died of meningitis. Hannah had totally lost her hearing, but she never gave up. Her sons and daughter heroically took over the farming, and they all survived.

When the youngest son married, Hannah came to live with my mother and father and helped with the care and raising of seven more children. Though I knew she was sometimes hurt by the unkindness of people, I never recall her blaming or retaliating. Rarely, I would see tears trickle down her lined face and watch her retire to her room where, in her worn Bible, she evidently found the peace that was endlessly restored to her faded blue eyes.

Her favorite comment about her deafness revealed gratitude that she need not hear the anger or the smutty stories that others must endure.

Stories of her childhood were an enduring source of enchantment, as she brought to life another era of time known only in the dullness of history books to my underprivileged friends.

The warp and woof of the tapestry of Grandma's life were her optimism, her patient acceptance of events beyond her power, and her boundless courage. Her creativity inspires me still. Some years ago, I faced the possibility of the deafness Grandma lived with for some thirty years. Even before I learned it could be cured by modern medical science, I knew I could live with the loss of that priceless gift of hearing, because I had seen Hannah overcome that very loss with joy!

A Negative Influence

By way of contrast, here is the story of another attitude and what it did to a family. Henry grew up an abused child, rarely experiencing gentleness or pleasure. To avoid the terror of punishment, he tried heroically to please his austere father and mother. By such extreme efforts, he did survive and grew to marry a warmly loving, laughing young woman. At first he experienced a happiness he had never known, but then came three children. They robbed him of the time and energy of his young wife. They made demands on him and did not always try to please him.

Unconsciously, Henry reverted to the austere attitudes and abusive ways of his parents. One by one the children lost their bouncy ways and bubbling joy in life, as Henry denounced them and then banished them alone to their rooms. When the troubled, confused children began to worry the school personnel, the family sought counsel. Ever so gradually, Henry came to realize the influence of his parents' attitude on his own, and how destructive that had become to his children. His description of his disciplinary mode is indelible in my memory. "I cannot rest," he said, "until I have symbolically torn my children to shreds and then mopped the floor with them." Henry's attitude demanded abject, slavish obedience in order to maintain his position of power. The exciting end of Henry's story is that he was able to change. He became positive, and in true strength, he developed a gentleness that restored the children's happiness.

Lack of Attitude Awareness

The problem with attitudes lies in the fact of one's lack of awareness about them. Since we grow up living intimately in a family, we assume that our parents' attitudes are normal—that the whole world is like they are. And by the time we leave home, those attitudes have become so embedded in us that we never actually think about them. Only if we see a striking contrast in someone else, or if life becomes so intolerable (as did Henry's) that we must find relief, do we stop to evaluate our attitudes.

Yet those unconscious attitudes set the mood of your home. Here are the most common attitudes. Which best describes you? Do you like what you see in this mirror? If not, are you willing to change?

Common Attitudes

The Critical Attitude. The person who carries this burden must always be on the alert for faults. The children's manners need mending, or they are too precise. They should study more, or they always have their heads buried in a book. John mowed the lawn, but he didn't pull the weeds in the corner. Sally baked the cake, but she left a smear on the oven door.

The critical parent, in the unbalanced sense, is likely to train children who rebel totally and quit even trying to please, or who become depressed over the failure of even their best efforts to merit approval. Such children learn to make excuses, become defiant, become passively resistant (often seen as stubborn), or withdraw in silent despair.

Let me hasten to explain that there is a healthy, positive criticalness that every parent needs. The ability to detect character weaknesses or habits that could hurt a child makes possible the early correction of these potential defects. It is the chronically negative, never-able-to-be-pleased attitude voiced in chronic anger or irritation that causes trouble.

The Depressed and Helpless Attitude. When you sit with a person who lives with this attitude for even a short time, you will identify it. Even the lines on his face slant downward in an expression of sadness. When Debbie brings home a grade card full of averages, the parent may make no comment but look distressed. Or he may say, "Well, I don't know why at least one of our kids couldn't succeed at something!" When Dale forgets to clean his room for the sixth successive week, such a parent will groan, "I just give up! I don't know what's gotten into you. You'll never amount to anything!"

All too often, that is exactly what happens. Dale catches the depressed, helpless mood of his parents and gives up, too. Debbie realizes that little is expected of her and she, too, really doesn't try very hard.

Such helplessness, often mixed with subtle anger, may breed contempt in the child. Often he will cause more and more trouble in a desperate attempt to get the parent to take action and bounce out of the intolerable gloom.

The Indifferent Attitude. In a society that has gone through decades of severe trauma, we may expect to see increasingly an attitude of not caring much about anything. I see this in children who have been abused or neglected. They cannot tolerate the pain of such treatment and their minds somehow become calloused, so they no longer can experience feelings.

A young, drug addicted mother of two little boys was abandoned by her husband. In despair, she gave the children lethal doses of drugs and ended her own life. The children somehow survived, and intense efforts were made to rebuild their wrecked little personalities. The most striking characteristic of their reactions was their nonchalant, totally uncaring attitude. In desperation, a counselor repeated to them their own predicament and asked them how they felt about their mother's attempt to take their lives and her own. With perfect poise, the eight-year-old replied, "Well, she was our mother. I guess she had a right to do what she wanted."

To be human demands emotions. And emotions are energy—they flow out of one's energy and stimulate energy in return. Children must have emotion to live and develop into human beings. They will do everything in their power to get some sort of feelings activated between themselves and their parents. When they cannot, they may withdraw in silent indifference or act out in futile rage at their world.

The Perfectionist Attitude. Not as common as the others, this attitude is seen in families where one or both parents need to have everything just right! They usually also need to have peace at all costs and would like to present a picture to the world of the ideal family.

The children in this family are always clean; they never fight. When one is sick, they all hover around, giving sympathy and understanding. The house is neat at all times (even the closets!), and the lawn looks like the cover of a magazine. When anyone has a problem, he wishes he didn't because he is overwhelmed with help and confused by all the ideas with which to solve it.

The problem with the suffocating attitude of perfectionism is this: it is not real. It denies the honesty of angry feelings and the motivation of good competition. It fails to prepare children to face a world full of less-than-perfect people—some, in fact, who are downright rotten! By denying the truth and indulging in wishful thinking about problems, such an attitude creates serious long-range problems.

The Healthy Attitude. Actually, this is a little bit of all of the others, and yet it is none of them. Healthy attitudes include a bound-to-win optimism and determination, as well as the acceptance of the fact that one hardly can expect to win all the time. They also face the fact that there are people in the world who are far from good, and one had better evaluate and figure out how to deal with them. There are still, however, many more fine people, and we need to look for them, enjoy them, and help each other create better communities. Good attitudes face mistakes and even deliberate sins for what they are and set them straight. They include compassion and empathy without pity or put-downs. Healthy attitudes can laugh at one's own goofs, while encouraging another who has failed. They brook no nonsense but have a healthy sense of humor. Good attitudes involve exploring until enough information is gained to make forgiving possible. And such forgiving lets go of the issues forever.

The clear thinking, warm understanding, and firm guidance of such a congenial, loving atmosphere can only produce healthy children. It's just too bad that so few families find out how to cultivate it!

Results of Poor Attitudes

Critical Atmosphere. When negative attitudes are allowed to go on, several damaging results will follow. First, *the child's inborn emotional needs will not be satisfied.* In the critical atmosphere, the child's need for approval may never be met. His self-worth and confidence depend on that, and without it, he usually will grow up nervous and uncertain. True, he may compensate for that and by heroic efforts become successful in the eyes of others. In his own estimation, however, he is never quite good enough. Studies show that such people are subject to depression or even suicide.

Depressed Atmosphere. In a depressed, helpless atmosphere, *the child commonly ends up trying to take care of the feelings of his own parents.* He often assumes responsibilities he can't fulfill and therefore becomes depressed and gives up. Often, such children learn to blame others for their troubles and find ready excuses for their failures. After all, they believe, they aren't very capable anyway.

The children of indifference may become successful out of necessity, but *they usually do not develop warm or tender feelings.* Their need for unconditional love is not met. They may experience rage but are incapable of true mourning. They inflict pain on others, but do not allow themselves to hurt. Compassion and tenderness for anyone, even the unfortunate, is beyond their capability.

Overprotective Atmosphere. Out of the perfectionist attitude, one sees children emerge who cannot cope in a real world. When she does not become a cheerleader or he is not accepted on the ball team, they are in despair. Of course, they are richly comforted at home, but someday each must leave home.

A dear friend grew up in a family whose mother had been selected National Mother of the Year. This notable mother had glossed over all the family problems, supported her sometimes incompetent husband, and faithfully helped her children through all of their struggles, even after they married and had families of their own. One month after this Mother of the Year died, my friend had her first mental breakdown. Her mother had done so much for her that she had no confidence in her own strength, and she simply could not make it without her mother. The "ideal" family is rarely ideal!

Both Caught and Taught. Attitudes are contagious; they are usually caught. They are taught, as well, but this takes place in disguised, unrecognized ways. When your attitudes as parents are less than healthy, your children will feel unloved, unworthy, and uncertain. The lack of congeniality is known to be an influence in the loss of self-esteem. When attitudes vary too much, the atmosphere of your home will be inconsistent, creating insecurity for your children.

How clear it becomes, then, that attitudes are powerful molders of children's troubles—or health. Make and keep your attitudes consistently positive!

3
Mental and Physical Problems

In the previous chapters we discussed the basic causes of trouble in the lives of children. These causes relate to the broad areas of discipline, communication, and parental attitudes. As troublesome as problems are in these areas of life, they can be corrected. With skilled guidance, open minds, and honest hearts, such troubles can not only be healed but can make of a family an even closer knit and more loving entity than those who have no such difficulties.

Such an optimistic outcome, however, cannot be promised to families who have a child with serious physical or mental handicaps. For such situations, families must find superhuman courage, wisdom, and endurance. Many do so—but some do not.

EFFECT ON FAMILIES OF HANDICAPPED CHILDREN

A colleague of mine has studied the families of multiply handicapped children for some years. Despite the most careful counsel, expert medical help, and the building of a support system, there is a tragically high divorce rate among these troubled families.

Reaction of Fathers

Commonly in my colleague's experience and in my own, the fathers of handicapped children experience similar reactions.

Apparently, feeling a need to be strong in order to cope with such heartache, they hide their sadness, worry, or feelings of guilt. Most parents of handicapped children do recognize such emotions at various times. Those who can talk, cry, or shout out these painful feelings find they recover from their grief more quickly, moving on to cope very well with the complexities of the problem. For various reasons, the mothers usually deal with these emotions more successfully, but they feel abandoned by or isolated from their stoic husbands. I have known wives to plead with their husbands to share their grief or express feelings in some way, but many times it seems impossible for these men to show their emotions.

Perhaps the apparent nagging becomes too much for the husbands. Perhaps facing their child's handicap demands too much of them. Maybe the problem lies in the attention that must be poured into a handicapped child and the drain this creates on their energy as well as their wives'. No doubt all of these factors have an impact, but the truth is, divorce is significantly higher in the families of seriously handicapped children, and it is almost always the husband who leaves.

There are many families, of course, who do not resort to a divorce even though they face the stress of a severely handicapped child. Instead, they draw together in mutual support and courageously work for the solutions to their problems. It is indeed the attitude of the parents that determines the ultimate outcome of the situation. How they resolve the loss of their dreams, and the grief this loss causes, sets the pattern for their children. It is not the handicap itself that is the major problem. Rather it is a bitter, negative response, which can so easily become a habit, that damages the families of handicapped children.

A description of all the various handicaps possible in children would be too tedious for most of you, but let's outline them broadly.

MENTAL AND NEUROLOGICAL HANDICAPS

These are certainly worrisome because they very often demand a life-care plan which may extend beyond the parents' life expectancy.

Retardation

The risk of a child's being born with a serious physical or mental handicap is one chance in fifty. Mental and neurological defects range from very mild forms to extremely severe ones in their extent. Minimally retarded children may attend regular schools and, with good social training, may fit in well. More severely retarded children have so much trouble in school that they cannot adjust and require special classes or even special schools.

Conscientious parents must make painfully difficult decisions about sending such limited children to boarding schools. Many times, however, the child's best chance to become self-employed and independent may rest in such a placement. I have equal respect for the parents who choose to train and educate their retarded children at home. Many of them do a heroic job.

A friend of mine goes out of his way to take his family's dry cleaning to an establishment owned by a special man. That man employs mentally handicapped people. One evening after a long day my friend stopped by to pick up his cleaning. In the process of paying his bill, he was a bit miffed as the shopkeeper stopped to pay a quiet compliment to the young man who was sweeping the floor. As the man turned toward his boss, his face, bearing the marks of Down's syndrome, beamed with pleasure. My friend's impatience melted and he now gratefully gives this great man his business.

Learning Disabilities

Much less limiting, but most irritating, are the problems of the child with learning disabilities. By all of our known intelligence-testing devices, these children are *not* retarded, but they cannot learn as others do. Some of them seem to have neurological "short-circuits" between the hearing and the thinking centers of the brain. Others have this mix-up between their visual and thinking centers. Still others can think clearly, but they promptly forget. And there are those who reverse letters and words to see *b* as *d* and *dab* as *bad*.

As these children see brothers and sisters or classmates getting ahead of them day by day, they become increasingly frustrated. And no wonder! They must feel as I did on a visit to

Japan. I could not recognize a simple street sign, or even a single letter! I felt very alone and gratefully stayed close to our guide.

Many parents find this handicap extremely hard to live with. They tend to scold and punish in the belief that the child is just lazy or stubborn. When an already-struggling child experiences such an attitude, he is very likely to rebel or give up!

Other Mental Disabilities

Other kinds of mentally handicapped children are the *schizophrenic* child and the *austistic* child. (These are discussed further in chapter 11.) Medical science still has much to learn about these tragic handicaps. We do know that a certain substance from the serum of a schizophrenic person, when injected into someone who is not so afflicted, will cause the major signs of schizophrenia to appear. After several months, the non-schizophrenic recovers. We also know that certain medications help the schizophrenic to feel better, be less afraid, and have fewer hallucinations.

We still know remarkably little about autism and its painful, frightening effects on children. The inability to communicate certainly is one of the most frustrating signs of the autistic child, with its attendant sense of isolation and loneliness.

The interaction of the physical handicaps these afflictions involve, with the stress that they cause, creates a complex situation. The best of medical and psychiatric help are needed. Most victims of autism and schizophrenia require periods of time in special hospitals in order to improve.

PHYSICAL HANDICAPS

Physical handicaps are still numerous in spite of years of research into their cause and prevention. They are of many types and degrees of severity, ranging from those that are fatal to those that can be perfectly corrected. (This subject is discussed further in chapter 10.)

In my experience, it is the chronic, long-term handicaps that are sure to end fatally that are the hardest to bear. Certain heart defects, cystic fibrosis, and the progressive neurological handicaps are examples. Yet even out of the hopeless anguish of these problems, I have seen parents and children muster the courage and energy to live lovingly and creatively.

Support groups, both local and national, have come together to help individual families and to raise vast amounts of money for research. Whether or not we understand the problem of pain, we can see remarkable good coming from it. Such support and caring are only part of that good.

Genetic Birth Defects

Medically, it is important that you understand the difference between inherited or *genetic* birth defects and those that are *congenital* (present at birth), but not inherited. *Hemophilia,* an abnormal bleeding condition, is a fairly well known example of a genetic, inherited birth defect. It is carried in the chromosomes of the mother, but it affects her sons. It creates such danger to life that its victims cannot engage in any activity that may cause a cut or bruise. Families who know of this possibility, therefore, may choose to bear no more children. Each family, obviously, must choose whether to take such risks and genetic counseling is available to help them.

Noninherited Birth Defects

Defects may be present at birth, however, that are not inherited. They could not be passed on to future generations and are not likely to happen in children born later. A friend of mine has a child who was born deaf. The mother had contracted rubella (three-day or German measles) in the first three months of her pregnancy, and the virus that caused the infection damaged the auditory nerve of that developing infant. That child has learned to cope with his deafness and need not worry about his children being born deaf.

Birth defects may be due to certain hormonal abnormalities in the mother. Though Down's syndrome certainly is known to be associated with chromosomal abnormalities, it is much more likely to occur when mothers are older than the usual child-bearing ages of under forty.

Then there are the tragically needless birth defects of babies whose parents have abused drugs and alcohol. Very recently a young couple, heavily drug addicted, lost their first child at only a few weeks of age due to a serious heart abnormality. Statistics are not yet absolute, but research strongly suggests that chemical abuse, even including nicotine and alcohol, will result in a major increase in birth defects.

Accident-Related Handicaps

Yet another category of physical handicaps is that related to accidents. The loss of an eye, a part of the body, or serious brain and nerve damage are known to almost everyone. Some of these are unavoidable by any human care or precaution, but many such accidents are due to carelessness or downright risk taking.

Most of the states in the U.S.A. are strengthening their laws and the enforcement of them, restricting and punishing drunken driving. Irresponsible driving is certainly a major cause of crippling accidents. Carelessness on the part of a child himself, or another person, is inexcusable at any time. The cost of permanent handicaps, or even death, is too high a price for irresponsibility.

Whatever the kind or the cause of a child's physical handicap, it is important that you avoid his becoming emotionally troubled as well. And this sort of trouble can be prevented.

GUIDELINES FOR PARENTS
OF THE HANDICAPPED

Here are some guidelines to help you in helping your child.

Deal with your own grief. It is very easy to become caught in the various stages of your own grief process. As a normal parent, you have dreams for your children. When a handicap prevents even part of those dreams from coming true, they are lost, and all loss involves grief. The process of grief includes anger, remorse, bargaining, some guilt, and often, blame. If you fail to finish your grief process, you are bound to transmit those painful, negative feelings to your spouse, and worst of all, to your children. If your handicapped child learns of or senses your failure to accept the inevitable, he, too, will waste time and energy in self-pity, anger, or blame. And he needs all of his energy, just as you do, to cope with and overcome *his* handicap.

Explore. Find out as much as you can about your child and

his handicap. That means you must discover your child's assets as well as his limitations. He can use them, with your help and encouragement, to compensate for the problems. Find out what resources there are to help you and your child and how both of you can draw upon them.

Repair. Many birth defects can be repaired surgically. Hearts that are seriously deformed can often be made nearly perfect. Defects of the bones can usually be straightened. Even hydrocephalus, once a horribly deforming, life-threatening, and protracted problem, can now be treated with amazing success. Some of you may wonder if you should risk such treatment. Whatever your reasons, I strongly urge you to give your child the advantage of every possible chance for reaching his maximum potential. Your doctor will advise you carefully. Seek several opinions if you like, but do take the advice.

Financial assistance is available through resources in your own locality or by contacting the Easter Seal Society for Handicapped Children and Adults. This nationwide agency is funded through donations by concerned people and is helpful to crippled children in several ways. Look in your telephone directory, or ask your physician how to contact the society.

Make a plan. Start, of course, with a day-to-day plan of living and coping with your handicapped child. But make the plan grow to include enjoying him and finally helping him develop to the fullest every asset he does have. Such planning will often include special therapy, both physical or psychological. It usually means special schools or training. It needs to be flexible to allow for the possibilities of both greater or lesser abilities than you may have thought existed. It must extend throughout the life expectancy of that child and may involve the need to plan for care that you, someday, can no longer provide.

Discipline and train. One of the most common pitfalls I have seen in the family of a handicapped child is that of pity. And perhaps the biggest danger of pitying is the unconscious lowering of healthy expectations. It is just as important to find the balance in expecting neither too much nor too little in your handicapped child as in your other children. It may be harder to establish this balance and even harder to accept it. But doing so will be a great advantage to him.

Once you understand what your special child can do, *require him to do it.* Use the basically sound principles of discipline that you would apply to any child. Do so consistently, and follow through. Teach him obedience, respect for others and himself, and help him to be proud of his accomplishments. These qualities of character will help him in his progress in therapy, in learning, and in life.

A good friend has worked as a teacher of retarded people for over twenty-five years. She tells me that the most difficult problem she had to overcome with those students was their lack of discipline. She found their families hard to convince that the same methods that made cooperative children out of a normal child worked just as well for a handicapped child. Once the families did believe in and practice consistency in their training, their children became productive students.

Consider your child as a whole person. There is no use denying that a handicapped child does, in fact, have special problems and frustrating limits. They are there to be faced every day. But you may choose to think of him as a defective child— or a lovely child who happened to have a damaged heart or nervous system. Your attitude will make a difference in how he sees himself.

If those of us who recognize this vital fact can educate others, our communities could change. Someday it may no longer be a shame or embarrassment to have retarded children. There are useful jobs they could do to earn self-respect and support themselves with pride and dignity—if people could accept and encourage them.

Having a handicapped child can be a burden and a blessing. It will bring you grief, but you can transform that into a challenge. You may react with anger or pity, or you may develop courage and poise. The choice is yours, but not yours alone. For your choice will transmit courage and determination to your child— or allow him to give up in despair. Bringing good out of pain is possible!

Part II

The Critical Need to Understand Your Child

4
The Foundational Makeup of Children

Once I watched a master potter at work. Disregarding clean hands or fingernails, he picked up a lump of gray, ugly clay. After feeling and shaping it in his dirty hands, he threw it on his wheel. While he carefully controlled the speed with which that wheel turned, his hands centered, balanced, and molded that amorphous mass into a graceful pitcher. Working inside and out, from bottom to top and back, he formed the lines and symmetry that identified his particular style. After the merciless heat of the oven and the penetration of the glaze, his pitcher, marked with his own insignia, commanded a great price.

PHYSICAL TRAITS

Whenever I see a child, I'm reminded of that artist. Each parent is a unique craftsman. The child at birth is already beginning to be formed. He has coloring, size, shape, and other characteristics that identify him. But there is still a great deal of molding and perfecting that will determine the ultimate quality of that life.

Just as the potter knew his clay and what its composition would tolerate in his working, so you as parents need to know your child. Even though he may have Uncle John's big nose, or Aunt Sarah's ears, he is not a carbon copy of either one! The sooner you recognize that, the more quickly you may quit worrying about whom he may be like, and enjoy him for who he is!

EMOTIONAL TRAITS

Not only does your child arrive equipped with his physical potential but he also is born with some emotional traits already in place. At birth, we can identify only two basic emotions. They are evidenced by facial expressions, body movements, and a special cry. Try as I can, or others have, we cannot see any other emotions at birth. The potential for others is there, but apparently they must be taught and molded later on.

Anger Is Inborn

One of these two inborn emotions is *anger*. If you have a new baby, you will be aware that hunger, wetness, a sticking pin, or other uncomfortable experiences will prompt identical responses. The child's eyes close tightly, his fists clench, usually his legs draw up and then extend, and he lets go with a loud and definitely angry-sounding cry.

You can see then that the angry cry of a tiny baby is his way of getting help for his pain. Milk for the hunger, a dry diaper for the cold, wet one, comfort and warmth for pain or loneliness— all come about from his angry cry. Babies are remarkably made—and so are parents!

Fear Is Inborn

The second inborn emotion is that of fear. A part of the complete physical examination of every newborn is the demonstration of this feeling. Babies at first are afraid of only two things: loud noises and falling. Making a sudden noise close to a baby's ear or causing a sudden jolt of his crib will prompt his expression of fear. We call it the startle reflex, and it means his hearing and nervous system are healthy.

The child opens his eyes wide in a look of surprise. His arms, legs, and hands spread out. Then, if the noise or jolt is strong enough, the baby will cry, but with a different quality to the cry than when he is angry. I saw that response often when our grandson was tiny. I would have rocked him almost to sleep, when our big dog would start barking. Sleep was gone, his eyes flew wide open, his arms and legs stretched out, and then the cry began. At least I knew his hearing and nervous system were healthy!

As a grandmother, I am a step away from the intimate involvement in child rearing that I knew with my own youngsters. It is becoming quite clear to me from the vantage point of experience that it is from these two simple, well-defined emotions that many others grow. From the inborn anger stems righteous indignation that can correct some of the painful injustices of life. So can the frustration and irritation that prompt parents to correct and discipline their children. So do the temper fits and fights of little children (and adult corporations!). The rage of murder, the vindictiveness and retaliation that cause so much anguish—all may grow from the simple anger, present at birth, prompted by pain.

From the innate fear, I see all of the vulnerable emotions developing. Worry, anxiety, panic, and phobias with all of their damaging effects; caution, concern, and protection with their lifesaving functions—all grow from the simple startle of a little boy at a barking dog!

Love Must Be Taught

It is of great concern to me that one cannot identify love in a newborn child. His advent will prompt intense love and fierce protectiveness in the hearts of his parents. But we cannot describe a look or a motion that reveals love in a new baby. Certainly, the potential to love is there. Like the clay, however, it must be molded if that potential is to become reality.

During my residency in pediatrics, I saw a sad demonstration of the end result of a child's failure to be taught love. An emaciated little girl of eighteen months was admitted to my ward from the emergency room. She was clean, and reports said that she had been fed a fairly adequate diet. But she looked like a victim of starvation. She never cried and did not smile. She couldn't walk and played with none of the most entrancing toys we could find.

None of our studies revealed a single reason for this child's serious failure to thrive—until we learned about her mothering. For reasons somewhat beyond her control, the mother had never wanted the baby. She was angry and depressed herself, and though she fed the child and kept her clean, she never smiled at her or hugged her. The baby had been so severely emotionally neglected that even her instinctive anger and fear were no longer expressed.

To my delight, we found that even at eighteen months, it was not too late. We assigned a special nurse to rock and feed the child. She sang to her, tickled her tiny toes, and taught her to play. Within three weeks, she was creeping about and gurgling with laughter.

Certainly the third basic emotion of love must be taught. Through the senses of touch, taste, sight, sound, and motion, the baby will be able to develop the imprint of his parents' love and joy at his presence. And normally by the age of two or three weeks, a baby will begin to smile back, reach out, and generally respond to love with love.

The case above is a rare one in our Western world. But another possibility for emotional trouble was demonstrated by my two-year-old grandson. I see this example magnified many times over in the troubled children with whom I work.

Anger's Effect

Andy's mother had to work all week long and he looked forward to the weekends with her. One Saturday morning, she had so many errands to run that I happily came to her rescue. It was my chance to spoil my first grandchild a bit. And I was busily doing just that—sitting and playing blocks with him.

Suddenly, Andy looked around, his face appeared troubled, and he abandoned both the blocks and me. He was gone altogether too long, so I went in search of him. He was not making the usual mess of the curious, exploring two-year-old. He was, instead, standing by his window, angrily surveying the empty driveway and street. He refused my invitation to come back and play by shouting, "Grandma, you get out of my house!" He had never talked to his loving grandmother like that before and, frankly, I felt downright angry at his impudence.

Fortunately, I took time to think before I reacted. In the direct, literal translation of those words I understood that if I were out of his house, his mother would be there. Obviously, she was the one he preferred—and wanted.

Instead of reproving his rudeness, I interpreted my guess: "Andy, if I were gone, Mommy would be here, wouldn't she? I think you're very sad and lonely for her, aren't you?" It was exactly right. He burst into tears and flew across the room to my arms just waiting to comfort him.

The frightening insight that grows in my mind ever since that scene is this: people, even at a tender age, learn to protect their vulnerable feelings of fear, worry, and loneliness with anger, and they learn to deny, in time, that they even experience those painful emotions. Furthermore, anger is contagious; it tends to cause more anger, which increases the original anger, and a vicious cycle is begun.

The Right Kind of Love

But the picture of that emaciated child, unable to express any feeling, is even more alarming. What a picture of living death she was! The hope for her inertia and Andy's protective anger alike, lies in love. And it must be the right kind of love. If it is too tender, a child will grow up too soft to cope in a real world. If love is too tough, the child will learn to be hard and calloused. If it is too protective, the child will feel helpless and become too dependent. But if parental love is composed of a uniquely individual combination of all three ingredients, perhaps it will be just right.

The protective element of love will help a child overcome his fears, and out of them he will learn caution, good judgment, and courage. The tough love will help the child learn to control his anger and use it in wise self-discipline and the fight for justice in our world. The tender love will keep softness, warmth, hope, and laughter alive in a child's heart. By the availability of flexible, complete love, both fear and anger can be kept in the finely tuned balance of emotional health.

Not only do children come complete with two very important emotions but they also arrive with four needs to accompany those feelings. We will discuss these needs next.

5

The Emotional and
Mental Needs of Children

Understanding these needs and their close interaction with feelings will help you not only to be better parents but better people as well! You may arrange these needs in any order you like, but these are my priorities.

FOUR EMOTIONAL NEEDS

Unconditional Love. Loving a child ought not to depend on the color of her hair or the way he behaves. Those are important qualities, but they dare not influence your love. The basis of a child's personality is his sense of trust, and a child cannot trust a parent whose love is conditional. Sooner or later, the child will fail, and so will conditional love. You can count on it! A child who lacks this total, committed love will be a troubled child.

How you demonstrate that love is important, too. Obviously, the tiny child needs to be cuddled, touched, smiled and cooed at, and in general, attended to. As children grow, however, sooner or later they climb down off the lap and go about finding and establishing their independence. They say, *"No!"* often and emphatically and sound downright rude! Now such negative behavior needs some teaching and discipline, but it never improves permanently by withdrawing love. Your love may become more protective and tough, but it still needs to be tender as well.

The two-year-old needs rocking and cuddling at times, just as

63

he did in infancy—but he may enjoy tumbling and playful rough-housing much more. Just be very careful that the roughness does not go beyond the child's tolerance, but do try out a variety of ways to express your love through physical means. Playing or doing creative activities together will become as much an expression of your love as rocking and cuddling or holding once were.

Only after the age of seven or eight do many children show embarrassment at too much physical affection. Especially in front of their friends, they begin to prefer that you not touch them. But don't let that fool you! They still crave your warm touch at bedtime or when you are all alone. And they need it. Just be sensitive to when and how each child wants that affection to be expressed. It's quite all right to ask, but don't ask when he is angry about something. He'll invariably feel he is getting even by saying, "Don't touch me!" even when he is longing for it.

When you feel angry with or worried about your child, both you and he may fail to really feel the love that prompts such concerns. Reassure him of your love, and then sit down and talk through your negative feelings. Express them clearly. Explain why you feel that way, and then come up with a plan to get the issue settled so you can return to feeling loving again. Encourage your child to talk out his negative feelings, too. You can teach him to do this with honesty and without being rude.

No matter how well you all know there is love among you, it becomes ineffectual unless both giver and receiver honestly *feel* loving—at least most of the time. In order to feel love you must unload resentments, hurts, and all bad feelings. In understanding your child's misbehaviors, you can forgive as well as correct him, and thus find release from the negative feelings.

Consistency (Predictability). I have already discussed this as a factor in problems relating to discipline and training. But predictability is vital in all areas of a child's life.

Love is hard to believe if it is not expressed in similar ways under similar circumstances day after day. A father who plays congenially with the children one day and snaps at them from behind his newspaper the next, will sooner or later be left to his paper.

A friend told me this insightful vignette. She and her friend were having lunch with their young adult daughters. As they reminisced of earlier days, they laughed and almost cried at times. The friend's daughter grew thoughtful and said, "Well, Mother, it sounds as if you were terrible. But at least you were terrible all the time!" She certainly knew, in that case, what to expect and survived to become a fine woman. It's *not knowing* that has such destructive effects on children.

You need to be consistent in fulfilling your threats. Children are quick to pick up any failures there and will push you more and more to see whether or not you will follow through. The sooner you do, the sooner such testing out will stop.

But you also need to fulfill your promises. I loved to make doll clothes for my children, and many an evening was spent designing and sewing high fashion! In our busy lives, however, interruptions were common, and often they had to go to bed with the project half-finished. Knowing how easy it was for me to postpone the completion, and how much they valued such a project, I would promise to have it done by morning. Many times I was up into the wee hours, but I tried heroically to keep these promises. I always placed the finished product where the children would find it the first thing in the morning. I knew the payoff of their trust in my word made it worthwhile.

Consistency also involves schedules and the structuring of a child's day. Having meals at widely varying times makes it hard to be prompt. And a bedtime that depends on the mood of Mom and Dad is tough to maintain. Certainly you needn't set the clock by a rigid schedule, but some semblance of sameness day by day offers your child the security of predictability.

Object constancy is an old term for a lasting value. Children do best when they stay in the same bed, in the same house, in the same neighborhood through their formative years. There are, of course, exceptions to this, such as neighborhoods where violence becomes a threat. The mobility of our society, however, has created the need to move all too often. I have seen children who go through the grief of losing their friends, their home, their own room and possessions, so often that they seem to stop caring.

Stay planted when you have the choice, for as long as possible. If you can plan a move, the year between grade school and junior high, or between junior and senior high may be the least disturbing. Due to boundary lines, most children are separated from some of their friends at those times anyway.

If you need to move a child to a new bed or a new room, try to do so gradually. When my daughter had to move Andy from a baby bed to a big one, she kept both in his room, crowded as that was, for a while. She allowed him to choose which bed he preferred and removed the crib only when he realized he had outgrown it. Patience and understanding about the security of sameness will help prevent trouble.

Whether you move or stay, allow your children to keep those special "security blankets" or toys. Only recently, a seriously troubled teen shared some bitter memories of her childhood with me. Her family was moving, and in a well-meant effort to clean out the junk, her mother threw away her treasured though tattered baby doll. When she cried, her mother assured her it was worn-out anyway, and she would buy a new one. My young friend did not even want a new doll. She felt so much a part of her old one, it was like throwing away some of herself. Though I tried to help her understand and forgive her mother, my heart went out to her. In that case, her mother was terribly wrong! Had she considered even a bit, she would have allowed the cherished old doll to stabilize her grieving daughter through the difficult transition.

Don't worry about taking away the tattered blanket or worn teddy bear! Your child will give them up when she is ready. The tatters and tears make them all the more comforting. Children need old, familiar articles in order to feel settled and at home.

Congeniality. Children must have free laughter if they are to be well-balanced, happy people. But different people have very different senses of humor. Coming from a given family, a child may not understand certain teasing or humor he finds in another situation. You need to be sensitive to the kind of laughter that occurs and what that means to your child.

Only recently, our adult daughter related a memory of her childhood. We were visiting her grandparents when she was only four. Being too short to reach the dining table, her grandmother suggested she sit on a telephone book. Our telephone book would have made an adequate booster, so Kathy agreed to the idea. Grandma came, however, with the thin booklet of their small, rural telephone exchange. Seeing the look of dismay on Kathy's face, Grandma laughed aloud. She had intended this to be a joke. The four-year-old, sensitive child, however, heard it as ridicule, and through over twenty years a twinge of pain had lasted in her heart. Even as her mother, I had been unaware of the pain of that moment. We need not try to protect our children from such moments, but a brief and gentle interpretation, had I realized her hurt, could have eased it then and there.

In your own home, work to avoid the inconsistency of moods. If special problems do bring concerns, explain them carefully and briefly, so the children will know why you are temporarily worried or upset. And return to your usual pleasant atmosphere as soon as possible.

Congeniality is a matter of attitude and self-discipline. It is easy to allow problems of the day or personal moods to dictate the atmosphere of the home. By carefully thinking through the problems and making plans for their solutions, you can keep your mind reasonably settled and open to good humor. Look for the funny events of your day and tell them to your family. Listen to the silly jokes of your children—many of them are worth a good laugh. It's usually your job, parents, to maintain the peace and goodwill of your home!

Approval. For emotional health and personal motivation, children must have approval. While love must be unconditional, approval is quite the opposite. It demands achievements that meet certain standards in order to merit the needed sense of pride. Almost always that demands good training and discipline.

Approval begins, however, with the natural course of a child's growth and development. Baby's first smiles are a joy to the family, and Daddy comes running to see them. (Hopefully!) The first tooth and first steps are worthy of a long-distance telephone call to grandparents. For older children, however, the excitement of the "firsts" is often diminished. And as a child reaches the difficult *twos* or finally trudges off to school, that sense of elation at his early events may dull to indifference or even chronic irritation!

Here are some guidelines for meeting a child's need of pride and approval, and your need for achievement by your child.

GUIDELINES FOR PRIDE AND APPROVAL NEEDS

Take the trouble to find out what each child is capable of at a given time in life. Watch his coordination, interests, and skills. Talk with other people who know and interact with him to find out how they see your child. Read about the normal capabilities of other children. Knowing what to expect of your child is essential in helping you set up goals for training and disciplining.

Take one goal at a time and explain to your child (and to yourself) just what you expect of him and how you will go about teaching him to accomplish that goal. Your best method is to go about this positively, with love and encouragement.

Follow through with firmness and patience. Correct the child when he fails and praise him sincerely when he succeeds. Now and then, in his hearing, tell someone else about his success, but be careful not to overdo it!

When he has established good habits in one area, move on to another. Not spilling milk is a major accomplishment for a two- or three-year-old. Picking up toys may be another, and going to bed without whining certainly would please many parents! Choose something the child is capable of doing, be consistent from your side of the plan, and don't go too fast.

Be alert for the time your child gets his own self-starter going. If you do your job well, at some point your child will want to get his own sense of pride and pleasure in what he does. He will always need yours to bolster him, but his real maturity will be there when *he* knows he has done well!

Understanding your child's feelings and needs can help you in preventing a troubled child. But if your son or daughter already evidences a problem, such basic understanding will also help you in the solving of that problem. Take some time and think about your child. Is she covering worry with irritation? Could she need a little more tenderness? Try a different approach, but be clear and honest with her so she will know what to expect and that she can count, absolutely, on your love!

If you are to understand anyone, you need to know something about how he thinks. For many decades now, people have been studying this process, so in these few pages, I do not intend to burden you with that complex information. But there are some practical facts you need to know in order to understand your children better.

UNDERSTANDING
THE THOUGHT PROCESS

Sight

In early infancy, children's brains—amazing computers that they are—"think" or register information only from their physical senses. An infant sees Mother's shining eyes and the lights reflected from her hair and cheeks. As his sight develops, he identifies her nose, mouth, and other features. It takes several months, however, before he can distinguish her from any other person.

Hearing

While baby's sight and visual recognition are developing, his ears also are at work. He hears soft sounds and experiences them as safe and soothing, because they resemble the sounds of his mother's heartbeat and movements before he was born. Loud noises, however, startle him, and too much noise in a baby's environment will make him nervous and hyperresponsive. Just as his eyes gradually focus enough to memorize and know individuals, so his ears learn to know and remember certain sounds. Daddy's sounds are different from Mommy's, and Grandpa is different still. And, of course, the cat is quite different from the dog.

Slowly at first, but with increasing rapidity, baby learns to put each sound together with the visual image to which it belongs. He then has a more complete mental picture that is slowly but surely becoming *thinking*—identifying, associating, remembering, visualizing. It's important that a baby have a nice balance in enough sights and sounds to stimulate that developing brain, but not so much as to overload or confuse it!

Smell and Taste

Perhaps earlier and more efficiently than the development of sight and hearing in a baby is the use of his senses of smell and taste. These go together so closely, it is a bit hard to separate them. There are only three kinds of taste sensations we know from our tongues: sweet, sour (bitter), and salty. All the rest of the enjoyment of food—the pungency of spices and the mellow, mouth-watering goodness of bacon and coffee—are strictly identified and enjoyed through the sense of smell. Try eating when your nose is stuffy from a cold, or hold it firmly shut, if you can, while you eat. You'll see!

Babies learn quickly to identify Mother through her smell, and Daddy, too. They soon taste the sweetness of the milk, and know the smell of bath lotions and soap. As babies begin to grow and explore their small worlds, they do so largely, at first, through taste. Every rattle, or other object they can grasp, goes directly into the mouth so that tiny tongue can taste and feel it.

Smells and tastes, then, are added to the increasingly beautiful picture of the infant's world. Even in old age, the memory of smells and tastes conjures up a wealth of pictures of special people and events from the past. A friend of mine has a box of mementos from her grandmother. Invisible, but most real to her, is the scent of Grandma's perfume, lingering on a scarf in that priceless box.

Touch

Have you ever had a person come up behind you, place her hands over your eyes, and make you guess who it is? In our big family that was a happy manner of teasing. When those hands are part of a person you know well, you will be able to recognize the touch accurately and quickly.

When I was only four, we attended a little country church where all the men sat on one side and the women on the other. One Sunday, I was allowed to go with my father to the men's side. I liked that a lot because he usually kept wintergreen candies in his pocket to tide me over the long, tedious sermon! On this special Sunday, I somehow lost my grip on Daddy's hand. In the men's coatroom, all was confusion and milling about. To my child's-eye view, all I could see was dark serge suits and the calloused hands of those wonderful farmers. I felt afraid, but soon picked a hand that looked like Dad's, and thrust my little hand into it. To my instant horror, however, I realized it was not my dad's hand. It didn't feel right! I felt sheer panic! Fortunately, my father was also searching for me, and I was promptly rescued. The sense of touch is accurate, indeed.

Tiny babies soon learn to identify touch. At first they know only if it is strong and safe or shaky and frightening because of their inborn fear of falling. When I was training in pediatrics in a large hospital, I was called one morning to see the baby of one of our hospital interns. His wife was rooming in with their very first baby, and it would not stop crying. She was weeping right along with him, obviously exhausted.

Gently and carefully I reexamined the baby. He was nursing well and had gained an ounce. There were no pins sticking, no rash, no problems to be seen. Still he cried. Finally I wrapped him snugly in his blanket and strolled about the room. To even my surprise, he was asleep before I finished the first circuit. He was able to rest in the strength of my experienced, untired arms. He sensed his mother's insecurity and fatigue and was afraid.

Kinesthetic Sense

We know that babies' learning to move, sit, crawl, stand, and walk has to do with still another sense called the *kinesthetic* sense. It is a combination of a sense of muscles and bones as well as the sense of balance from the inner ear and the brain. This enables a child to know where he is in his environment. As we watch our astronauts in the atmosphere of weightlessness, we know our earth's gravity has much to do with that kinesthetic sense. But a baby need not know that in order to stretch and flex those muscles and begin to explore yet another facet of his world and himself.

Dreams

By a year and a half of age, children have put together a fairly complete picture of their lives. About then they begin having dreams, and waken at night, sometimes terrified. By then they have had some tumbles, have been scolded and punished, have experienced scares with animals or people, and they relive these events in their dreams.

When our oldest child began to have such sleep-disturbing (for me as well as her!) dreams, I did not understand what was going on. Night after night one hot summer she would waken, stand up in her crib, and scream. I began to think she was just spoiled and considered spanking her. But finally I opened my own tired eyes enough to really look at her face. What I saw there was obviously an expression of terror. That sight made it easy for me to gain control over my fatigue and frustration. I spoke to her gently and rocked her until she felt safe enough to go back to sleep. She was a bright child and her mental pictures of her world were a bit too clear—certainly too alarming. And she had too few words to explain it.

Speech

After dreams, in the child's thinking development, come words. Words are a major step in the child's progress. Many children seem to pick these up almost automatically. They hear parents use words repeatedly and suddenly a light dawns! *That silver thing they use to stuff that gooey cereal in my mouth is a "poon." The scary thing that barks is a "dog,"* and on it goes.

Late Talkers. Some children are so adept with body language they don't need to talk. A look or a gesture tells someone what they want and they are content to hear others talk of "poons" and "dogs." In fact, it can get to be quite entertaining to watch people mouthing words over and over trying to teach these relaxed children to talk.

Don't worry too much about your child's talking. Keep talking to each other and to him, but don't get too pushy until he is four or older. By then he may become socially ill at ease if he can't talk. In fact, it often helps a slow talker to put him with children his own age. They learn more naturally, perhaps, from each other, than from adults.

From saying words symbolic of objects to words describing actions, to words explaining needs, to words describing feelings—these are the usual stages of learning to talk—comes a reflection of learning to think. You can see how nicely this progression works. Thinking is connected to pictures, to objects, to mental memories of visual, auditory, smelling, tasting, touching, and motion senses.

TEACHING WISDOM

Most parents may not realize, however, what it takes to teach a child wisdom—the application to life situations of all sorts, of the important facts he learns at a given time. That takes patient explaining, persistent teaching, and reminding. It is in this area of a child's life that consistency and following through really pay off.

Importance of Reading to Your Child

Reading to children has the advantage of teaching them to think and understand. As you read to your child, you are brought close together. Physically, that is great for developing your child's sense of touch and feeling, and you are likely to feel emotionally close as well. In this loving nearness to you, your child's total sensory awareness can stimulate the interest that will motivate him to learn to read later on.

Early Learning: Good or Bad? There has been a great push for early learning, and I am for that. But I am not for preschoolers learning reading and mathematics. Certainly many of them can. But studies show that by the third or fourth grades, when most children master reading skills, the youngsters who started to read at three were no more advanced than those who started at six. The few exceptions to that are the gifted children. It is alarming to see so many children hurried out of childhood in our society, and it seems to me that pushing academics on a young child is one more giant step in that direction.

Selecting Books. Another advantage in reading to your child is the opportunity it gives you to interpret ideas and values as you read. In order to do that, select books carefully. There is a collection of books that contain rhyming sounds that may teach a child to read phonetically. But they are total nonsense—disconnected gobbledegook that has no relationship to real life except some slapstick humor. If you and your child understand and enjoy that sort of humor, these books may be harmless.

Some tried and true stories, however, are those in which animals or fictional people live out the conflicts and discover the values that apply to the lives of your child, his friends, and your family. Seeing the pictures, hearing the stories, listening to your interpretations will help your child develop the rare and price-less quality of *wisdom*. When situations arise that relate to the story, you may wish to review it, or remind your child that this is an example of the moral of that story.

I'm seeing troubled young people who cannot connect one life experience with another. They do not learn from experience and seem devoid of any wisdom. You can prevent such trouble in your child by teaching him to think and by making learning a daily process.

Concrete and Abstract Thinking

Children think very much as they experience life in their early years. As mentioned earlier, a doll with a broken leg has actually lost the leg. When a young child hears of a friend with a broken leg, she will instantly envision that friend with a leg bro-ken off! We call this *concrete* thinking, and it is normal until the late preteen years.

There is, however, a gradual process of learning to think more symbolically or abstractly. The various experiences of life grad-ually teach a child that a broken leg is still attached and that *broken* may mean several things. Still later, she may find that *broken* applies to her emotions when her boyfriend jilts her!

By the tender age of seven or eight, children make some major decisions about life. They may decide to be like their par-ents, or quite different. They decide the world is a fine place, or quite scary! Their parents' attitudes, the way they have been disciplined, the way relatives, neighbors, and friends treat them, along with individual experiences in school and the community, all add up to teach each child what he or she believes about the world and his place in it. Be sure you give your child a healthy, balanced view of herself and the world!

6
The Social Development of Children

Troubled children nearly always live out their problems in society—both acting them out and ultimately having them reflected back. Such negative interactions worsen both the troubled child and the society in which he lives. It will be helpful, therefore, to understand a child's social development.

For varying periods of time, a baby's first social contact is her mother and (somewhat less) her father, brothers, sisters, and grandparents. Fairly early her social world enlarges to include neighbors, friends, baby-sitters, and a parade of curious and interested strangers.

INFLUENCES ON CHILD'S SOCIAL DEVELOPMENT

There are several factors that influence a baby's adjustment in his social environment. Perhaps the most obvious is the *baby's own personality and temperament*. If he is full of energy, curious, and feels somewhat safe, he will reach out to others and explore them in a way adults describe as friendly or outgoing. If people whose noses he tweaks and whose glasses he grabs respond with smiles and warmth, he will become even more outgoing. If they howl in pain or yank their spectacles away, the child will probably retreat from such an unfriendly attack and may become shy.

75

An innately quiet child who is content to be still and ponder his own toes will usually be seen by others as unresponsive or even unfriendly. Some mothers even describe such infants as not wanting to be held from birth. They experience these babies as hostile and tend to distance themselves from such "indifferent" babies, thus pushing them into further isolation.

It is clear, then, that the *temperament and personality of the parents and close family members* will be another vital factor in a child's social security or lack of it. If Father (or especially Mother) are quite different in their natures from their child, they may subtly and unconsciously reject him. Or, of course, if the child's behavior is desirable, they may admire and dote on him. In the first instance, a child will probably withdraw into loneliness or become, on the other extreme, aggressive enough to make himself noticed. Doting parents are in danger of hero-worshiping their child, giving him too much power and spoiling him into being obnoxious.

In most cases, neither extreme happens at birth. Healthy parenting instincts enable the mother and father to accept the child into their hearts, to love, protect, and nurture him or her until struggles appear later.

Baby's sensory makeup is another element in his social growth. Babies who twitch and cry with even slight sounds, who cry loudly with their discomforts, and react intensely to all stimulation, are likely to be hard to live with! Tired mothers may yell at such babies and handle them with rough, jerky movements. Warm, loving feelings may be rare, and the security these create missing. Being high-strung already, the baby's intense reaction to a tired, irritable parent may create a lifelong vicious cycle before the child can even sit alone!

Fortunately, most parents become more patient with time and experience, and most hyperactive babies begin to calm down, becoming more human and less monster by three or four months of age.

Still another important piece of baby's social adjustment must be his *physical environment.* Inner-city apartments are surrounded by intense sounds: the wail of sirens, screeching of brakes; sometimes violent arguments and fights are common in many city neighborhoods. How can a sensitive child adapt to such a world? And yet he must.

Overcoming Your Environment

If you are parents in such an area and you cannot escape, here are some ideas. Keep your own minds and hearts as peaceful as you can. Babies sense that calm strength, and it helps them feel safer. Keep quiet music playing to muffle some of the external sounds. Use as many heavy curtains as possible to block out loud noises, at least in the baby's room. A folded handkerchief or diaper laid over baby's ear (if she will sleep with her head on one side) is also an excellent sound muffler. Be sure to move it when she is sound asleep, so it won't slip over her nose and bother her breathing. Be grateful for the adaptiveness of babies! Sooner or later, they get used to almost anything.

Handling the Curious Stage

About the time parents and baby have adjusted to each others' personalities and idiosyncrasies, the baby has reached another stage. He has climbed out of the crib and up the wall into the medicine chest or the bookshelves. His boundless curiosity (if he is that sort of person) will drive him to explore—and you to distraction. Herein lies another challenge to meet in helping your child socially.

Remember, the foundations of any child's social structure are built at home. During the first three years of a child's life, he needs to learn to trust others, to like himself, and to find out for certain what he may and may not do. The way you supervise his activities, encourage his healthy exploring, and stop his dangerous adventures, will help him learn those essential lessons.

INTERACTING WITH OTHER CHILDREN

Most children are so busy with these lessons that they are not able to play with other children of their own or younger ages. They are actively taking away toys from each other, poking one another's ears and noses, pulling hair, and biting. And few children are benefited by such aggressive interactions. At best, a very adaptive child will learn to play quietly in the midst of others, but he truly cannot cooperate in play. (That's not quite true, for I *have* seen two-year-olds roll a ball back and forth a few times, but that soon ended in one's possessing it and the other's running, screaming to repossess it!)

By three, however, a miracle happens with some rapidity. Most children settle into being amiable, sometimes cooperative and helpful human beings! They can share building blocks, cars, or dolls with grace, and may even forget what belongs to whom. Be aware, however, there are limits to such kindliness, and determined children, born and bred to be leaders, will do less cooperating than others! If you have one of those, trim her down a bit, but don't destroy those good qualities.

Courtesy

Today's society seems to have given up teaching good manners and I, for one, deplore it! There are people, of course, who have only superficially good manners and are rude or even cruel behind others' backs. To live in a pleasant social environment, however, I am convinced we need certain rituals and rules.

It is never too early to teach such courtesy. Begin, if you don't already have the habit, to speak to each other, Dad and Mom, as if there were guests around. Saying, "Please," "Thank you," "I'm sorry," and "Excuse me," are much more loving than "Give me that," or "Get out of my way!" If you talk gently out of love and respect, not sarcasm, you will begin to set the congenial atmosphere so conducive to confidence building in children. As your child learns to talk, it will be relatively easy to teach him and her these social graces if you are already in the habit of using them.

Just because your child is three and even has learned some good manners, however, don't take for granted that she will sail on her own steam socially! She needs lots of supervision in order to establish balances in her interactions. Some children are so adaptable, they let others run riot over them. These children can become fearful, shy, and may lose their own sense of initiative. By being there, at least now and then, you can help her know how and when to protect herself, and keep others from taking unfair advantages.

Sometimes the child who seems gentle and passive at home is an absolute tyrant with other children. You may not like seeing that, but you certainly can't correct it if you avoid looking! Such a child needs firm correction and must be taught how others feel when he tyrannizes them!

In school these days, believe me, the child who demonstrates respect and social graces will go far! The teachers will love him because his kind is rare. And other children will respect him if you have balanced his training in considerateness with the will and skills to deal with bullying by others.

Avoid Snobbishness

Do help your children to avoid snobbishness and cliques. In my experience, these are signs of basically insecure, unworthy-feeling children. By "lording it over" others, they can feel superior for a little while and alleviate their true sense of inferiority. Truly great people never act superior to others—no matter what their age!

You can avoid or stop such behavior by listening to your children talk, watching them interact with friends, and by asking their teachers. Simply be aware. Watch the faces of children who are rejected by such snobs, and I suspect your own basic feelings will tell you how to handle your child. If your son or daughter is the victim of such rudeness, simply help him see the real fear in the snob or bully, and help him find better friends.

Entertaining

No matter what your income or where you live, help your children plan parties now and then. Parties teach children to be gracious and thoughtful of guests and give them a sense of importance. They need cost very little, but with imagination they can be superb! A walk can collect acorns, leaves, interesting rocks, or a variety of delights to children. Crackers or fruit are fun when served in doll dishes for small children, or on napkins your child has decorated. Be sure your child invites all the children in her class or neighborhood (in small groups, of course!), so no one will feel left out.

Please avoid the middle-class competition for the best and biggest party. Children need to play creatively together, win small prizes, and hunt treasures much more than they need clowns, magicians, and hot-air balloon rides! Children who are given too much lose appreciation for the value of what they have!

Your modeling of healthy social interaction will be the ultimate learning tool of your children. How you talk with each other, Mom and Dad, how you talk with your friends on the phone (and what you say after you hang up), whom you invite to dinner, and how you serve them—these are the living demonstrations of happy, loving, social interactions, or the opposite! Watch how you live!

7

The Spiritual Nature of Children

Philosophers have argued for ages about the existence of God or the nature of God. It is an ongoing discussion. But one of the most convincing experiences I have known, about the presence of God in this world, is the sharing of a sense of awe and wonder in the face of a child.

THE WONDERS OF NATURE

We lived near a large medical center in a big midwestern city while our oldest daughter was a preschooler. There were bright lights all around us and Kathy went to bed early. Late one evening we left the city and drove along a highway on a welcome weekend visit to relatives. It became dark as we drove, and Kathy grew more and more silent. Thinking she was sleepy, I started to lay her down, but she persisted in sitting upright on my lap, her little nose pressed against the window. At last, very softly, she pointed her finger asking, "Mommy, what's that?" For a moment I could not follow her careful pointing, and I was puzzled over which "that" in a dark countryside she meant. But finally I realized she was seeing the stars for the first time. The sky was clear, and the stars very bright. While I was startled and sad because our three-year-old had never seen stars, I was excited with her discovery. But I was made reverent by the awe and wonder in her voice and eyes. Stars are a source of wonder so lovely and so precise that we measure time by them.

Taking my grandson for a ride in his stroller one evening, I became aware that he was nearly tumbling out of it in eagerness. My eyes focused in the direction of his energy, and there was a gray squirrel. Boldly chattering away at Andy and flirting his tail, he was like a stuffed toy come to life. Andy was enchanted, but I had taken squirrels for granted.

KNOWING GOD THROUGH HIS CREATION

After realizing that I had failed to teach Kathy about nature, I hastily mended my ways. We walked to clearings to see the sunset, and wished many wishes together upon the evening star. I looked for rainbows and explained thunder and lightning. We looked for dandelion flowers in the spring and made snowmen in the winter. It was a wonderful day when she found me fixing dinner and said, "Mommy, come see the clouds!" The afterglow of the setting sun had illuminated them in brilliant rose and purple and accented them with gray.

Certainly one of the ways we may know God is through His creation. But few people in cities see enough of nature to look for Him there. If you parents will look for and relearn His presence, you may teach your children about Him in a way their freshness can absorb like a sponge!

He was busy and worked long days, but my father remembered to teach me. Though we lived on a farm where we shared intimately in creating gardens, crops, and raising the animals carefully, he never took for granted that I would value nature.

THE MASTER PLANNER

When baby chicks were about to hatch, my father watched for the right moment. He came to find me and, with the familiar twinkle in his eyes, told me he had a surprise for me. Excitedly I skipped along to the hen house, and he stood while I watched, in breathless wonder, the ancient process of the birth of a new life. The unborn chick would peck away at the shell until a piece fell off. Then it rested, but soon it pecked again. It seemed to my childish eagerness to be an endless process. At one point it rested so long, I feared it had died. I reached out to help remove the stubborn shell and set the baby chick free. My father knew best and gently pulled my hand back. "No," he said kindly, "pecking his own way out of that shell is what makes the chick strong. If we helped it out, it would be too weak and might not live." He made me understand more than a baby chick. His gentle teaching and his own interest in God's creation helped me see that there is a big plan that guides and controls nature. We can work with that plan, but we must never think we know better than the Master Planner.

TEACHING TRUST

Nature was a tool in teaching me, but Dad was the artist who used that tool. I adored him and went everywhere with him that I possibly could. At the end of a ride on a wagon or other vehicle, Dad would dismount first. Planted firmly below me he would call, "Now jump, Gracie!" With absolute confidence, I would sail into his strong arms. He never let me fall! Trust, for me, therefore, was natural.

Mary Anne was not so blessed. She became my patient when she tried to take her life when she was twelve. One day she told me this story of her childhood. Her father was a fireman, big and strong. He loved to sit on the floor and play with her. He would call, "Run to me, Mary Anne!" She ran as fast as her chubby legs could go. He would hug her, and then she wanted to do it again. If he were tired of the game, he would call, "Run to me, Mary Anne!" but he would slip to the side and allow her to crash headlong into the stucco wall behind. She showed me the scars that were silent proof of his cruel humor.

Like it or not, dads, you are a model of the heavenly Father. What will He look like to your children? Or will He be there at all?

Part III

The Most Common Childhood Problems

8
Behavioral Problems

Problems do not seem, on the surface, to have any good components. They produce pain, and all living creatures instinctively shrink from pain. Through many years of experience as a physician, however, I have learned that it is pain that prompts people to seek the help that will heal their ills and restore wholeness.

It is, then, the pain of a child's problem that often reveals some malfunction of an entire family. And the parents' awareness of and response to the pain of the child they love can result in the healing of that child and the enrichment of the family as well.

This chapter is a compilation of the major concerns parents share with me about their children's behavior. Some are serious; others are transient and will go away with time. All of them need your understanding. Their listing here is alphabetical and has nothing to do with the seriousness of their effects.

CAUTIONS FOR PARENTS

In dealing with behaviors that create problems for you as parents, your children, or those with whom they relate, there is a need for special caution. It is tempting to believe that a good, sound spanking will drive the behavior out of them. And—at times—it will, just as touching a hot stove produces pain enough to keep a child from touching it again.

The older a child becomes, however, the more complex will his life and all of its branchings become. The way people treat a child, therefore, teaches him a way of responding—gentleness and reason, or harshness and impulsivity are certain to prompt a similar reaction. Furthermore, as a child develops, the reasons for specific behaviors become increasingly more important than the behaviors themselves.

In discussing these problem behaviors, therefore, please bear with the explanations. I am not against discipline, or even spankings. The biblical command for this is clear and correct, but it also commands fathers to avoid provoking their children to be angry. So I do ask you to understand the deep needs and feelings that prompt a child's problem behaviors. You may well change his behaviors by punishment alone, but if his feelings are unrecognized and his needs unmet, other problem behaviors will crop up. Leaves from a bindweed root may be chopped off daily, but more will grow until the root is removed.

Children's problem behaviors are often like the leaves growing out of a root of harshness and deep criticalness in the hearts of their parents, though they certainly have their own foolishness and ignorance as well. So please think deeply and circumspectly about each issue that may involve your child before you plan a way of overcoming it. Very likely some part of each one has something to do with *you*. Now let's consider the various types of behavioral problems.

BABYISHNESS

This is acting like a baby or a child considerably younger than a child is. The symptoms include crying with little provocation, whining, acting more helpless than the child actually is, tattling and otherwise seeking adult intervention, or regression to earlier patterns of thumb sucking, wetting, or soiling.

Causes of Babyishness

The causes of such behavior are:

1. Being treated like a baby by a parent who is overprotective and anxious, or by grandparents or others.
2. Feeling pushed to grow up too soon before a child's baby needs have been met. The arrival of a new baby may temporarily cause it just as the start of kindergarten and first grade may provoke this behavior.

3.   Grief or anxiety in a child may be manifested in babyish behavior. This is especially true if divorce is threatened. A child may hope his parents will see how much he needs them.

4.   Certain illnesses may cause some of these behaviors. Allergies, anemias, and some chronic toxic illnesses, such as lead poisoning, are examples.

Treatment of Babyishness

First, be sure your child has a thorough physical checkup before you decide that babyishness is just a behavioral problem.

Second, do an inventory of your child's present life-style.

1.   *Has there been a big change in his accustomed amount or kind of attention?*
2.   *Has he been around someone who has treated him like a baby? Have you done more babying than you realized?*
3.   *Has there been a change in the family, such as Dad's changing jobs, Mom's going to work, or a death in the family?*
4.   *Has there been extra worry or arguing between you parents? (Little ears hear and sense many things you may not realize.)*
5.   *If your child is in school, is there a problem with a teacher or other children?*

The precise way of dealing with this problem must be related to the cause. Try matching these suggestions to the results of your inventory.

1.   Get medical care, if that is indicated.

2.   Explain your understanding of the problem to your child. Even when he can't talk, he will understand more than you think, and you will be developing the habit of fairness and reasonableness.

3.   Make it clear to the child that both he and you will be making some changes and describe those simply.

4.   Explain these changes clearly and emphatically to older children and any adults who will be dealing with your child, and request their help. This will provide consistency.

5. Decide on a proper response to the behavior. For example, ignore it or put the child in his room or a special chair where he must take time out from activities to think (called a "time-out" chair or other special location). Firmly tell him to stop the babyish behavior, but tell him what he may do instead. (Spanking, in this situation, usually prompts more crying and babyishness, so it is not likely to work very well.)

6. Be careful to lavish positive attention and love on your child when he is not acting like a baby. Let him know your pride and respect for his efforts to control such behavior.

7. Be persistent. Too often parents give up just short of success and try something else. Inconsistency causes confusion and defeat.

BED-WETTING (Enuresis)

This is the continuation of, or the return to, nighttime wetting after daytime bladder control has been mastered. It may occur at any time during the night, and it may take place once or more often. Do not be concerned if your child is three or under. Many children do not quit nighttime wetting until they are four or five.

Causes of Bed-Wetting

The causes of enuresis are one or more of these:

1. Slower neurological development makes bladder control later and more difficult for some children.

2. The size of the urinary bladder is too small to hold a night's quantity of urine.

3. Excessive fluid intake in the late evening, especially those liquids containing caffeine, such as chocolate milk, colas, or tea. Caffeine strongly stimulates urinary output by the kidneys.

4. Profound sleep, so deep that the discomfort of a full bladder does not awaken the child.

5. Dreams in which the child goes to the bathroom—in bed!

6. Extreme dependence on the parents' help or reminders, instead of assuming personal responsibility.

7. Emotional distress, including grief, anxiety, and anger.

Here are some possible distressful situations:

1.   The birth of a new baby, with the loss of a child's secure position in the family, often causes a temporary return to earlier habits. This is especially likely if the older child is just getting bladder control.

2.   Beginning of a new life-style that is frightening to a child, such as moving, the divorce of parents, starting school, or being placed with a new baby-sitter.

3.   Overly harsh punishment of a child or a brother or sister may sometimes result in wetting.

Treatment of Bed-Wetting

How can you handle bed-wetting so it will stop, without emotionally damaging your child? Both physically and emotionally, bladder and bowel control are difficult for children. They must give up their carefree state and take on new responsibilities. It's easy to forget the new habit or to prefer the old, easy life of wetting whenever he feels like it. So be thoughtful of your child while you are helping him to form or regain his control.

First, *have a thorough physical evaluation and remedy any problems that can be treated.*

Next, *evaluate your child's toilet habits during the daytime.* If he empties his bladder every hour or so, it will not stretch enough to hold a full night's quantity. Help your child wait a few minutes longer than he thinks he can during the day, when he needs to void. As the time between voidings lengthens, and his bladder can hold a cup and a half of urine, he should be ready to stop wetting. Sometimes letting him measure the amount of urine can involve the child in the process of gaining control.

Notice how many liquids your child is drinking after the evening meal. Limit his drinks for the last two hours before bedtime to a single drink just before retiring. Avoid coffee, tea, colas, and chocolate. The caffeine in these stimulates the secretion of urine and is not good for your child, at any rate.

There are mechanical devices that set off a buzzer or bell as soon as the first drops of urine moisten the sheets. The noise, of course, awakens the child; usually the startle response stops his urinating, and he can get up and go to the bathroom. Only a few such awakenings usually teach or condition a child to awaken before he wets. These devices are perfectly safe and are successful in stopping all but the most difficult cases of enuresis.

The only concern I have about these devices is the one regarding a child's emotional needs. When enuresis is a manifestation of such needs, simply stopping it will almost always be followed by some other manifestation of those needs.

When, and if, your child does not respond to the electrical device, or if you become aware of personal problems your child is experiencing, you will want to use the other suggestions that follow.

Be sure your child completely empties his bladder just before going to sleep.

If possible, have the sound sleeper take a short nap or retire earlier, so he won't be quite so tired.

Get the child up and to the bathroom before he wets. If he urinates at the same time every night this works, but often the time varies. If you get him up, be sure he awakens, so he can form the habit of awakening himself.

Take stock of the emotional stresses that are affecting your child.

How to Take Stock of Your Child's Emotions

Encourage the child to talk about any and all of his worries and feelings. When he has trouble doing so, start talking about such events yourself, but wait for long enough periods to allow him time to open up.

Throughout the day, as you see emotions registered on your child's face, remember them. Try to get him to verbalize these feelings, and help him find the words to do it. Even if he must be angry or cry to get such feelings out, allow that and help him to do it appropriately.

Saturate this child with love, patience, and attention. Rocking and cuddling even an older child may give him enough security to enable him to stop wetting. Sometimes growing up implies the loss of such loving attention, and a child may prefer staying "little" and bed-wetting because of his need for babylike attention.

Help the child find answers to his needs and problems. In listening, asking, and suggesting, you will help him know he and his needs are important, and that he can learn with your help to take care of them.

Stop any anger and punishment for wetting. Your very anger produces fear and resentment in your child which may, by their unconscious effects, increase his wetting, which produces anger in you, which makes him more afraid—a vicious cycle indeed! Sometimes parents' anger sets up an unconscious power struggle. Your best maneuver, if this is your problem, is to give up. Strange as that may sound at first, it gives to a child the sense of positive power he needs. He's been using his power to resist; by stopping the fight, he may decide to use it to control.

I do not recommend bribing a child for controlling a biological function. Some parents have, however, found that it works!

Once in a while, I have found that *telling a child firmly and positively to quit wetting the bed has worked wonders.* For this to be successful, the child must believe that you mean it and that he can, in fact, quit.

While it is annoying to parents, *remember it is the child's problem.* Give it to him, when he is old enough, teach him to change and wash his own linens, and rejoice when he stays dry!

Take heart. *Your tenacity will win out!* I rarely see a college student wet the bed.

CHEATING

This is the practice of deception or fraud. It usually involves taking advantage of another person. In preschoolers, cheating begins when a child secretly refuses to play by the rules of a game or take turns. As a child grows older, he may cheat in sports and in classwork, as well as in games.

Reasons for Cheating

The reasons for cheating are numerous. These are the most common ones and should help you to understand and deal with this issue:

1. Some children are just naturally aggressive. They have an inordinate need to win. If it takes cheating, they may even do that.

2. A younger child may see an older or more manipulative child cheat and win, and may believe it pays. He cannot see

far enough ahead to realize the ultimate problems that cheating involves.

3. A child may feel so compelled to measure up to an adult's expectations that he will do anything for the approval that brings. (Parents who demand As from a child who is truly not capable of A work may unwittingly tempt him to cheat.) Expecting achievements in sports or other areas in life of which a child is truly incapable may prompt cheating. Severe disapproval or punishment for falling short may prompt anger or fear and cause a child to cheat.

4. By failure to recognize or admit that a child is cheating, parents unwittingly give their consent to it. I find that to be all too common! The parents' intention is to support their child, but they often end up permitting very negative behaviors.

5. Most children have a natural laziness. They prefer to find an easy way; cheating may seem to offer that.

6. Being too trusting of a child who is struggling with problems can allow him to get by with cheating until it becomes a habit.

How to Deal With Cheating

This, of course, depends on the reasons for doing it.

For all children, *be aware of their being tempted to dishonesty.* No one is above it, even adults. Be clear about your values and time-honored laws demanding honesty.

Take a look at your expectations and demands of your child. When you do this, be honest with yourself:

1. *Are you expecting more in behavior, performance, and grades than your child realistically can do?*
2. *Are you so harsh in your discipline that you prompt fear instead of respect?*
3. *Are you too lenient, allowing your child to get by with cheating without your knowledge?*
4. *Are you in touch with your child's teacher, coach, or counselor enough to know if he is cheating?*

Having noted these, what next? Once you are aware of a mistake or imbalance in your expectations or discipline, plan for changes.

Rearrange your priorities. Honesty means more than the recognition of top grades or winning and deserves top billing on your list.

Talk with your child about his cheating and your mistakes and make both clear. Your mistakes do not justify his!

Make it absolutely clear that cheating will not be tolerated, and set up some consequences if it happens again. Those should be directly related to the event. For example, cheating in a game means no more playing today. Cheating in school may demand extra schoolwork or taking an *F*. Don't be too easy on him if you expect your child to take you seriously. Repeating a course in school—or even a year—may be a small price to pay for acquiring honesty.

Make it equally clear that you will be fairer, less angry and demanding, or whatever you need to do to create a secure environment for your child. To cheat or not to cheat is, in the final analysis, each child's choice, but whatever you can do to make his environment fair and encouraging will help him to choose honestly.

Once your plan is made, *follow through!* Habits are hard to break and you or your child may slip back into old ways. If that happens, don't give up. Just get going again.

Be sure to praise your child for his efforts to reform. (And encourage each other as parents.)

CHILDHOOD OR PREADOLESCENT "CRUSHES"

These are unsually strong, dependent feelings toward another person. While it often seems like love, such a relationship is almost always based on needs and may become a serious problem when the other person either rejects your child or becomes overly attached to him or her.

Crushes, when they exist, usually begin at about ten to twelve years of age. They may involve another child of the same or opposite sex or an older person, such as a teacher. While many such relationships are platonic, they may develop into sexual ones rather suddenly. We once believed that before puberty, children did not have sexual feelings. That is not true, and we now know children develop strong emotional and sexual feelings rather early.

Causes for Crushes

The reasons for such crushes are not always clear, but we do
know the child sees in that other person certain powers and at-
tributes that are meaningful to him. These qualities may not
actually be present, but are imagined, or at least exaggerated.
Knowingly or not, as this type of relationship develops, the
other person takes on an unhealthy degree of power over a
child. The one who is the focus of the crush may seem to have
the positive traits of a parent or other relative with few of their
negative qualities. He or she meets a deep craving by the child
for security, significance, and seeming love. Some people see
this as normal, but I see it as risky at best, and it may be downright dangerous.

Often such a relationship takes place just when a child is
struggling toward independence. The other person may seem to
be the gateway to that independent state, but actually he more
often becomes a prison—a confusing blend of friend, good parent, and sweetheart.

Recognizing a Crush

The characteristics of a crush may vary, but you will recognize them clearly.

How They Start. Crushes usually start with respect, admira-
tion, and trust. Usually there is a lighthearted fun side as well.

Desperate Preoccupation. As the relationship grows, one
usually gives the other too much power over his feelings, and
there creeps into the friendship a desperate preoccupation with
one another.

Here are some signs to watch for:

1. Your child may talk or seem to think of no one else but
this friend.

2. He worries about the other's safety, activities, or
friendship. He seems afraid of "losing" the person. There is
none of the carefree joy of a truly trusting friendship.

3. A child neglects other friends and activities, mopes
about the house, becomes moody, and seems happy only
when he is with this special person.

4.   Such a relationship carries the risk of sending a child back into a "symbiotic" life-style, such as he knew with his mother as a tiny baby. He depends excessively for his emotional existence on someone else.

How to Handle a Crush

This is not an easy question to answer, so first of all slow down and *do nothing* until you have evaluated the entire situation. It may be the child's feelings are only temporary and will flicker out promptly. Often the other person is not even aware of the child's feelings, and this will cause them to burn out with no trouble. When such is not the case, however, consider these steps:

Get acquainted with the person who is the other end of the relationship. You can soon tell if this is someone who will fit into a good friendship or help create a dangerous relationship.

Take a close look at your child's unmet needs, and see where these may be feeding a problem. Meeting a child's emotional needs demands a balance in affection, approval, consistency, and enjoyment. If there is too little of one of these qualities in your relationship with your child, correct that!

Rarely, you may need to call off the relationship abruptly and completely to protect your child or the other person. Usually, however, it is better to move slowly, help your child see the dangers, and choose to get out himself.

Sometimes there are good aspects to a crush type of relationship. A shy child may become more outgoing through the other's example, or one who is bored with school may become motivated to learn through sharing the friend's interests.

If It Is a Healthy Relationship. When there are such positive and healthy features in the relationship, try these steps:

1.   *Sit down calmly with your child—and, if possible, the friend.* Explain the risks and problems in the relationship as you see it: the exclusion of others, the loss of personal freedom, the worry, and the risk of getting tired of one another.

2.   *Point out the positive factors of sharing interests, feelings, and experiences.*

3.   *Try to gain their cooperation in "cooling it."* Once they

understand these issues, many children are relieved to have
someone help them do this.

4. *Together, outline a plan that will limit their time
alone, include some other friends, cut down on phone calls,
and replace their dependency needs with you (Mom and
Dad) again.*

5. *You will need to enforce the plan because most children won't have the willpower or maturity to follow through
alone.*

You'll be glad you accomplished this difficult task! It can save
some real heartaches for all of you.

FIRE SETTING

This is the habit of playing with matches, cigarette lighters,
or other incendiary materials, or using them to start fires, large
or small. Throughout known history, people have been fascinated by fires, and children are no exception. They simply are
not ready to handle fires, however, and the ultimate problem
becomes the serious risk of destruction and death through arson
or pyromania.

Reasons for Setting Fires

Most fire setters begin this interest simply out of curiosity.
They excitedly follow a fire truck on their bikes, or are intrigued
with the flames in a fireplace or trash burner. They may discover, however, that such excitement can be duplicated through
building their own fires. The more angrily a parent tries to stop
this, the more secretive a firebug may become. At such a point,
obviously, danger sets in. Secret fire settings all too often get
out of control by accident, and become seriously destructive.

*Fire setting may be due to emotional problems, such as
deep-seated anger, a need for parents' attention, or an imagined need for respect from friends.*

*Fire-setting children often see their parents as threatening
and angry people.* Sometimes there are severe arguments in
their families.

*Children who become confirmed or stubborn in their fire-
setting patterns may have strong but confused sexual feelings.*

They sometimes hear their parents argue or fight in their bedroom and may believe that sexual issues are at stake in those troublesome problems. To these children the excitement of a fire is an escape from their worry, but may in time arouse sexual feelings.

Dealing With a Fire Setter

This demands real caution to avoid sending the habit underground. Here's what to do:

1. *Keep all fire-starting materials away from a child.* Small children can be cured by this simple process.
2. If you can see that your child is simply fascinated with the mystique of the flames, *schedule some times for a bonfire and a wiener roast or a fire in a fireplace.* Teach him how to build a fire and control it. Tell him the extreme danger of fires that are out of control. Let him see pictures of a devastating forest fire. Be with your child at all times around a fire until you are sure he is old enough and responsible enough to care for it properly.
3. *Look for emotional problems or symptoms that could result in fire setting.*

Along with exploring and working on these issues, remember this: *Tell your child to stop setting fires!* Let him know you simply will not tolerate it. Then go ahead with the more involved processes below.

Possible Emotional Problems. Are there *angry arguments between you and your spouse* that could frighten your child and make him angry, as well? If so, control those and keep them totally out of your child's hearing. You can argue and discuss issues successfully without being loud or explosive.

Are you *too angry with your child?* He may be angry with you but afraid to tell you. *Control your anger* and learn to be reasonable and fair by dealing with issues early, before you get to the boiling point. Encourage your child to talk out his feelings, even anger, rather than act them out.

Serious fire setters have *strong sexual feelings* that they do not understand. With sensitivity, check this out. Keep your own sexual issues more private, but teach your child wholesome attitudes toward sex, so it will not trouble him.

Sometimes a child has too much or too little freedom or power. He may need more supervision or, on the other hand, you may be too controlling of him. Try to balance those issues in proportion to your child's capabilities.

Discuss your child's feelings as you see them expressed in his eyes and on his face. Help him understand and talk about his loneliness, fears, angers, or any unhappy emotions. Help find the answers for his needs through your protection and love.

If you need to, *seek professional help.* Some of these issues that read rather simply can be most complex. It is never a shame to need help. Ask your doctor or pastor for a counselor who is experienced in child and family problems.

HAIR PULLING

Hair pulling and nail biting are both common manifestations of nervous tension in children.

Causes and Treatment of Hair Pulling

Pulling His Own Hair. This is usually an outgrowth of the infant's tendency to rub his hair while nursing or sucking his thumb. He likes its soft feel. As he grows old enough to coordinate his movements, he may begin, accidentally at first, to pull rather than stroke his hair when angry or frustrated. This can become a habit, and children sometimes produce bald spots from pulling out their hair. This is not dangerous, and the hair will grow out again. The frustration, however, needs some healthier outlet.

Eating Hair. Once in a while, a child will eat the hair he pulls out. Now hair is not digestible, so it may collect in a child's stomach to the point that it has to be removed surgically. Such a habit is quite rare, but since its consequences are fairly drastic (surgery), it's better for you to prevent it. Just watch your child, and if you see him pulling hair out, distract him. Give him a doll, a blanket, or some soft, stuffed toy that he can stroke or even pull on. The doll should have short hair, since it's less likely to form a hair ball in his stomach.

If your child swallows his hair, you may need to give him a pacifier or some other means of biting and chewing. Especially look for signs of needing more holding and gentle nurturing. Since hair pulling is most common at bedtime, hold and rock the child until he is nearly asleep so he won't have time to pull out his own hair before he sleeps.

Hair pulling is an aggressive and angry act. Since anger in children is caused by pain, physical or emotional, firm and gentle attention is usually curative.

Pulling Other Children's Hair. This is an outward expression of aggression. It is common in two-year-olds who are not yet ready to play with other children, but are put in the midst of others. Usually the pulling of a playmate's hair occurs as part of a struggle over a toy or a turn at playing. While most children lay aside such childish practices as they mature, some people carry the habit into older years. They punish their children, a spouse, or another person by grabbing a handful of hair.

Treatment. Treat this habit early by stopping such behavior in your child as soon as it begins. Supervise his interactions with other children, and help him learn to share and take turns. Teach him how to stand up against other children's selfishness, as well, without hurting them.

LYING

This is a deliberate denial or misrepresentation of the truth. Sometimes it involves withholding part or all of the truth in a misleading way.

Causes of Lying

These are similar to those of cheating.

1. In childhood, there is a period of "yarn spinning" or fantasy creation that is not lying. It may, however, lead to lies later on because a child learns to get attention in this way. The boundary between reality and pretense may be harder for some children to find than others.

2. Lying often begins by its usefulness in getting a child out of some punishment or responsibility.

3. Boasting may become lying, and is always due to a child's need for a sense of importance.

Treatment of Lying

Stop the Payoff. When you have figured out the reasons for your child's lying, sit down ceremoniously and tell him these benefits have stopped paying off. Let him know that you will no longer tolerate dishonesty from him for any reason. He will no longer get out of jobs, discipline, or the responsibilities of his life by lying. This is to include school responsibilities as well as those at home. Furthermore, if he does lie, tell him there will be a consequence. Decide whether that will be a spanking, an additional job, or some other fitting discipline. *Ask your child what will help him most in breaking the habit of lying.*

Cooperation of Others Necessary. Get the cooperation of all the involved adults or older siblings in making this regimen work. Consistency and a united front will make the cure much faster.

Follow Through. Be sure someone is assigned to follow through with this plan. One of you parents needs to check regularly to see if the lying has stopped. If not, has someone failed to carry out the discipline? Or is it just the rare backsliding of anyone who has to break a longtime habit?

More Recognition? If your child needs more recognition or less severe punishment, provide that. His importance to you as parents is paramount, so be certain he knows it. You can punish him when he needs it without devastating him.

Getting Rid of the Guilt. Help your child get rid of his guilt over past lies. Teach him why lying is wrong: because it takes away trust, hurts others and himself. This bad habit lets him be irresponsible. If you believe in prayer, lead him privately in a prayer of confession, and assure him of both your and God's forgiveness. Help your child to ask forgiveness of those to whom he has been dishonest, if possible, and then bury the past.

Slipups. Begin a new era with a clean slate. But remember that old habits are hard to break, so don't feel all is lost if there is an occasional slipup!

MASTURBATION

This is the touching or fondling of genital areas for pleasure or sexual orgasm.

Causes of Masturbation

These vary with the age of the child and with the way parents treat sexual matters.

In the Infant. Masturbation is the simple discovery of the anatomy, which also includes the ears, nose, fingers, toes, and navel. Touching the penis or clitoris may cause an erection, which is a pleasurable feeling. Some infants learn to repeat such touching, just as others suck their thumbs—because it feels good.

Preschoolers. These youngsters sometimes masturbate at bedtime, after they are out of diapers. It is a comfort to them and helps them relax and go to sleep. This is usually a transient habit and is commonly outgrown. When there is too much punishment for this (as for any misdeed), it may become secretive, willful, and guiltproducing. It may become a habit that is complicated by setting up a power struggle. This makes it very hard to stop and produces serious emotional problems.

Curiosity About Others. A by-product of masturbating may be a natural curiosity about the genitals of a child's playmates. It is quite common for such inquisitive children to have exploring parties. Usually this is remarkably innocent and purely curious. They take down their pants and look at each other's genital areas. When you act shocked or punish and shame a child for doing this, you may unwittingly heighten his curiosity and again drive him to secrecy. On the other hand, this practice invades an important area of privacy and can lead to excessive interest in sexual matters, prematurely.

I suggest that you deal with sexual curiosity by calmly getting the children's clothes back on, and then conducting an impromptu sex-education class, touching briefly on these ideas:

1. Let them know that curiosity is normal and healthy.
2. Tell them that taking off clothes and exploring each other's bodies is not the best way to learn about such ques-

tions at this time in their lives (or really until they are ready
for marriage). Tell them not to do that again.

3.   The best way for children to find out about most things
is to ask their parents. Suggest that they talk with their parents that day.

4.   With your own children, find out their questions and
then, with the help of books, or in your own words, explain
their sexual anatomy and the differences between boys and
girls.

5.   Assure your children that they may come to you at any
time for further information. (*See* my book *How to Teach
Your Child About Sex* for your own resources.)

School-Age Children. These youngsters generally stop masturbating because their interests and energy become directed to
areas beyond their own bodies. They may practice this a bit
during bathing or at bedtime, but it is rarely significant.

If a child masturbates at school or becomes preoccupied and
withdrawn to do so, it usually is a sign of emotional problems.
*These problems cause the practice of masturbation and not
vice versa!*

In Late-Grade-School Years. At this time, masturbation may
be a sign of too much sexual stimulation from television, magazines at the local drugstore, or from classmates. You need
to give your child healthy sexual attitudes and a good sex
education.

Treatment of Masturbation

This depends on the age, the causes, and the quality of the
habit.

Infants and Young Children. These children do not merit your
worry. Do nothing about it because it will stop as soon as the diaper goes on. Do be sure your baby has plenty of colorful toys,
sights, and sounds to keep his interests focused mainly on areas
other than any part of his body. Do not punish an infant for discovering the genital area, and do not treat it any different from
his discovery of the rest of his body.

Preschoolers. These children need to have their energies and
time devoted to exploring the big world outside their bodies.

Keep toys, activities, and your involvement such that they will forget themselves and their bodies most of the time. When a preschooler does masturbate, watch to see if it is brief and casual. If so, I strongly recommend ignoring it. If it is intense and habitual, causing frustration to the child, I suggest you help him stop by the following means:

Explain to the child that such frustration and effort must be tiring and even painful to him (or her). Ask him to stop it, and find out if he feels he can stop by himself or needs help. Some ways of helping are:

1. *Allow him to stay up until he is tired enough to sleep readily.*
2. *Give him a sleep toy to fondle.*
3. *Read to him until he falls asleep.*
4. *Give him plenty of parental affection and encourage social interaction with friends during the day.*

On a daily basis, do anything you can to get his interests transferred to the world outside himself. This is a gradual process of education and training toward external more than personal occupations.

Grade-School Children. Those who are having problems with masturbating will sometimes be reported by school staff or neighbors. Sexual issues are private and it is understandable that they may be troubled by such an experience. Please do not allow their anxiety to upset you, or cause you to be rude to your child or to them. Let them know, however, you appreciate their concern. Here are some suggestions to help you in such a situation:

Explain to your child, if he needs it, that others are uncomfortable with such behavior, and tell him you expect him to stop playing with his body, especially in front of other people.

If he is a nervous child and expresses this through genital touching, *help him find a better way* to communicate his needs and feelings. Teach him to draw little designs on scratch paper. Give him a "pet rock" or "worry stone." Children and adults do feel nervous and need some outlet for that.

Find out why your child is emotionally troubled and get relief for him from his anxiety and concerns. If your child is de-

pressed, lonely, or worried, deal with whatever is troubling him in a loving way.

By developing wholesome sexual attitudes yourself, you can become so comfortable that your child will talk with you. He can then satisfy his curiosity from your teaching, relieve his fears through your protection, and can put sexual matters aside until he is ready to handle them.

At All Ages. In every case, avoid placing guilt upon a child who masturbates. This can cripple a successful sexual life in marriage later on. Helping a child understand his feelings and needs can do the most to stop wrong and harmful habits and replace them with good and healthy ones!

Confession and Forgiveness. When your child feels guilty, help him determine whether he has actually harmed himself or someone else. If so, he needs to make it as right as he can. If not, he needs to stop blaming himself. The ancient practice of confession, forgiveness, and restoration can relieve all guilt! Be sure your child knows God as a forgiving, healing Being who will help him in every struggle.

NAIL BITING

Nail biting is the habit of biting off bits of one's own fingernails. It may start from a need to smooth a rough spot, but it often becomes a prolonged habit, extending even into adult life. Nail biters are nervous people. They really are upset or angry with someone else, but they are too controlled and considerate to hurt others, so they bite their own nails. They often do this to the point of biting nails off to the quick. Both nail biting and hair pulling are always signs of stress.

Usual Causes of Nail Biting

1.   Too many demands or too high expectations at home or at school.
2.   Discipline that is more punishment than teaching, and is done with too much harshness or anger.
3.   A child may have had to grow up too soon and may

need more nurturing, cuddling, and affection, such as he had when he was little.

   4.   There usually is too little laughter in the life of a nail-biting child—he takes life seriously and reacts with frustration.

   Your child's stress may be from one or all of these factors. If you are a conscientious parent, you may overreact and blame yourselves for all of them. Or you may discount all of these reasons, and even the whole problem. So that you can more objectively see the whole picture, ask a trusted relative or friend to share his point of view about you as well as your child, but don't get angry or hurt when he tells you the truth!

Treatment of Nail Biting

Eliminate Pressure. Once you locate the stress points, plan to eliminate or reduce them. You may not be able to entirely remove the pressure, but you may be more encouraging and supportive—and less critical or angry about situations. Do avoid going to the opposite extreme of permissiveness or pampering.

Nail Care. For nail biting, I suggest filing or trimming the nails daily to keep them smooth. A soothing, undelicious cream rubbed into the cuticle will help heal irritated fingertips, and will discourage the habitual biter. Nail polish can make the nails so smooth it will be hard to bite them.

Sugarless Gum. This can help satisfy a child's need to bite something and help break the habit of chewing nails or hair. I suggest using gum for the shortest time possible during the hardest part of breaking an old habit. It can become a habit itself!

Child's Cooperation. Ask the child to stop, and seek his cooperation. This is last because it is so important. All of the above measures will fail *unless your child puts some willpower into deciding to stop and then doing it.*

BITING PLAYMATES

Biting other children is another obnoxious habit, and one that will bring down upon you the wrath of other parents as well as their children.

Causes of Biting Others

Starts at Teething. I believe biting starts at the time of teething. It feels good to bite on something then, and many parents encourage it. They even allow an infant to bite on their own fingers in order to soothe those aching gums.

To my knowledge, no one has officially studied this, but it is very likely that two-year-olds who bite are those who "bit" or "gummed" someone while they were teething. When a child suffers the pain of frustration or anger, it will help him feel better to bite. To a child, it makes sense to bite the one who causes the pain.

Dealing With Biting Others

This cannot, of course, be tolerated, so you need to stop your child's biting. To do that, one of you needs to plan a day or two during which you focus on this problem. When you see an angry storm building up, take the child out of the situation, calm him down, and teach him an acceptable way to let out the normal frustrations he will feel. A pounding board, or yelling, will be better than biting.

Biting Back. If he does bite you, another child, or himself, it may be a good idea to firmly but lovingly swat him or allow the other child to bite him back. Sometimes knowing how it feels to be bitten will help a child stop. This does not always work, and if you do physically punish him, be sure you do not do so in a childish, getting-even fashion. That will only make the situation worse, and he will feel even more like biting. Be firm, take charge, and simply do not allow the biting. Punishment will rarely be necessary if you do this well.

SELFISHNESS (Also Bullying)

Definition

Selfishness is the habit of being too concerned with one's own desires and welfare, and showing too little interest in others. In my experience, selfishness is a symptom of emotional hunger, and often covers very low self-esteem. It evidences a lack of trust in others, so that both caring and sharing involving another person are absent.

Grabby Twos. In normal two-year-olds, there is an intense struggle to define some sense of personal power. Twos become very "grabby" and seem selfish in their attempts to test out their own versus someone else's power. Usually they give up such practices when they resolve the power issues, and I do not consider them truly selfish—simply *two*.

Causes

Other reasons for selfishness are these:

1.   A child is spoiled by being given his own way too much. He can quickly come to expect it and demand it in selfish ways.
2.   Giving in to a demanding child by an adult is almost always done out of frustration and fatigue rather than love. Hence the quality of the enjoyment of getting what he wanted is tainted but not destroyed. He, therefore, will often continue his demanding ways, getting a little satisfaction and searching for more.
3.   There may be too little adult supervision, so a demanding child is able to continue his bullying habits and getting his own way.
4.   Sometimes adults see this as strength and feel the child is exerting leadership. They, therefore, may even encourage selfish, bullyish behavior, through their misinterpretation.
5.   No one has taken time to teach a child to share, give in, or take turns. Few children do so naturally.

Treatment of Selfishness

This gets more difficult the older the child becomes. So start as early as possible.

Talk to Him. Talk with your child about selfishness, and how much it hurts other people; tell him you will be watching for signs of it in order to help him understand and correct the bad habit. Seek his cooperation to overcome this trait.

Remove Him. When you see your child being selfish, remove him kindly from the presence of other children. Explain what he did and how it hurt the playmates. Tell him what to do instead, and then go back with him and help him do it. If he is about six or seven, he probably can and will do it without your help—so don't embarrass him needlessly. Embarrassing a child is more likely to cause rebellion than cooperation.

Disciplinary Action. If this direct and positive approach does not take care of the problem, establish some disciplinary action that will be meaningful to your child, and enforce it consistently. This may mean removing him temporarily from playing with friends when he is selfish. It may be requiring him to give up a possession for a time, so he can learn how others feel when he grabs their things.

Watch for Unselfish Acts. Watch just as carefully for any *un-*selfish act, and let your child know your respect and pride in his efforts to change. It may help to make your child aware that he even *feels* better when he is unselfish than when he gets his way—at the cost of angering or even losing friends. (While one must do the right thing because it *is* right—and not because of how one feels—yet good feelings do help!)

Takes Time. Forming new habits takes most children several weeks. Stay close by to help your child really finish the job of forming new habits of generosity.

Your Example. Your example of sharing, taking turns, and putting your child or spouse first can be a marvelous teaching-learning experience. Avoid, however, taking this lovely practice for granted! Express appreciation!

His Own Turf. Each child needs some territory and certain things that are his very own. It's easier to be generous with most things when a child is allowed to protect these few things.

In teaching about any problem behavior, try to help the child see its importance in all of his life. It is easy to allow life to be a series of disconnected, senseless episodes, unless you take time to put them into a meaningful perspective.

SIBLING RIVALRY

Larry and his sister Melissa were always arguing, it seemed. All the kids in her third-grade class liked her and she had more friends than she had time to play with. Larry, on the other hand, was regularly in trouble. He spent long hours after school to pay for his misbehaviors or to make up his carelessly done schoolwork. Their parents smiled warmly at Melissa and often thanked her for her helpful ways. Larry, in contrast, learned to expect their frowns of disapproval or at least their worried looks at him.

Larry, as he grew older, often worried about himself, but he avoided that painful sense of anxiety by becoming angry at Melissa. He did anything he could to tease her, and he especially seemed to enjoy making her angry at him. Only when she ran crying in frustration to their parents would he stop his tormenting.

Larry and Melissa are typical of countless children who experience the painful problems of sibling rivalry. They compete with one another constantly, frustrate their parents and baby-sitters beyond endurance, and may even threaten one another's safety.

Causes of Sibling Rivalry

Healthy Competition. There is a normal and healthy sort of sibling rivalry that promotes motivation and ends in a successful spirit of competition. Some children who live the most competitively when they are young, grow up to be the best of friends later. They often are, in fact, each other's staunchest ally among their friends. Such sibling competition only requires some supervision to keep it within safe limits, and the passage of time, with its maturing processes, to become the asset it will be.

Adult Partiality. Melissa was an example of the angelic child who seems to have been born pleasing almost everyone. She knew what to do and say and was rewarded for that with the love and warmth of her parents and friends. Larry, by contrast, was abrasive and constantly annoyed or worried people. He did not fit his parents' values and earned their attention negatively.

When parents, grandparents, or other adults find more qualities to respect in one child than another, it usually is due to one of these reasons:

1. *The favored child manifests the traits, interests, and qualities they happen to value greatly.*
2. *The favored child resembles someone of whom they were very fond.*

The approval of the adults will consistently prompt even greater positive efforts by the special child, still further enhancing the favorable relationship. The contrast of this good child with the one who is less favored can only serve to accentuate his negative qualities.

Child's Own Unfavorable Comparison. Larry knew how well his sister got along with people, how successful she was in school, and how happy she made their parents. Even if those parents had not worried and fretted over him, he could very well have felt angry because of his own unfavorable self-evaluation. It seems to be instinctive for children to retaliate. They want to get even for their hurts by hurting the other person. And children are usually unaware of the dynamics of the pain process. They only want to pull down the other person to their own level (as they experience life), now and then.

Attention Getting. I am seeing a large number of children who learn early in life that they can get their most intense attention from their parents by fighting. In their cases, sibling rivalry means some intervention, with time and emotional interaction, by their parents. In such families, I discover that the adults are very busy, hardworking people who feel that their work evidences their love for the children. Certainly they are right, but providing for them is only one facet of the love children need. And when they can find no way to achieve that loving attention, they will settle for even scolding or punishing rather than no attention at all.

Treatment of Sibling Rivalry

Harness Healthy Competition. Parents, you need to understand how to help your children compete, like a good team, to work and play together for everyone's good. Teach your youngsters that they can get work done more efficiently by seeing who can do it faster and better. Finding more time to play can be the reward for such work. And teaching them how to compete at play but also to be good sports, win or lose, can exalt that sort of sibling rivalry to a high and lofty interaction.

Check Out Your Feelings. As you examine your child's behaviors and your responses to them, you will quickly discern the presence of an attitude of partiality if it is there. When you reprimand one child more often than the others and find your feelings toward him are irritated and anxious more than proud and happy, it is likely that you are unknowingly feeding into a vicious cycle of defeat.

Notice the reactions of other relatives and friends and help them to stop treating one child more kindly than the others.

Know Each Child's Good Qualities. When all of you become aware of the assets in each of your children, you can learn to value them equally. As you consistently express your pride and love, you will discover that the love grows, and your child's efforts to earn more of your approval redouble. Be careful to keep your training and discipline firm and clear, but not angry or hurtful.

Help Children to Feel Equal. While all children have different assets, each one has some gift that is unique and special to him. Help each child to value himself, and also to be proud of his siblings. As the more gifted child learns to sincerely compliment his siblings for their successes, they are likely to learn to be proud of him rather than resentful. Parents must be aware of the need to teach such sensitivity and responsiveness to all of their children. It does not happen automatically.

SLEEP DISTURBANCES

Jeff was five, and he had just seen a horror movie for the first time. His father, perhaps unaware of the nature of the film, had taken him. That night Jeff awoke screaming in terror. The story of the movie had locked itself in his mind and invaded his dreams. His sleep was troubled for several nights, until his mother was able to encourage him to talk about it. For a long time, he poured out the weird and frightening events as she listened. Her calm reassurance and understanding, simply expressed, provided relief and Jeff had no more troubled sleep.

Causes of Sleep Disturbances

Nightmares. As early as one or two years, we know children begin dreaming. They rarely, however, have a vocabulary to describe the events of those dreams, so they only cry out in fear or frustration. When parents, understandably tired from several nights of such disturbed sleep, react in anger and punish the wakeful child, his fear and its accompanying stress will mount and can cause still more troubled dreams.

Other causes of bad dreams that disturb children's sleep are overly taxing days with too many activities (even happy ones), too many expectations of their performance of any type, too much anger or harsh discipline, fighting or arguing (their own or others'), stress related to school or social experiences, and anxiety about problems.

Physical Problems. These can also disturb sleep. A cold with stopped-up nose, earaches, or cough may cause distress enough to awaken a child. In fact, I found that the most common cause of lengthy periods of wakefulness and crying at night in our children was an earache. Gentle pressure over a child's ear will elicit loud crying if it is infected. Such a condition deserves a visit to your doctor the next day!

Little children with wet or soiled diapers and irritated skin will often awaken at night. Being cold, hungry, or thirsty are also likely causes of disturbed sleep, as is the need to go to the bathroom in an older child. A fear of the dark may trouble some sensitive children.

Loud noises will awaken many children, especially if they are strange sounds. A barking dog, siren, or thunderstorm still awakens me at night.

Treatment of Sleep Disturbances

Obviously, the cause of the sleeplessness must be discovered if you are to help your child, and yourself, back to sleep.

Check All Physical Areas. Be sure to find out if your child is wet, cold, hungry, thirsty, or in some kind of pain. Be sure to feel the child to detect fever and take the temperature if he feels unusually warm.

Take any measures necessary and possible to restore the greatest possible comfort. Give some children's Tylenol or baby aspirin if your doctor has previously recommended this, when there is evidence of physical discomfort. Clean the nose if it is stuffy, and administer cough syrup your doctor has prescribed. I believe in keeping such simple remedies in your medicine chest.

Quiet Atmosphere. If you live in an area where loud noises are common, I suggest a radio with soft music be left playing quietly. It will muffle outside noises and help the child to sleep through many of them.

Think About Child's Life-Style. See if he is stressed more than he can tolerate. Is he with a baby-sitter too much, or when there, is the environment one that is too loud or stimulating? Could the discipline be too strict or the protection too lax? In older children, are the school demands too great or is he threatened by other children? Is your own discipline too rigid or your attitudes too harsh? Remedy any of these out-of-balance situations as soon as you can.

Soothe Fears. If your child awakens in fear, reach out to hold and comfort him. Speak firmly and gently to him. Offer him a drink, and perhaps a short rocking time. Avoid playing, turning on lights, or stimulating him, and lay him back on his bed as soon as he is quiet.

When children who are out of a crib come to your own bed at night, do not reject them. I shall never forget awakening one night during a severe thunderstorm. I was terrified and felt so comforted and safe as I crawled in bed between my parents. They later returned me to my own bed gently and reassuringly, and I quickly fell asleep. You will recognize real fear as compared with the manipulations of a spoiled child.

The Manipulator. It is not uncommon for children to learn to love the extra attention of a parent at night. They can form a habit of awakening simply for that. If your child has such a habit, I suggest you help him break it. I do recommend you talk with your doctor or have him see your child to be certain he is in no physical distress.

When you are ready, explain to your child very firmly that you need your sleep, you will not be getting up with him, and you do not want him to get up. Then plug your ears and harden your heart! Allow the child to cry alone until he returns to sleep. The first night this will last from one-half to one hour. Most parents will sneak over and check on the child. If you do, it will lengthen the process, so do not stay long. Simply reassure yourselves and return to bed. The second night, the crying time will be cut in half, and usually, by the third or fourth night, it will stop. If your child cries longer and takes more nights to stop, don't worry. Just stick it out until you both win.

Keep Child in Good Health. Enjoy him and play with him every day. Soothe and relax him at sleep time. Avoid high stress levels for both you and your child, and be gently firm when you must.

Your child and you will survive and will laugh someday about those troubled nights you spent.

SOILING (Encopresis)

This is the habit of having a bowel movement in his pants *after* a child has been well trained to the use of the toilet. This distasteful habit, in my experience, is always related to emotional stress that makes a child wish he were a baby again.

Causes of Soiling

Harsh Discipline. Severe discipline and expectations that are too high—from the child's-eye view—may contribute to this problem. And *there,* of course, is where a child must live—on his own level! Worry, fear, and resentment, triggered by such treatment, may understandably create some resentment and the wish to be little again.

New Baby. The birth of a new baby may threaten an older child's security. One way to be sure of some personal attention is to mess himself. True enough, it's bad attention, but to a child it is better than none.

Change in Life-Style. From the age of four to six, a major change in life-style may trigger this regression: starting school, a family move, or a divorce may also result in this habit.

Anger Reactions. A child may begin soiling from fear or worry, but when parents react in anger, a child may react to the parents' anger with more anger, compounding the problem. You will understandably be angry at a soiler sometimes, but be sure to build a loving, positive relationship in all other areas of his life.

Physical Reasons. There are, rarely, physical reasons for soiling.

1.   Discomfort from constipation, diarrhea, rectal gas, or rectal irritation may all cause soiling at times. This is usually temporary, unless you overreact to it.

2.   Irregular toilet habits and poor hygiene, such as failure to wipe after a bowel movement, or careless bathing, can create the personal odor and offensiveness of soiling.

3.   Almost all birth defects that may cause soiling will show up within a child's first year of life.

Treatment of Soiling

This is demanding and may go against all of your instincts!

Checkup. Have a good physical checkup and follow through with any medical recommendations.

Review Past. Think back to the time the soiling began.

1. *Was there any big event in the family, such as a new baby, a move, a big argument, a job change, or Mother's starting to work?*
2. *Did your child start school, get a new baby-sitter, suffer an illness, or experience a great fear?*
3. *Is your child going through any other problem that involves severe discipline or fear of rejection?*
4. *Are the disciplinary measures you or a teacher are using too harsh or unfair to this special child?*

Communication. Does this child talk about his problem or his feelings? Most children who soil keep their feelings strictly inside. A child needs a healthy outlet for anger, fear, and worry, as well as love. Teach your child the language of feelings and give him permission to use it properly. (This does not mean that he is to be impudent or rude.)

Dealing With Stress. Teach positive ways of dealing with stress:

Give extra play and cuddling time to the child without commenting on the soiling. Let him know he is secure in your love.

If necessary, with a child under five, use diapers again. It's easier in the long run and may help the child know he can regress if he needs to. Often paradoxically the need subsides with the permission.

Any child who is capable should be taught to clean his clothing and himself, and be required to do this. It's best to be matter-of-fact, rather than shaming.

Cut down on stress—try a little less responsibility; less severe discipline; give more encouragement; talk about school adjustments; and give lots of chances to discuss any family changes.

Believe (and you can!) and tell your child that you know he has a need to be little for a while. Tell him that he may be little by asking you to hold or spoil him, and that he need not mess his pants to be little. Tell him that as soon as he is ready, he is to use the toilet again. (You are all too aware by now that he is not going to do it until he is ready.) He may realize your wisdom from such a statement.

Be certain that the child has permission to use the toilet as needed. At school it can be embarrassing for a five- or six-year-old to have to ask permission to go to the toilet. He may need someone to reassure him about the high-pressure water system at school. He could fear being flushed away!

It has been my experience that shaming or spanking, by their very nature, increase the stress and actually aggravate the soiling.

Every time your child uses the toilet instead of his pants, quietly compliment him.

It takes great willpower and effort for a child to overcome soiling or wetting. You may be justifiably proud of your child's improvement, and if you have weathered it, I am proud of you!

SPEECH DIFFICULTIES

Stuttering and Stammering

These are problems in speaking that involve involuntary pauses and the repetition or prolonging of sounds or syllables. It occurs much more commonly in boys, though no one knows why.

Causes of Stuttering

These are thought to be mostly emotional.

In Children Under Four. Stuttering at this age is quite common, and is usually due to a child's inability to think of the words to use. Along with his limited vocabulary, a child may have trouble keeping the attention of his listeners. Older children and adults commonly fail to see a younger child's conversation as important. They often give a child the brush-off, so he may try to keep their attention by continual talking. Being unable to think of enough to say or the right words to use may initiate stuttering, and then it becomes a habit.

Fearful Child. A child who is afraid of the anger or disapproval of his listener may stutter because of that anxiety.

Traumatic Experience. A serious loss, accident, or illness during the period of developing speech can result in stuttering, which is also related to fear.

Parental Anger. During this same time, a parent's intensely angry scolding and demanding of a child to give a reason for misbehaving may result in stuttering.

Change in Handedness. There is still some belief that trying to change a child's handedness from left to right may result in stuttering.

Treatment of Stuttering

This is difficult because of the tension the problem creates on both sides. The listener will become tense and try to help the talker, who is tense and embarrassed by his problem. Neither knows how to help his own nervousness, let alone the other's! Here are some suggestions to help the sufferer and the family:

In Early Childhood. Simply ask the child to slow down in his talking. Give him your calm, undivided attention. If he seems to be groping for a word, supply it. Reassure him. Oftentimes he will stop stuttering in a surprisingly short time.

In An Older Child. Practice similar attention with a calm, reassuring manner. In addition, be careful to avoid scolding or irritation with this child. The more irritation he feels, the more nervous he will become, and the more he will stutter.

Discipline. In any discipline of such a child, avoid intense anger. You can use firmness, yet be gentle. Stutterers are exceptionally sensitive people, and usually will respond best to that approach.

Communication. Help your stutterer to admit and describe any fears, anger, or nervousness he feels. Avoid nagging, but remind him of your interest in his concerns. Then listen when he does talk.

Patience. While you need to help a young child to find a word, this practice is not so good with older children. Just patiently give them time to find the word. *They* will need to do so to overcome this problem.

Don't Pity. It is very hard, but try not to pity the stutterer. The more truly you can accept him, the more relaxed he can feel, and the less he will stutter. Pity can be felt as a put-down.

Don't Change Handedness. Do not force a strongly left-handed child to become right-handed. As long as possible, offer a child his spoon, crayons, and other tools in his right hand. As he develops, however, and simply cannot use that right hand as well as his left, do not insist on the right hand.

Speech Therapist. Do not wait long to seek a speech therapist. If your own efforts have not relieved the stuttering in a few weeks, get help. The longer a child goes on stuttering, the harder it will be to stop the habit. Practice patience, be deliberate and slow, and be *encouraging* with your stutterer. In such a warm, positive atmosphere, he will have the best chance to recover.

Delayed Speech

This is the refusal or inability to talk well past the age when most children are talking. That time is hard to define because there are large variations in so-called normal times to start talking. Most people would not blame you, however, for seeking advice if your child has not done some talking by three or three and a half years of age.

Most children will say a few words by a year of age. They will use short sentences by two, and are able to talk a great deal by three.

Causes of Delayed Speech

Physical Causes. These are a major worry and include the following:

1. *Brain damage to the speech area of the brain.*
2. *Most parents worry about mental retardation, and it certainly can slow down the development of speech.*

3. *Deafness also will slow down or prevent the learning of speech, depending on how severe it is.*
4. *Being tongue-tied or having an abnormally shaped palate may delay speech, but these defects are more likely to cause abnormal sounds in talking.*

Nonphysical Causes. These include extremes of several kinds.

On one hand, *you may pressure your child so strongly to talk that he may rebel and stop.*

On the other hand, *you may not realize that you need to teach your child to talk,* and you may leave him too much to his own devices.

Sometimes a clever child can get whatever he wants without talking. He gestures, points, or in other ways makes clear what he wants. Older siblings are especially bad about waiting on a younger child. Third and later children are notably slower to acquire speech.

Sometimes parents do not spend enough time talking specifically with a child. Therefore, he has no incentive or opportunity to develop verbal skills. On the other hand, parents may talk too much, too fast, or in words the child cannot understand. To learn to talk, a child needs live language directed pointedly to him, listening and waiting for his response, as well as talking to him.

Treating Delayed Speech

This requires sensitivity and patience.

Consult a Physician. This is to be sure there is no physical defect. If there is, correct it.

Next, a Speech Pathologist. If the correction of physical problems does not cure the child, consult a speech pathologist and follow his recommendations.

Start spending enjoyable time with your child, and center this time on words. A-B-C books with attractive pictures of things your child likes are a good place to start.

Look for an item your child may get excited about. *Show it to him, say the word slowly and clearly, and repeat it,* as you hand it to the child.

Ask the child to say the word with you, but do not act irritated if he won't. Be patient.

When you feel certain your child knows the word, require him to say it before you give him the item. If he won't say it, calmly put the item away, and tell the child when he is ready to say the word, he may have it.

Avoid Punishment. Punishment for something you cannot really enforce is useless, and will only create a lifelong battle. Save it for situations that deserve it.

My husband had a patient who would not talk. His parents took the child, at his recommendation, to every major speech-and-hearing clinic in the area. Each was, in its turn, futile. He would not talk. He functioned well in kindergarten—but he would not talk. Finally, in the first grade, he talked. He asked a question in a perfect fashion and has talked ever since. He now is a fine teenager in every respect.

"Be patient. Don't worry!" I suspect you will resent reading that again, but sometimes that's all there is to do.

TV Helpful. Television may come in handy for the learning of words. "Sesame Street," "Mr. Rogers' Neighborhood," or your own local children's programs are excellent teaching tools. *Watch such shows with your child, and say the words for various things as both of you watch television.*

Read stories, sing songs, and talk to your child. Someday he'll respond.

Be sure your child has time with other children. Very often a child learns better from another child than from adults.

Abnormal Speech

This speech is difficult to understand or is "different" from the usual sounds of a given language or dialect. Common sounds that give children trouble are *S, R,* and *L.*

Causes

The reasons may be physical, and these include being tongue-tied, having some weakness of the fine muscles used in speech, or some neurological "short circuits" through which sounds are heard, interpreted, and reproduced. Partial deafness may also lead to abnormal speech sounds. More commonly, children are inadvertently taught or encouraged to use so-called baby talk. Children's talk is uniquely charming, but such charm is lost when the baby talk continues after babyhood is over.

Treatment

This demands patient teaching. Many children who say *wabbit* instead of *rabbit* learn correct *R* sounds as they hear them and are required to practice talking properly.

Physical Problems. Correct any physical problems your doctor thinks need help.

Teaching. When you are ready to devote some time to teaching, help your child to focus on his particular problem sounds one at a time. Exaggerate your own mouth, tongue, and teeth components in saying the sounds for him, and ask him to copy you. When he succeeds, praise him. When he doesn't, tell him, encouragingly, that he will be able to do so later on. Avoid nagging, ridicule, or punishments.

Be Consistent. Be careful to avoid a double message by thinking your child's baby talk is cute, and yet expecting him to use adult talk on demand.

Encourage Playmates. Encourage your child to be around other children enough to learn from them.

Speech Therapist. If the problem really interferes with clear communication, consult a speech therapist. As with stuttering, don't wait so long for such help that your child forms bad habits.

STEALING

This is taking something by force or secrecy and claiming it for your own.

Reasons for Stealing

Some of the reasons for stealing are similar to those for cheating discussed earlier, but here are some specific aspects you need to understand.

In Younger Children. Especially in this age group, stealing is an aggressive act for getting an object a child wants. He does not usually realize that such an act is stealing.

Attention Getter. Children may steal in order to get attention from parents or teachers.

In Older Children. Stealing is commonly a way of gaining favor with other misbehaving young people. One girl proudly said that she was the "best shoplifter" in her crowd. Unfortunately, stealing has become a way of getting money for drugs or alcohol for many addicted young people and, yes, even children.

Treatment for Stealing

The treatment for stealing is *urgent,* and as with most other troublesome habits, it is easier to prevent than cure.

In a Young Child. Be sure that he understands the *mine* and *not mine* boundaries in life. If a young child starts to take an item from a store, you need to teach him the concept of purchasing things, instead of taking them. Help him select a small, inexpensive item, and go through the entire process of purchasing it. Make it clear that this process is the only way to take anything out of a store. (Do not think, however, that you have to buy something every time your child wants or grabs it. Just be certain that he knows *that is the only way to get something from a store.*)

Children may similarly pick up toys or other items from homes in which they may visit. My husband and I established this helpful policy regarding items from another home. *We did not allow our children to borrow or accept as a gift anything from friends' homes.* If a gift was purchased for the child, of course, it could be a happy treat, but to take any other item home was forbidden. That saved a great deal of trouble in deciding whether a toy had been given, borrowed, or stolen. Anything that did show up in a pocket was promptly returned.

Just as we expect each child to respect others' property, we need to respect his. Give him some space and things that he need not share. Require other children to respect that, too.

Unmet Needs. See if your child may have some needs that are not being met. Such needs may make stealing a temptation. This investigation is not to excuse the stealing, but to make the cure more thorough. Consider these possibilities under "unmet needs":

1. In the busy whirl of providing materially for your child, you may have inadvertently robbed him—of the time and love he needs with you.
2. Does your child feel so inadequate that he may have settled for friends who think stealing is brave or smart?
3. Have other children threatened him to make him steal for them? (There are many bullies in your child's world.)
4. Is your child using stolen things to "buy" friends? Every child wants to be liked and to have friends. It can be deceptively easy to be popular by giving gifts. You will need to tell your child how frail such relationships are, though he may have to find that out the hard way. Do help your child develop skills that promote healthy friendships.
5. Check out your child's social contacts. Even in the fifth and sixth grades there are children who are addicted to drugs and alcohol. Be sure your child is not stealing to support such a habit—for himself or his friends.

Kleptomania

This is a special kind of compulsive stealing. It often is a means of getting attention or expresses the need for being loved by some important person.

Treatment of Kleptomania—A Serious Psychological Problem

Discipline and understanding alone will rarely cure kleptomania. *Do seek qualified counseling. This should involve you parents as well as your child.*

Importance of Child's Cooperation. Get your child's cooperation in breaking a habit of stealing. In the final analysis, you cannot make him stop (short of locking him up) without that willingness. Then follow these steps:

1. *Establish the fact of his stealing—either by reliable witnesses or by the child's own admission.* Try to keep an open mind, without prejudice, regarding possible guilt or innocence, until the facts are clear.

2. *Tell the child you will do whatever is necessary to help him stop stealing and ask what he needs in order to stop.* Do not ask him at first *why* he stole, because he probably won't know. The stealing must stop while you and he are working out the basic problems.

3. *Let your child know you still love him and that God loves him.* You will forgive him, and so will God, but he must forgive himself. Let him know how hard that will be until he can understand himself. At this point, help him start to explore why he stole.

4. *If you and your child cannot discover why he began stealing, seek outside counsel.* This is such a serious problem that it could land your child in prison when he is older. Do not take a chance that it will pass.

5. *It is tempting to believe that a sound thrashing will cure stealing.* Perhaps in a very small child, it will. In older children, however, I have seen physical punishment cause more estrangement and rebellion than cures. So if you do try it, be prepared to seek other help if it fails.

Bad Influences. If your child is involved with friends who are a bad influence on him (or he on them!), you will need to help him break off those relationships. This, also, demands your child's understanding and cooperation. Help him see the dangers to himself and his future. Your child deserves more from life than the consequences of a habit of stealing. If he is lonely or feels inferior, help him to begin to succeed and teach him how to make better friends. Unfortunately, this takes time, and all too often parents of "good kids" are afraid to let them associate with a child who has had problems. Teach your child to be patient, steady, and earn back the respect of others.

Develop a Friendship With Your Child. He still needs you as parents, but he also needs your love and support as friends through the struggles of changing. Have some good times, get him busy with a job, and remind him proudly of his successes.

Pocket Money. Be sure your child has a little money of his own—not so much he can buy things he ought not have, but not so little he'll be tempted to steal things he could have.

STUBBORNNESS

This is the refusal to obey, yield, or comply with another's commands or wishes. Synonyms for *stubborn* are *obstinate, determined, doggedly resisting,* and this trait can be extremely hard to live with!

Causes of Stubbornness

Some of the causes of stubbornness can be outlined as follows:

Power Struggle. Stubborn children often are bright, energetic, and inquisitive. When such a child happens to be born to critical, unbending parents, he can even start right out in life with an ongoing power struggle that is intrinsically a part of stubbornness. It takes two parties (parent and child) to keep such struggles alive. I seriously doubt that a strong-willed child exists, who does not have at least one strong-willed parent!

Disciplinary Problems. Some that increase stubbornness include:

1. *Failure to start early in teaching obedience.*

As soon as a child is able to move about on his own, he will invade areas or objects that are dangerous to him. It is then that you need to set limits and enforce them. Waiting for the child to get older will allow habits to form that reinforce his power and stubbornness, so they will be even harder to change.

2. Failure to follow through sets the stage for a complication of this already tough struggle.

When a child is told to do something but finds out he really doesn't have to do it, he becomes confused. Usually he will learn to test out the situation, and by this testing out feeds into the struggle even more. *It is essential that you understand the difference in testing out behaviors and rebellion.* In the first, the child needs you to be firmer, more consistent, and to follow through on your requirements to the finish. In *rebellion,* parents are too rigid and harsh, so the child feels imprisoned. In this case, he needs more flexibility.

3. Expectations are unrealistic.

Asking more of a child than he can do, or expecting less than his abilities indicate, are both frustrating to him. He needs to be understood and challenged.

4. Discipline through emotional explosions can set up a child-to-child combat that no one wins.

Or your child may even win (thereby losing!) by being stubborn.

5. Power struggles are the building blocks of stubbornness.

The more of these you allow to develop, and the more in which you give in, the more likely it is that you will have a stubborn child.

Treatment of Stubbornness

Treatment is obviously based on stopping those damaging power struggles. Now that does not mean you should go to the other extreme and allow your child total freedom to become a little dictator! Take these steps:

First, decide between yourselves, Dad and Mom, whether or not you are willing to be in charge. That requires time, energy, and real commitment. Being in charge automatically rules out childish arguments and fights, and sets up clear authority.

Expect your child to test out your authority, and do not allow that to stop your plan. He needs you to stay in charge.

Lay aside past failures, fears, and resentments caused by your child's resistance. This will avoid the angry sort of unconscious retaliation that feeds power struggles and stubbornness.

Select one issue at a time, and work on that alone. It may be picking up a messy room, or doing homework, but set up a plan. Ask your child what he is willing to do in order to stop fighting and take care of that problem. Have some ideas about what you will do. (It may help you to know that your child really doesn't like the fights either.)

State clearly what the goal is, how you will stop the old defeating habits, and how you plan to establish new patterns. Give your child the respect of recognizing his importance by seeking his help and ideas. Use them in formulating your plan.

Think often of your child's good qualities and tell him about these. Let him know how much you love him in positive ways as well as in discipline.

For a strong-willed child, a reason or explanation is helpful, but beware lest he trap you into an old habit of arguing.

Wait it out. This is the most difficult but most important part of the plan. Giving in is hard for a stubborn child, and he won't be able to do it quickly. If you will firmly hold to your plan and be patient, you both will make it.

Carefully balance consistency (avoid being rigid) *and flexibility* (but do not be permissive).

Remember, your child wants you to be stronger than he is! Many of the things he does are a test of your strength.

SWEARING

This is the use of crude or downright profane words as exclamations or in routine speech. It never occurs until the child hears and can repeat such language from another person.

Causes of Swearing

Hearing Others Swear. This may intrigue your child. Friends, especially older ones, may swear in a childish effort to prove their "toughness." This can be done with such a show of strength and energy that it invites duplicating.

Need for Peer Approval. This may prompt your child to adopt the coarse talk, and other habits, of "tough" young people. If your child seems to need the approval of such friends, you need to explore his own self-concept. He may feel very weak and inadequate. Tough associates can seem to offer safety and power to such a child.

Need to Rebel. If you have been too strict and perfectionistic, your child may feel he has to do something drastic to break away from your hold over him.

Temporary Fascination. Oftentimes, a child's swearing is a passing whim, started by fascination with the swagger of the one who teaches it. Give it some careful ignoring and a chance to die a natural death. If your child does not stop by himself, however, *do* pay attention.

Dealing With Your Child's Swearing

Discuss the issue, person-to-person, with your child. Explain your values and your reasons for wanting him to stop using bad words.

See if your child can figure out why he is swearing and recognize the reasons as being unworthy of his own values. If he can't explain the reasons, give him some ideas, and ask him to think them over. Allow your child time to think through the values that are at stake here. These concepts are usually complex and deep. The more he can really comprehend them, the more likely he will be to truly adopt them as his own.

If he is feeling weak or inferior, think out a plan for reflecting to him his strength, so he can believe it. Be aware that telling this to a child never really convinces him. He has to see it for himself in his own behavior and successes. The best way I know is for you to point out to him regularly the good qualities he shows and the achievements he has made.

Help him set up a plan for breaking the habit. Fining him a nickel or a dime and having him work at a special job to pay that off sometimes works. (Children often have very respectable ideas for discipline that works for them!)

Help your child find some acceptable word he can use to express strong feelings. Everyone needs some means of expression.

I know some of you will say, "Just whip him and make him stop." Perhaps that will work for you. I never argue with success. *But I can show you countless young people who have been driven by angry whippings into secret rebellion.* Gentle spankings are superb for smaller children, but in older ones, the loving but firm approach works far better and more often.

Help your child see for himself, then, the crudeness of bad language and how quickly its use becomes a habit. Tell him clearly but kindly that you want him to stop, and then work at the plan for doing that.

TATTLING

This is the practice some children develop of telling the misbehaviors of another child to an adult who is in charge. It has, as its aim, the often-unconscious wish to make one's self look good at the expense of the other person. It involves a desire to get that other person in trouble in order to get even for some reason or other. Eventually, a tattler ends up alone and miserable.

Causes of Tattling

These relate to the child's sense of insecurity.

1.   *He needs a great deal of adult attention and protection and feels anxious or afraid when he is on his own.*
2.   *Many times a tattler has been treated unfairly by an adult who may be partial to another child, but does pay attention to him under duress. Tattling may be an attempt to get the adult to recognize his value and the other child's faults.*
3.   *If a child has been hurt, he may feel a bit avenged and powerful by hurting someone else.*
4.   *The tattler is often a timid child who discovers how to be aggressive in a passive way, and protects himself with the adult to whom he goes. As with any bad habit, tattling has some benefits to the child who does it.*

Dealing With a Tattler

This rarely requires professional help.

Pay attention to him and find out why he is tattling, or if, in fact, he is tattling at all. Sometimes a child is truly mature enough to see another child getting in a dangerous spot, and really reacts from caring and protection.

Stop the payoff for tattling. Even if the victim deserves a punishment, make that become secondary to the act of dealing with tattling. Tell your tattler that you will not hear any more such reporting.

Observe closely your child's interactions with playmates. If they need supervision, step in quietly before the child feels a need to tell.

If one child is trying to get another in trouble because of a need to get even, find out how he was hurt. People almost never hurt someone unless they have been hurt first. It is an instinct to lash out when we have suffered pain.

Help the child talk about his feelings, and explain the situation if possible. Comfort him and then help him see how his habit of getting even in this passive way hurts the other person, who will hurt him even more. The eventual rejection of a tattler is painful to see, but in itself, this may cure him.

Teach him how to forgive, understand, and turn his hurts into a strong effort to stop pain rather than inflicting more. Help him understand that he must choose whether his anger will produce lots more anger, or whether it will be used to stop the fight and restore fun.

If the child tattles because of a need for attention, help him see that such attention costs too much. He is likely to lose friends and may even lose his own self-respect. Find the time to supply his needs for attention in a satisfying way.

Tell your child there are three things he may do instead of tattling:

1. *Handle the situation himself by helping the children do the right thing.*
2. *Trust an adult to handle the problem in his own way and time.*
3. *Let others make their own mistakes and learn from them—unless this involves real danger. If a truly risky*

situation arises, the child needs to report it. Be watchful lest in stopping tattling, you inadvertently destroy your child's healthy concern about the misbehaviors of his friends.

TEMPER TANTRUMS/ BREATH-HOLDING SPELLS

These are quite common in the two-year-old world. Sometimes such tantrums begin earlier than two and extend on into early school years. (In fact, you have probably seen some adults having tantrums!)

Symptoms

Tantrums are uncontrolled expressions of rage and frustration. They are expressed by screaming, kicking, hitting, head banging, and throwing things. Sometimes the child holds his breath, and may do so to the point of a brief convulsion and loss of consciousness. Such a spell rarely lasts over two or three minutes, and is self-limiting. As soon as the waste gas (carbon dioxide) builds up in the bloodstream, it serves as a powerful stimulant to breathing. The child quickly revives and is fine. *So do not panic about such an attack.*

Causes of Tantrums

Reflex Action. Children's fits begin almost as a reflex reaction to fatigue, pain, or the inability to make something "do right." Blocks that will not stay stacked, or the stopping of play (which a child likes) for a nap (which he abhors) may be enough to precipitate the throwing of tantrums by some children. Others may work for a long time on a special project with great patience, but then some relatively minor frustration will, like the proverbial straw that broke the camel's back, cause a fit.

Not Fatigue. Fatigue does not cause a tantrum, but it may shorten a child's "fuse" and make him more likely to explode. (It is tempting to excuse a child's problem behavior on the basis of his being tired and not teach him the controls that are essential.)

Manipulative Use of Tantrums. While the original tantrums truly are beyond a child's control, he will quickly recognize the "fringe benefits" that are associated with them. Few expressions get the rapid response of adults that tantrums do, and these childish tantrums then become manipulative trickery, which is much harder to eliminate.

Treatment

This should include the prevention of habitual "fit pitching," as well as curing it.

When a child is young, tired, and has had an obviously difficult time that results in a tantrum, I believe in holding, soothing, and protecting him. Our son had an especially short "fuse" and would go into an agony of frustration when something he was working with wouldn't work. Spanking only enraged him more intensely. Ignoring him was impossible for me. I learned, by trial and error, to pick him up and wrap my arms gently and firmly around his body and my legs around his (to avoid bruises). I would quietly rock him, still crying and squirming, saying something reassuring. In a very few minutes he would relax, cry instead of yell, and I could both comfort and reason with him. Many two-year-olds just need the strength of a parent's physical control.

When a child throws a fit just for attention (and it *is not hard to recognize that*), it is best to ignore it. Even if you have to call on someone else for your courage, do not give in to a manipulative tantrum. Giving a child his way in order to stop a fit reinforces this behavior so well that it will become extremely hard to break. Do not let this type of behavior gain any benefits for a child. In such a case, put the child in his bed or on a rug, so he cannot seriously hurt himself. Tell him firmly that you are not going to talk with him until he calms himself down. Then simply walk away. (Do not look back, or he will probably redouble his efforts!) When he is calm, hold him, talk over the issue at stake, and find the answers.

In breath holding, lay the child down so the head is on its side and slightly lowered. This prevents the tongue from falling back and choking him. If he does not start breathing in a minute or two, do not hesitate to take him to an emergency room. You certainly would not be the first parent to do so for this reason.

You may even use artificial respiration or mouth-to-mouth resuscitation, but I have not seen this become necessary, except for the parents' peace of mind.

Prevention of Tantrums

This can often be accomplished by the following measures:

Whenever you feel your child is becoming exceptionally tired or irritable, gently stop his activity, or sit and help him with it until the difficult part is worked out.

When it is time to change one activity for another, give your child a forewarning. Rather than calling to him from another room, go to him and help him "shift gears," until he learns to change from one activity to another independently. I see this as teaching him and not spoiling him. You will not need to do this very many times before he will be able to handle transitions in his day all by himself.

With a child who is under three, help him adjust to the other children. Before that age, a child may have extreme difficulty in sharing, taking turns, or playing in general with another child. After three, children do this fairly automatically.

As your child grows older, you may need to speak very sternly to him, telling him tantrums are not to be tolerated. Decide then if he is to go to his room, be spanked, or lose some privilege. Be sure to carry out your plan *consistently,* and do not give up too soon. It is tempting to feel that a particular plan is not working and stop, just short of success.

Help your little fit thrower to find an acceptable way to get his understandable frustrations out. A pounding board, crying, or—best of all—talking about whatever is wrong, will give him something constructive to do with his pent-up feelings. The goal in dealing with tantrums is to help your child become aware of his feelings and needs, express them appropriately, and ask for the help he needs to take care of the situations that produce such problems.

THUMB SUCKING

This is a big worry for parents of small children—and sometimes older ones. It is common in infants, but many of them give up the habit in favor of the increasing number of external interests that take their attention away from their own bodies. It is only in children older than two or three that most parents worry about thumb sucking. A child may become attached to a pacifier, as well as to his thumb or fingers, and many parents dislike the use of such a gadget because of the picture it presents of an overgrown baby.

Causes of Thumb Sucking

Sucking Reflex. Babies start sucking their fingers or thumb in a reflex manner. They accidentally discover that this brings some of the pleasure that sucking on a nipple brings. Since babies can't cry and suck at the same time, many parents are all too happy for them to suck their thumbs at first. Only later do they (the parents) discover that habitual thumb sucking is a problem and even an embarrassment to them.

Oral Needs. We know that babies have strong oral needs. That means that they need to have something in their mouths to feel content. When babies nurse slowly enough, the satisfaction of their oral needs should be about the same as the satisfaction of the hunger needs in their tummies. When they eat too fast, however, they may get full before their mouths are satisfied. For such babies, thumb sucking meets that need.

Comforting Habit. As a child gets older, the sucking becomes a habit that is associated with sleeping, the relief of boredom, or comfort. The more parents try to force him to stop, the more unhappy the child becomes, the more comfort he needs, and the more automatic is his habit of thumb sucking for comfort.

While parents worry about the deformity of teeth by thumb sucking, dentists tell us this rarely is a danger. Only if a child persists in sucking with strong pressure against the gums while he is cutting *permanent* teeth is there likely to be a problem. Permanent teeth usually do not erupt before six or seven years of age.

Treatment of Thumb Sucking

Prevention First. Once again, prevention is better than the treatment of thumb sucking. Allow plenty of time for sucking during feeding time from birth on. Stop the baby briefly, if you are nursing, to prolong the feeding process a bit. Be certain the nipple holes on the bottle, if you are using bottles, are not too large. A slow, steady drip from an inverted bottle usually means the flow will be about right. Stronger babies, however, may need slower flow, and weaker ones a faster or easier flow.

Cover Hands. Keep baby's hands and fingers away from his mouth at first. There are baby shirts with long sleeves that have cuffs. Your baby's hands may be tucked inside that sleeve like a mitten, so the fingers or thumb can't get into the mouth. Be assured that this does not seriously inhibit your baby's motions. He can move those fingers as much as he wishes inside those sleeves. After only a couple of weeks, the hands may come out.

Pacifier. If your baby seems to have a need to suck, I believe a pacifier is permissible. In fact, it may be a blessing. The newest ones are especially designed to avoid pressure on the developing gums, and they do not extend far enough back to gag a child as the old kinds sometimes did. When your child no longer needs the pacifier, it can conveniently be lost—a thumb cannot!

Some people object to pacifiers on the grounds that they are unsanitary and they look bad. Frankly, I feel they look no worse than a thumb. You may keep several and have them disinfected, but after a few weeks, your child does not need a strictly sterile environment anyway. You, of course, must decide whether to use this gadget or not.

Treating the Older Child

As a child grows older and is still sucking his thumb, you will need a different solution. Here are some useful ideas:

Give him plenty of cuddling, rocking, and happy physical contact, so he feels very safe. As you hold him, place a toy or your own hand in his to transfer its habitual position from the mouth to an external interest. To avoid boredom, babies need plenty of stimulation of all their bodies' senses.

Spend time with your baby in play to draw his attention outside of himself. Keep his hands busy doing active things—holding toys or teething biscuits. Use the hand to put eatables into the mouth and substitute them for the thumb.

When a child is about four, he can often successfully chew gum—without swallowing it. And this can give his mouth a real workout. He may not even want his thumb!

When our oldest child was four, we talked about the need to stop sucking her thumb in order to keep her teeth straight. She decided to work with us, and all by herself made up a game. She pretended to hide her thumb under her pillow at bedtime, so it wouldn't sneak into her mouth. It worked!

On the other hand, my little sister sucked her thumb, and my parents made a real power struggle out of that. They used every known device to stop thumb sucking, and probably created a few! She outwitted them all and chose to quit sucking her thumb only years later—another example of the destructive effect of power struggles and the effectiveness of the child's own decision to cooperate. Stay calm, firm, creative, and above all, *loving,* and you will work out the problem.

There are a number of devices designed to make children stop sucking their thumbs. A heavy coiled wire slipped over the thumb and tied to the wrist was one of those my parents tried. My sister found ways to remove it. Splints on the elbow and other restraints aimed at breaking this habit seem cruel to me. I do not recommend them, and I have found the measures suggested above to be so highly effective that I feel the mechanical restraints arc not necessary.

TICS OR HABIT SPASMS

These are jerking movements of a muscle or set of muscles that start voluntarily as a reaction to a tense situation, but come to be beyond the control of the victim. They begin during an experience of intense fear or anxiety, but can become a habit with amazing rapidity.

Causes of Tics

Stress. To my knowledge, tics are always a sign of extreme intrapersonal stress. They are a child's involuntary reaction of fear to the pressure of intense anger, disapproval, or punishment. They usually begin after school age, and commonly are related to school and social problems, though they may involve a parent's reaction to these problems.

A Vicious Cycle. Adult reactions to tics unwittingly feed into the vicious cycle that keeps them active. Tics are so grotesque and annoying that parents often react to them with irritation or even punishment. Remember that tics *originate* as a reaction to anger and punishment, and you will quickly see that more anger and punishment are likely to make them worse. You must also understand that *these are truly beyond a child's control.* They are as automatic as blinking an eyelid to help remove an irritating grain of sand.

Treatment of Tics

This sounds simple, but it takes heroic self-control. I believe this will work in almost every case.

Avoid commenting about or reacting to this tic as you would avoid the plague. Do not respond to it!

Use your energy, instead, to *understand and emphathize with your child. Find out what is hurting and frightening him and stop it.* Here are some possibilities:

1. *Perhaps a teacher or cruel child is making it too tough on him in school. Visit your principal and seek his help in dealing with that.*
2. *Perhaps you have been too hard on your own child. Don't stop disciplining him, but tone down your anger. Real strength can be gentle!*

To help find the cause of your child's tic, *take note of when it happens.* After several times, you will begin to understand the specific stress that contributes to it and can reduce that or even remove it.

Teach your child to trust you with his troubles and to talk with you about them. The more he can discuss them, the more you can help find the answers to them—and the less those troublesome tics will happen.

It is not uncommon for adults to have some habit spasms such as a nervous cough, a grimace, or exaggerated blinking of the eyes, yet they function very well. So you need not be overly worried about your child. The less you worry, the calmer your child will feel. In this case, *the less you do, the better he will be.*

9
Emotional Problems

THE INTERACTION OF COMPONENT PARTS

Marie was a shy child. She often felt lonely, misunderstood, and even angry. She was a gifted child, though she did not realize that until much later. School and books were an escape from her loneliness and a satisfying resource for her curiosity and creativity. When others failed to think as she did, she felt that she perhaps was at fault. The confusion this created kept her even more isolated.

Socially, Marie felt at ease only with a select group—her sisters and brother, a few girls from her church, and occasionally children of her parents' friends. When other children said, "Hi!" she replied, "Hello." Once the other girls giggled at her stiff response. Not only did she not talk like other children but she also dressed differently, and was not allowed to take part in many of their activities.

During one period of Marie's life, she had a serious illness that threatened her life, and she was afraid, but received unparalleled attention. After her recovery, she gradually, unconsciously, sought attention through a variety of physical and emotional symptoms—a typical neurotic sign.

Through all of these sad times, however, there ran a bright thread of love and hope. And eventually Marie gained the understanding and strength, through counseling, searching, and maturing, that stabilized her life.

Example of Such Interaction

Marie is an example of the complex interaction of all the component parts of one's being. Certain *social factors* within her family and community created her loneliness. Her *childish helplessness* added to that and created a *neurotic pattern of depression.* Her *giftedness* often set her apart still further, and her *physical illness* taught her to relate with others through problems. Yet even for Marie, there was hope.

In the next chapters, I will outline the major types of troubled children with whom I have worked. They are listed under *Emotional, Physical, Psychological,* and *Social* headings, but remember, most problems could easily be placed in another category just as logically. Marie illustrates emotional, physical, social, *and* academic problems. People are, like Marie, unbelievably complex creatures, and all facets of life merge imperceptibly into the others. Like a fascinating kaleidoscope, the same parts are constantly changing into similar but different patterns. Life is never static, but it always is dynamic. In that fact there is frustration, because just as one thinks he understands, the design changes. But in that very change there is hope: making the changes for the better in your troubled child is your exciting option!

ANGER

The Angry Child

No matter how she tried, Brenda could not seem to please her mother. The dusting she was assigned, and rather liked doing, was never quite perfect. When she redid it, Mother's comment, "Now, why didn't you do it right in the first place?" left her feeling resentful. Her school grades were not the best, and Brenda realized sadly that every day she failed to do as well as almost anyone in her class. She tried her very best, but her parents didn't believe her. They wanted her to do even better.

Often when Brenda walked into her home after school she would overhear her mother talking about her to a friend. She always sounded irritated, or at least worried. As soon as her mother noticed her presence, she would change the topic of conversation.

Through all of her mother's disapproval, Brenda somehow kept some hope for herself, because she sensed that her father still believed in her and was not too disappointed in her accomplishments. She devoted herself to him and kept trying. But a day came that Brenda had dreaded. That day, even her father seemed to turn against her! She blamed her mother for feeding him lies, but nevertheless, Dad was scolding and grounding her, and worst of all his eyes looked angry. Brenda had no more allies and no hope. She was full of anger at the unfairness of her parents. By the middle of the her sixth-grade year, she found some relief from her distress in the deceptive high of marijuana, and for several years rebelled in dangerous ways.

The Expressions of Anger

Angry children may express their anger in two basic ways: actively or passively. The *aggressively angry child* explodes regularly. Such explosions may be verbal, with screaming, swearing, name calling, and insulting anyone and everyone with whom he is upset. Or he may explode physically by throwing things, hitting, or kicking like a two-year-old in a tantrum.

Recently a single mother, struggling to raise her preadolescent son, came home to find an expensive and treasured vase broken. Her son admitted that he was angry because she was not at home when he arrived. He deliberately broke the vase to get even with her! This boy almost certainly was also feeling helpless, lonely, and perhaps worried. He may (as children and adults alike will do) have been acting angry to cover these painful emotions.

The *passively angry child* usually withdraws and sulks. He refuses to talk, won't do what he is supposed to do, and may sit alone for long periods. He may make faces at the person who is the focus of his trouble, but usually this is done behind the person's back. He waits for his quiet resistance to wear away at the parent's authority until he or she gives in. He may take out his anger at Mom on his dad, or maybe on his little sister, or the dog. Sometimes the passively angry child gives vent to his anger through tears. It may be difficult to know whether he is angry or really sad. And usually, he is both.

In newborn babies, we identify anger as a response to pain. In older children, this fact is also true, but the pain is usually emotional and is often disguised or covered up, and we adults forget to look for it. We react instinctively to a child's anger with our own frustration, thus feeding a vicious cycle that all too often ends like Brenda's—in tragically destructive behavior.

Causes of Anger in Children

Let me remind you that anger is, in itself, a *normal* emotion. It is a natural response to pain. What one does with and about the anger, however, can make it destructive, and therefore wrong.

Anger Is Prompted by Pain. Even tiny babies soon learn that their cry of pain brings attention, and it should. The child's indignant cry at his pain is his only way of communicating that he is in trouble. A tender, strong hand and proper attention will relieve most discomfort promptly, and the baby's anger subsides.

Uncertainty in Parents. An indecisive, anxious parent, however, may fail to reassure the child and make him even more nervous. Such parental uncertainty comes from the confusion of baby's angry feelings with his fear. Babies must wonder, *What if Mommy never figures out that my diaper rash hurts?* An upset infant can therefore result in the parent's increased anxiety, creating more fear in the baby, setting off another vicious cycle.

Insufficient Response by Parents. A parent on the other end of the spectrum may be imperturbable! No amount of crying will worry her (or him)! That baby will cry himself into an absolute rage before he gets the care he needs. As he grows, he is quite likely to continue the rage.

I hope you can see, then, that troublesome anger in a child is related to, if not caused by, the type of parental response to the infant's anger. And that response is prompted by the meaning of the baby's anger to the parents, which usually, in turn, reverts to the response of the parents' parents when they were angry. Habits of recognizing, interpreting, and responding to anger are transmitted from generation to generation.

Fringe Benefits of Anger. As babies grow, they learn quickly that they can use their anger to *control and even tyrannize others.* They find out how to bully and manipulate their families, then their friends, and finally almost everyone who touches their lives. Such children are truly emotionally troubled.

Parents' Anger. Children and parents become mirrors of each other in many ways. What the child sees in Mom or Dad, he learns to imitate, and many parents see an image of themselves in their children. Such reflections can be lovely, but they can also be ugly caricatures!

When parents communicate in unreasonable anger, their children will learn those habits. They will see the benefits of getting one's way, developing power over others, and seeming to be strong. In self-defense, children learn to fight opponents with their own weapons. So beware! You may unknowingly teach your child anger that he could use against you.

Frustration at Their Limitations. The well-known story of Helen Keller is a prime example of the anger of a child who cannot communicate. All limitations that children experience can cause some degree of anger. Again, the underlying pain at not being able to do or express what he wants so badly to do can truly cause the tantrum of frustration. This childish anger can be quickly helped by supplying words, helping with the play project, and explaining the parents' awareness and understanding.

Dangers of Mishandling Anger

Expression Is Forbidden. Many parents see anger as sinful, undignified, or inappropriate, and punish the child for being angry. Since anger is always caused by some sort of pain, such punishment compounds the problem by adding more pain. The child's pain and anger are there, demonstrable, and real. Parents need to learn to recognize and heal the pain first, and *then* teach the child how to understand and express both the pain and the anger constructively. When the direct expression of anger is forbidden, it will inevitably be turned inward or shoved underground, where it seethes away beyond the reach of the child's conscious mind. Such anger sooner or later will cause physical illness, such as high blood pressure or ulcers. Or it may come out in the disguise of depression or self-pity. It may explode in violence when too much emotion accumulates. Hidden anger may come out in later years in joining so-called causes that are aggressive and destructive.

Placating. While it is dangerous to drive a child's anger underground, it is equally risky to try to placate an angry child. A friend described a bout with his two-year-old daughter. She awoke most mornings acting grouchy, but on this particular morning, she was a real bear! Her parents offered her some fresh orange juice, which she refused but asked for grape juice. It happened they also had grape juice and brought her that. She hit the glass, splashing purple stains generously about the kitchen. Thinking milk would surely please their baby, they tried it next, but again she turned it down. It was my impression that this child did not need pleasing. She needed strong limits set. A choice between two items is enough. If she had refused even those, she should have been firmly put back to bed or left in her chair to await a better mood, with a firm, clear warning that even parents will not tolerate such actions.

When parents fall into the trap of placating an angry child to gain peace—no matter what the cost—that price is too great! A child sees such a parent as weaker than himself—a child-parent. He really knows, in spite of his bullying, that he is quite inadequate, so if Dad and Mom are weaker still, it's a very scary world!

Child-to-Child Combat. Related to the placating role in dealing with an angry child is hand-to-hand or face-to-face combat. Acting more like brothers or sisters, such parents engage in a fight to the finish. As long as the parent is bigger, louder, and stronger than the child, he may be able to get the child to give up his anger and give in. But sooner or later, the child is likely to grow up, and then his anger will win out. Such combats, verbal or physical, can result in permanent damage to the child and to the family relationships.

Acting Aggrieved. Some compulsively patient parents, in desperation, may try to make an angry child become nicer by acting very hurt. And they may honestly feel hurt! But over a period of time, children come to see that as an act or manipulation. To them it seems weak and ineffectual, although they also feel guilty at making Mom cry or seeing Dad worry.

If we had the opportunity, we could learn many lessons from animals. I once watched our mother cat with her litter of kittens for several long periods of time. There were five of the soft, purry things, but two of them especially caught my attention. One was shiny black and white. He was always on the go and especially playful. But he constantly picked on the other, a soft, gentle, gray-and-white kitten. It seemed to be quite unable to hold its own and would scurry to the mother for protection. To my surprise, she quite ignored the helpless one, but she grasped the aggressive one firmly between her paws and held him face to face. She licked him and meowed at him, and in a moment he was settled quietly in a corner of their box. She did not cuff him and did not seem to sympathize with his victim. Such wisdom!

How to Help Your Angry Child

Here, then, are my suggestions for helping your angry child. Whether he is a few weeks or several years old, I have found they work.

First, recognize your own anger. Like it or not, anger generates anger, just as certainly as a mirror reflects exactly what lies in front of it. If you deny your anger, or try to hide it, it will come out in disguised ways. If you do not control it, it may cause you to explode, and possibly abuse or terrify your child.

Next, make yourself take control of the situation so that you will have time to think. Firmly place a small child in bed or hold him in your own arms. Older children should go to their rooms, or to a time-out place, if you have one. At any rate stop the violence, and give yourself some space and calmness as well!

Then, find out what caused the anger at this time. Whatever your habits of the past, or your child's, a time of violent anger is not the time to react. It is a time to listen quietly and look for the initial pain. Whether that is physical or emotional, you can always find it. If it involves a fight between two children, talk to them separately. Neither one will be able to give you the whole truth, but between them, you will come close! Be careful to avoid taking sides or rescuing the so-called victim.

Help each child put into words his tender, vulnerable feel-

*ings and teach him the skill of figuring out why he feels as he
does. Next, help him decide what to do about the situation.*
Perhaps he needs to keep special toys out of the reach of an inquisitive younger brother or sister. He may need to come to you
for help or advice, or perhaps he can now reason through a
problem rather than fighting it out.

*Explain to your child as often as you need to, what anger
is—the cry of pain. Teach him the words with which to express
the anger and understand the hurt that causes it. Then teach
him what to do about the problem.* As you go through these
steps with your child, learn them, so *you* can put them into
practice with your spouse, people at work, or in the neighborhood.

Serve as a model for your child. This method of constructively dealing with anger will be your prize teaching tool. With
this plan, you can avoid childish, bullyish, or guilt-producing
methods. You will find you quickly return to loving feelings, and
certainly so will your angry child.

FEAR

Being born with fear is universal, as you will recall from earlier chapters. Caution and healthy carefulness may be lifesaving, but irrational fears often preoccupy a child's attention and
cripple him emotionally.

Development of Fear

The following example illustrates the complex development
of fear and how it can become a phobia. Such extreme fears are
not uncommon among children.

Resentment. Commonly fear is accompanied by anger or resentment and guilt. Mark tried very hard to please his parents.
He was bright, worked hard in school, and tried to put up patiently with his curious little sister. He felt that she was taking
away most of his attention, and resented being blamed for her
screaming. True enough, he did pinch her now and then, when
she broke his carefully built block houses, but it seemed she
never was caught or punished.

Loss of Parents' Approval. Furthermore, Mark could see his mother giving less time and affection to him and more to that troublesome sister. Even his dad was so busy, he rarely had time anymore to play with him. No matter how hard he tried, nothing pleased Mom and Dad. Even if he missed only one problem in math, his parents scolded him and rarely praised the rest of his excellent schoolwork.

Guilt Feelings. Gradually, Mark became discouraged, and then downright angry. *It isn't fair!* he thought, and silently he sometimes wished Mom would *drop dead!* Actually, however, he still loved her and his dad and worried lest his angry wishes come true. If anything happened to his parents, Mark believed it would be his fault.

Anxiety. Mark began having terrifying nightmares of monsters out to get him. He dreaded going to bed. He was afraid to go to school lest something happen to his mother and little sister while he was away, and he worried about his dad having an accident.

Compulsive, "Undoing" Behaviors. In order to relieve his mounting panic, Mark tried to be extremely good. He washed his hands many times every day, put everything exactly in its right place, avoided his little sister, and even his parents. He became worried about getting cancer, and was so afraid of death that even the insecticides in the fertilizer on his lawn scared him. He wiped his feet over and over after walking on the grass, and the hand washing became a ritual.

 Mark's fear had become a phobia. Both he and his family required prolonged psychotherapy in order for him to return to being a happy child.

How Children Cope With Fear

 Over a period of time, childhood's understandable fears may become anxiety and cause actual physical symptoms. A rapid, strong heartbeat, heavy breathing, and tense muscles are common signs of prolonged fear. So are nightmares, certain school problems, and many behavioral disorders. Frightened children will try almost anything to alleviate their fear. Keeping very active and getting into trouble that will result in punishments will

help a child forget his fear or relieve, at least temporarily, the
guilt that accompanies it.

Methods of Dealing With Fear. A young boy I know slept with
his flashlight and baseball bat under his bed. He felt that he
could protect himself from any threat with these familiar tools.

Yet another boy shared his secret world of fear with me. He
kept his active mind constantly geared into two levels of thinking. One was the world of actuality, and he worked in school, in
sports, and at home with some energy. With the rest of his
mental capacity, however, he was always alert to potential danger. He developed a complete list of plans for coping with these
frightening possibilities. This extreme pressure built to the
bursting point, and he suffered a mental breakdown. He, too,
required intensive care to break out of the vicious grip of his
fear.

Witchcraft and the Occult. A tragic by-product of fear in the
lives of children as early as preadolescence is the interest and
involvement in supernatural, occult phenomena. Ellen had
learned of witchcraft from a superstitious grandmother when
she was only four. As soon as she learned to read, she studied
articles and books on occult beliefs and practices. Her inner and
outer worlds became weird and extremely frightening to her. By
the time I worked with her at the age of twelve, she was convinced that love and caring were weak. She was so entrenched
in fear that she actually practiced a form of Satan worship.

I find a startling number of young adolescents and preadoles-
cents who place great credence in witchcraft. There are many
serious books and articles promoting this practice and promising supernatural powers through its use.

Now, parents, don't go on a great witch-hunt, but do be aware
that such ideas are not uncommon. When you have an opportunity, teach your children of the error and danger in such beliefs,
and protect them from any belief in the occult that can only
compound their fear.

Causes of Fear

You have already understood that fear is inborn and instinctive. It can be lifesaving. *This healthy fear should be taught
and encouraged by parents.*

The crippling fears just illustrated, however, are a problem to children and eventually will cause trouble for the entire family. Such fears are actually taught to a child by parents or other adults!

Fearful Parents. Jimmy's mother was afraid of heights. As a child, she had climbed a tree against her mother's orders, and she fell, causing a serious fracture of her left arm. Her guilt and pain, as well as her mother's angry lecture, left her afraid of high places. When Jimmy began to climb, as most boys do, she panicked. She simply would not allow him to explore any high places. Even climbing the steps to speed down a slippery slide was too much for her to bear. She strictly forbade any climbing. Jimmy was quiet by nature, and gave in to his mother. His occasional attempts at healthy exploring became further apart, and finally Jimmy adopted his mother's belief. He, too, became afraid of heights.

Whatever your fears are, parents, try to overcome them. Your children sense your feelings accurately, and they are likely to adopt them. Their love and respect for you includes your feelings of fear. If you cannot promptly overcome your fears, I suggest that you be open and honest about them. Tell your children as much as you can about the beginnings of your fears. Explain that you know it is not a reasonable fear, and that you are working hard to overcome it. You may explain that this fear is one you want your children to avoid and that, in this case, they really must hear your words and not be influenced by your example.

Such honesty, accompanied by your efforts to overcome your fear, can be a marvelous example to your children. If even parents must work at personal growth, certainly children can do so without shame!

Unfair or Angry Parents. In the story above, Mark's parents were unfair. In their well-intentioned efforts to help Mark develop his fine mind, they expected absolute perfection, without any praise for his efforts or his unusual successes. No matter how understandable this was to me, their counselor, it was simply unfair in Mark's estimation. Had he been able to express his resentments at the unfairness, he would never have needed to feel guilty about his anger, or afraid of the fancied consequences of it.

By their size and strength, which are disproportionately huge to a small child, parents become awesome at best. When parents evidence great anger, a child may feel overwhelmed. I have seen children actually look terror-stricken when their parents scolded them. In such cases I know those parents have disciplined their children with excessive anger.

At times, children become afraid of the anger between their parents. In a serious argument, parents may forget the presence of their children. Be sure, however, your children cannot forget you! They overhear, even at night, the loud, harsh tones of unhealthy arguments. So learn to fight fairly, and avoid scaring your children.

Discipline by Fear. A family once came to me for help with their two daughters. Both of these basically healthy youngsters were having frightening dreams. They were biting their nails and beginning to worry about things that were beyond their concerns.

Very carefully I reviewed the areas of their lives that could bring about such anxieties. School was going well. They both had reasonably good friendships. They had no serious problems with their parents, and Mother and Father had a good marriage.

In their case, it was a baby-sitter who had created the problem. Due to their financial needs, the mother found it necessary to work. She had found a mature woman to care for their girls, but this woman had a set of superstitions that came with her. She taught these, along with their fears, to the children. Furthermore, she used her beliefs to threaten them into absolute obedience. These girls improved quickly with a new baby-sitter.

Fear and Real Danger. Many parts of our world today hold very real dangers for children. We are hearing of children's anxiety about war, famine, and disasters on a wide scale. When newscasts on television show starvation and actual battle scenes, this is not surprising. My concern, in fact, in this area of fear, is that our society may become so calloused as to lose it! Seeing terror routinely can eventually make terror routine.

The real dangers to our children, however, do need to be understood. In any large city there are robberies, abductions, murders, and family violence every day. Such tragedies are extending into smaller cities and even rural areas.

Teach Caution. It is necessary, therefore, to teach caution to your children. Try to avoid making them suspicious or afraid of everyone by developing their judgment. Children intuitively look at people's faces and eyes (unless they have learned shame and fear). Use this to teach your child to read faces. The angry, "evil" look of a threatening person can be detected readily. Children can avoid such people. They must be taught to never go anywhere with a stranger. Many potentially dangerous people do not look evil and may entice a child with toys or food. It is not cowardice for a child to run from danger. Teach your child to run into a house or store or any sheltering place, if he is accosted by a stranger.

Avoid Gangs. Many children form groups or "gangs" for self-defense or aggression. Teach your child to avoid such groups. Children may need to be taught some form of self-defense or how to reach protective adults. Be sure your child knows his strengths and weaknesses in this area! It is far better to risk being a coward by running from a group of bullies than to try to fight them off and be hurt in the process.

Teach Your Child the Dangers of Nature. Recently I learned of an adult who picked up a rattlesnake and was badly bitten. It required heroic measures to save his life. Children may be fascinated with snakes, spiders, or any wild animal. Some of these are harmless, but many are dangerous. Teach your children the difference—especially if you visit or live in areas where these dangers exist more freely.

Storms involve certain dangers, too, that need to be explained to children. Depending upon where you live, storms may include hurricanes or tornadoes, with their destructive wind force. In almost any area, lightning can cause serious injury or death. *Earthquakes* are localized and, fortunately, scientists are often able to give some forewarning of them. Each of these natural disasters has its own safety and protection rules. Learn and practice them, and teach them to your children. But avoid unnecessary fears!

Helping a Frightened Child

Identifying a Frightened Child. A truly frightened child may be recognized at once by looking at his face. Before they learn to mask their feelings, children's eyes, faces, and bodies reveal their emotions, quickly and honestly. A frightened child will reveal that fear in these ways:

1. *His eyes will be open wide, and the black center circle may be dilated and large. You will not miss the fear in his eyes and entire face.*
2. *His muscles will be tense, and the fists are often clenched tightly, as are his jaws and mouth.*
3. *If you hold a frightened child, you can feel the wild pounding of his heart and the heavy breathing.*
4. *He may cry or tell you he is scared, if you listen or ask him.*
5. *In older children who have been abused or overpunished, a fearful child may run and hide and will refuse to look anyone directly in the eyes!*

Responses to a Frightened Child

Comfort. A frightened child desperately needs comfort and reassurance. When I was only four, I went with my older brothers and sisters and their friends to see the early construction of a new schoolhouse some distance from our farm home. They helped me into the basement, and in my excitement over such an elaborate new building, I failed to realize they were all back in the car, and *I* was still in the basement, alone. In my panic, I could not find a way out, so I screamed until they finally came to my rescue. They had no awareness of the depth of my fear, but when we finally returned home, I was still sobbing.

My mother was busy, but a dinner guest sensed my needs and took me to a big rocking chair in the living room. Quietly she spoke to me as we rocked; she understood my feelings and assured me I was all right now. Then she sang a lovely song to me about a mouse that was afraid of a kitty, until finally I laughed.

Information. Once the emotion of fear has subsided, the child can think again. Do not make the mistake of trying to explain or teach a frightened child before she is comforted. She will not be able to think well enough to remember until the fear itself has been relieved. Then, however, be sure to use this time to teach invaluable lessons. When an experience is new and the feelings are fresh, is the prime time for an object lesson. You may be certain I did not play alone when I was far from home after my basement experience. I stayed within close touch to whomever I was with. So, explain to a frightened child what he needs to know to avoid a repetition of the fear. Ask him what he has learned from the experience and help him to mentally engrave that lesson in his memory. Do avoid, of course, any sense of shame or stupidity in this process.

Protection in the Future. Sometimes fearful experiences are due to a child's disobedience or carelessness. Such experiences themselves are often the best of disciplinarians to a child. In other cases, however, it is up to the parent to provide protection for the child. Finding and knowing that fact will help you to be good parents and to avoid overprotecting or babying your child. Use good judgment, observe your child, and know his capabilities or weaknesses. These facts will guide you regarding his self-protection and further a healthy caution.

Responding to the Specific Causes of Fear. When he was three, our son began awakening at night in terror. He would cry out and then run to our bedroom in obvious panic. For several nights, I assumed he was having bad dreams, so I would comfort him, put him back in bed, and usually he slept on peacefully. My sleep, however, was suffering, and so in desperation I finally asked, "Son, why are you so afraid?" We were sitting in a rocking chair by his bed. Nearby was a big *ABC* poster with charming animal pictures for each letter. He sat up, pointed one chubby finger at the *T,* and said, "Dem tigers!" The poster came down at once, and to my surprise those bad dreams stopped. Perhaps it wasn't just the poster but my loving and caring that helped; however, objects can scare a young child at night.

I strongly recommend night-lights, going to a child, and being with him when he is frightened. If he is anxious about dark areas, go with him until he knows it is safe. Never accuse him of cowardice, but be certain that your protection and example of courage will in time help your child overcome fear.

A friend recently told me that her son returned from a Cub Scout overnight event with fear that she hadn't noticed previously. He finally shared with her some scary stories the boys had made up. Her son had a vivid imagination, and these stories seemed all too real and possible to him.

Television Programs and Movies. Both of these "entertainment" forms seem to take a macabre delight in competing for ever greater horrors. Even the brief promotions of such programs can terrify a child. Be careful to monitor your TV viewing until your children can separate truth from fantasy, and be sure they talk over with you any programs that leave them uneasy.

Guilt. Real or imagined, this is a serious cause of fear. Parents punish their children for doing wrong, and as they grow, they fear that God will punish them in some monstrous way. That fear can cause tragic symptoms. If none of the more common causes of fear seems to fit your child, see if he or she is harboring guilt over some secret or past misdeed. This gives you a marvelous chance to teach your child about learning from mistakes and being forgiven, rather than staying guilt-ridden.

Be an Example. Overcome your own fears by understanding them, facing them, and taking action about them. This may be possible simply by practicing self-control and courage in the face of fear. It may take the help of a counselor, but do whatever you must to enable you to stop teaching unhealthy fear to your child. Once you have overcome an area of fear in your life, use that experience to teach your child how to overcome his fear.

What to Avoid With a Frightened Child

It is common for a parent to try to reassure a child by *belittling his feeling or minimizing the whole problem.* I have even heard parents lecture and shame a child for being cowardly. Such an approach is always intended to cause the child to make a heroic effort to be brave and strong. Personally, I have not seen this work. It makes children stop telling their fears and withdraw or cover them with false bravado. But the fear is there, and it will come out.

Don't Be Fooled by a "Faker." A child may like the attention he gains through real fear so much that he learns to "fake it." His face, however, will tell you the difference, or you will find that intuitive sense within you warning you that this is not real. Be firm about explaining your suspicions to the child, and tell him to stop such dishonest faking. If he needs attention, tell him how to ask for it without such dramatic pretense.

Do Not Overprotect Your Child. Comfort and reassurance can feel great to the parent as well as the child. You may unconsciously encourage fears so you can feel strong or close to your son or daughter. Your biggest job as a parent (and often the most painful) is to teach your child to be independent of you.

Never Punish a Child by Fearful Threats. I actually overheard a tired mother tell her crying child in my waiting room, "If you don't stop crying, I'm going to have that doctor give you a shot!" Threats with fear attached create many more problems than they cure.

Seek Professional Help

When you are unable to find or cure the cause of your child's fears, don't be afraid to seek the help of a counselor. It does not mean that you are bad parents or that your child is bad or crazy. It often *does* mean that you are so close to the problem you can't see it quite clearly. It always means that you care and, with outside help, the problem can more quickly be solved and happiness can be restored to you and your child.

By your example, your protection, your guidance, and your courage—slowly and surely—your child will learn to understand and conquer his fear!

GRIEF

The first encounter with grief I can recall was, paradoxically, involved with the birth of my baby sister. My family was quite reserved about things they considered private, and the conception and eventual birth of a baby was, to them, highly private. I was not told there was a baby on the way. Those earlier years of my childhood, before baby, were golden years, and I may very well have been so intent on keeping them that I ignored as a threat the signs that should have told me she was expected.

At any rate, that May morning came when she appeared in the baby basket at our house. My father took me to see her, and for the first time in my life I felt angry with him. Why was he telling me that I now had a baby sister? I neither needed nor wanted any baby at our house. It seemed as if all the attention once so delightfully focused on me was suddenly gone, without warning. It didn't make any sense at all!

I was angry, sad, lonely, and silent. I did not then know the words to describe the unbearable pain I felt. When I tried to explain how I hated to give up my time to entertain this usurper (later on), I was scolded for being selfish and learned that most children would love to have a cute baby sister to play with. Though my troubled feelings were hidden, I remained resentful for many years, both feeling and quietly acting out the anger and sadness of my grief.

Too many parents, like mine, fail to comprehend the grief of children. They expect their children to be always happy and make great efforts to keep them so. But they do not realize that children cannot be happy until they finish the process of grief. Whether childish griefs are big or small, they follow a similar pattern, and helping a child through this painful sequence is a responsibility of every parent.

The Stages of Grief

These have been studied and described by many people. Let me summarize them for you.

Denial. The first stage of grief is denial. There is an instinctive reaction to shrink away from pain. And grief—big or little—is *pain!*

I once knew a young boy who lost his father. He knew his dad had died and he attended his funeral; but he could cope with his grief only by pretending his father was away on another business trip. He denied the death for many months, until he finally grew strong enough to cope with the pain.

Usually denial lasts a shorter time. My brother was accidentally killed when I was a teenager. I still recall my first words upon hearing of his death: "Oh! No!" But my denial was for only a few seconds.

Anger. The second stage is usually anger. We wonder, *Why? Why me? Why now?* and with these questions we feel angry with God, the doctors, the persons responsible for a loss, or even ourselves. Anger makes people want to lash out, and in this stage, grief may be confusing to the victim and the observer.

A child whose friend is moving away turns into a monster

overnight. He breaks things, kicks his sister, yells at his parents, and refuses to do his work. Before disciplining such a child, try to help him recognize and express the pain of his impending loss. Parents often fail to see the immensity of a child's grief because to them, it is a small thing. You must remember to take a child's-eye view of what is happening if you are to understand the anger of grief.

Anger in the grief process is best understood if you recall the frustration or rage you may feel at times when you are helpless. Many people do experience that at times, but children face it regularly. Certainly they do in the process of loss and grief. Understanding and talking about the angry feelings will resolve them fairly soon.

Sadness and Preoccupation. These are usually the third step in grief. One's thoughts tend to revert constantly to the pain and loss and there is a continual feeling of desolation or profound sadness. In children, as with anger, the sadness may be disguised by mischievous or naughty behavior or a pretended indifference. By such a masking, the real feelings become buried and are prolonged. The best answer is to encourage the child to talk or to cry about these feelings.

Guilt. Children develop, very early, a sense of omnipotence. The world revolves about them. When anything happens, good or bad, they feel they are directly responsible. In some of the small griefs of childhood this is true. A child's irresponsibility may result in the loss of a pet, or his carelessness may allow a special toy to be broken or lost. So it is understandable, in a child's system of logic, that he feels responsible for bigger losses as well.

When he is truly guilty, he must be taught the vital lesson of restitution, but he also needs to find forgiving and the security of your love. Unconditional love is tested at such times!

In events where the child is not guilty, be sure to explain the true facts to him and reassure him that he is not at fault. This can help a child to learn an invaluable lesson: the difference between real guilt and false guilt. And perhaps, as parents, teaching your child will help you to find release from false guilt you may have carried.

Fear. Many people experience fear as a part of the process of grief. *What if this happens again?* A few years ago our home was robbed, and I had a very hard time getting over the fear of the return of the robbers to get the few items they had left! When there is a death, one may be plagued with the fear, *It could have been me!* Children sometimes fear the loss of a parent after losing another relative.

Blame. Closely related to anger is the common tendency to put the blame for a loss at someone's doorstep. A child who broke a special toy was heard to say, "Suzy bumped me. She made me drop it!" Whether it is a child's need to blame his sister, or an adult's need to sue someone for his accident, blaming is common. It is not a healthy step, because it projects the fault onto someone else, keeps people from assuming their own responsibility, and sets in motion a system of destructive anger and bitterness.

Resignation. Guilt, fear, and blame are all highly destructive detours of grief. Be aware of them and cut them short by explaining the truth to your child. When they are over and done, the healing processes can begin. One must finally admit that which most people so despise: that the loss has, in fact, taken place, that we can do nothing to stop or reverse that fact, but that life will go on. And we can transcend the pain and finally return to the joy and zest of life—sadder but wiser!

Common Types of Loss and Grief in Childhood

Grief always results from loss. I can think of no exception to that, but there are losses that are not material loss, and so people tend to overlook them and miss the normal grief process. I am convinced that understanding and working one's way through these many small griefs can restore the joy and peace of life much more quickly. Many people live much of their lives in denial and anger, preventing pain but never really finding joy.

Loss of Freedom and Dependency. Let's face it! It's easier to let parents pop a bottle or breast in the child's mouth than to teach her, laboriously, to work the spoon and feed herself. It's easier for a child to use a diaper than to stop her play to go to the bathroom, especially if she is afraid of falling into that cold water in the toilet! No wonder most two-year-olds are so negative! They give up a lot and take on a lot of responsibility in a short time! More of these losses happen when a child learns to dress herself, pick up toys, go away to school, and face an increasing array of duties.

Help your child through such losses by explaining, loving, comforting, and then praising her for what she must do!

Loss of Objects. To feel secure, children need a certain constancy or sameness in their possessions. A pacifier or bottle, Mother's breast, a special blanket or teddy bear, are examples of the great significance of an object to a child. A friend recently took away her child's bottle and found that he really grieved over that loss for several days. One does not want to encourage a focus or dependency on *things,* but remember, these things are symbols of security, dependency, and the child's love of you, the parent. Don't be in a hurry to take those or other special things from your child. But don't, on the other hand, unduly prolong their function. Do explain to your child what you know he will feel, that you know he will recover from that pain, and that there will be new and better things for him to enjoy as he grows older.

You may not believe that a two-year-old or younger child will understand such ideas, but my experience shows they understand more than one thinks through your voice, your face, and the love that prompts such understanding.

Loss of Pets. Sunny, our dog, had been a part of our family for nearly eight years when she developed cancer and had to be put to sleep. We had loved her puppies, saved special scraps for her to eat, and worried over her when we were on vacations. Even I mourned her death. Little children become quite attached to pets. They feel, as did I, that they are part of the family. In fact, they are. Be sure, then, that you and your child will feel the loss of such a pet, and will need to comfort one another.

There is a special danger of guilt and blame in the loss of pets, for most children neglect the care of their pets. When one dies or strays, the child will likely feel responsible.

Loss of Friends. The average family in the United States moves about fourteen times in the course of being a family entity. We are a mobile society, and that brings about a major area of loss and grief.

By the time you become parents, you may have learned to cope with the loss of friends and environment through moving. Most children, however, do not learn that for many years, and you need to understand and help them through this type of loss and grief.

Our youngest child lost so many friends through their moving away that she stopped going out to play. She did not want to love any more friends only to lose them. After I recognized what lay beneath her silent withdrawing, I talked with her at length. I explained the fun of her memories of each friend and we discussed the fact that those memories would last forever—that the play and love they shared had become a beautiful part of each one's whole life. The more people she loved, therefore, the richer and better would she and they become—even though many friendships would only last a little while. Those words, by the way, have echoed back to comfort me many times!

Death. Rarely do children lose friends in death, but sooner or later they will lose grandparents or other relatives or friends. Because of its profound meaning of our own mortality and enormous and ultimate helplessness, few people face death with much equanimity. It is, therefore, very hard to help a child cope with death. Do avoid, however, the temptation to shield a child from death. Each child deserves a chance to know about it and the ultimate grief process it involves. You can handle your own grief better if you know there is a child watching you. And a child, surprisingly, can bring great comfort to you when you grieve.

Lost Hopes and Dreams. School-age children, or even pre-schoolers, begin to develop certain dreams and wishes. They will become the fastest runner, the best speller, or the best-liked person in school. But only a special few can actually reach such dreams in today's average school. The rest become the necessary (but unnoticed) "ordinary people." The disappointment of not making the team, not scoring the point, not being popular, is all too common—and all too often overlooked.

One mother I know felt keenly her daughter's disappointment at not being chosen for an important part in a school play. The girl took a lesser role, however, with grace and did her best. When the girl went to her room after the performance, she found a special bouquet of flowers by her bed with these words on a simple card: THANKS FOR BEING OUR SPECIAL STAR! Family recognition and efforts can help children through these painful losses of dreams!

Loss of Eras of Time. Many children cry when they start kindergarten. And so, may I add, do their mothers! Some of those tears are for fear of a new situation and the loss of freedom and being taken care of. But some are due to the loss, forever, of a unique era of time. Never again will your child be as carefree as he was before starting school; and, in turn, as he was before starting first grade, and going on to junior high school, and senior high. There is no returning. You know it, and part of you rejoices; but part of you grieves. And so it is with your child. There's no way to undo it or prevent it, so again—as with all grief—you and your child must endure it. Do so together— knowingly and lovingly!

How to Help the Grieving Child

Accept the Fact of the Loss. Some months ago, a child of ten lost her father. He died suddenly from a heart attack, and the family was in shock. In their well-meant efforts to help this young girl through her grief, they sent her with friends to an amusement park the next day. She tried bravely to be happy, because she knew that's what her mother needed her to be. But how and when she was helped with her grief and loss, I never found out. Here are some suggestions for helping your child at this difficult time:

Avoid denial. Do not aid any child in prolonging the denial stage of grief. Strength comes with coping, and there is an instinctive survival urge in all of us that will help your child as well as you to make it.

Share the child's stark grief, and he will be through with it sooner. There is a strong urge for parents to replace a broken toy or lost pet with a new one. Do not yield to that urge until you are sure your child has finished grieving over the loss. To survive in today's rough world demands strength, and strength comes from coping (with guidance and support), not from being overprotected.

Talk it out. Repeated experiences verify the fact that talking about a loss and its grief helps the healing to be faster and more complete. In the small griefs of every day, healing can occur in even a few minutes if the episode is explained and discussed. Teach your child the language of feelings, and encourage him to use them. If that language includes angry yelling or tears, help him to express those, too, in your own best way.

Tell your child some of your own sad times, and how you felt. The fact of your survival will be as encouraging as your understanding of his sadness.

Comfort him. There are many times when a child needs and wants to be held and comforted, just as I did when I thought I had been abandoned as a five-year-old. Be aware of that need and meet it! It does not spoil a child to meet his honest emotional needs. Even if he or she is older, offer the warmth of physical comfort and nearness. If they prefer not to be held and rocked, offer to sit near them. Stroking a head, squeezing a hand, touching a tense shoulder—are all symbolic substitutes for the cradling of a younger child. Just be there—with all of your energy and attention focused on your grieving child. Be sensitive to his need for silence a well as talk. If you aren't certain, ask. Children are likely to be honest.

Recognize the need for privacy. Most people who grieve need some time alone, as well as some time to talk and to be comforted. Children, too, may need some time to be alone. When you have held them, listened to them, and talked gently with them, ask if they would like this private time. Tell them you will be back, or where you may be found if they want you.

Avoid hindrances to recovery. Whether it takes a few hours or many months, recovery from grief does occur, unless it is hindered by self-pity, guilt, or blame. Allow this recovery. When there is a death or other serious loss, it may be tempting to feel that one must stay sad to honor the departed one. Please do not accept that as a fact. Any loved one would want you to be happy and to finish the grief. Do so as soon as you honestly can, and teach this to your child.

Recovery from grief takes place in cycles. On anniversaries or other reminders, a loss through death will be remembered. The grief feelings are likely to recur for a while. But each time they do, the time period will become shorter and the recovery more lasting.

One day you will be aware of only bittersweet memories. Then the healing is complete.

Spiritual Aspects of Grief

There is a tendency in some religious circles to comfort grief quickly by assuring the victim, "It was God's will. You mustn't question it!" I have heard people say to a child, "God wanted Grandma in heaven!" These people mean well, but such answers may cause more pain than comfort!

Children especially do not find comfort in the thought of Grandma's being in heaven if they loved her and wanted her with them. They may even feel God is cruel for taking her away.

Be Honest. Admit to the child who is grieving that you don't really understand all about his loss. But share with him, when he can listen, some of what you do know. For example:

1. *The more we learn to cope with pain and trouble, the stronger we become.*
2. *The more we learn about grief and pain, the more we can help and comfort others.*
3. *There is healthy growing that takes place when we learn to accept the limits of our power.*

Be an Example. Your presence, strength, honesty, and comfort with your child can teach him what God is like. Someday you will no longer be with your son or daughter. Then they will need to know where to turn for help. Brief prayers with and for your child are a fine means of touching the infinite power of God's help.

Grief and loss are normal. Your understanding and acceptance of that fact will guide you in teaching your child to cope. As you master the entire grief process, share your progress with your family. Then when they must encounter their own griefs, they can face them with skill and courage.

GUILT

Fear and anger can be both constructive and destructive in the life of a child. This polarity is equally true of guilt. Psychiatrists have spent many decades trying to learn how to help people deal with guilt, and we have gained some helpful information.

Examples of Guilt-Ridden Children

Lynn was a child who always longed to please her parents. She watched their eyes for every sign of approval or disapproval, and quietly acted according to the signals she saw there. Lynn did not talk much, but that was because she was afraid of interrupting her parents or of saying something that could upset them.

Her father, especially, wanted her to be a good student, and her mother expected her to help about the house. When she scolded Lynn for failing to do her household chores, Lynn made up her mind that she would do a super job and spent several evenings getting the house in perfect shape. But then her father asked her about her school grades, and due to the time she spent cleaning house, Lynn had forgotten to study for her tests and did rather poorly. So the next week she studied every evening, and her mother lectured her again about the housework.

Poor Lynn! No matter what she tried, she was always in trouble. She constantly felt wrong and anxious. As a child, she could not realize that the problem lay with her parents. If they had talked together, they could easily have laid out a plan with their daughter that would have enabled her to schedule enough time daily for both duties and even some time for herself. They simply didn't realize that the predicament had caused their daughter to become a troubled child—troubled by guilt.

In Lynn's case, her guilt came from her long-term failure to please her parents—whom she loved and respected very much. She gave them the power to control her feelings and she was depressed as well as guilt-ridden.

Carl, on the other hand, felt that he had great power over his mother. He could make her cry or rarely, laugh. His antics often gave her a headache. And she repeatedly said, "Son, you'll be the death of me yet!" When he was only ten, Carl's mother died of heart disease. He was inconsolable and believed absolutely that he had caused the death of his own mother. You may be certain, Carl became a very troubled child.

Most children, as I have explained earlier, develop a sense of omnipotence. In children like Carl, that sense is reinforced by their parents' attitudes. When a parent, bigger, wiser, and stronger than the child, verbally gives him that power, the child believes he actually does possess it! Such authority is frightening to a child and when he sees it hurting his own parent, he will certainly feel guilt as well as fear.

Furthermore, guilt is often accompanied by anger. Lynn eventually resented the constant bind her parents kept her in, and Carl was angry at his mother for being so weak and for finally leaving him.

The powerful triad of *guilt, fear,* and *anger* commonly go together, and create a vicious cycle that often explodes into serious emotional illness.

Sarah's parents were exceptionally rigid about many rules. It was rare for her to believe that they were pleased with her. Since she tried as hard as she could—and much harder than her friends tried for their parents—to make them proud of her, she began to feel very angry with them. But she believed it was wrong to be so hateful to her parents, and began to fear she would be punished for her anger. She became afraid when the lights were turned off at night, and her heart beat very hard if she ever had to go into the shadowy basement. What if some monster popped out and grabbed her? Sarah was so angry with her parents that she would not soften enough to admit her guilt and fright. So she carried these painful feelings silently until her school grades fell, and her friends rejected her since she was no longer fun to play with.

Misunderstandings with parents, then, unknowingly cause hurt in a child, and pain, right from birth, that results in anger. Anger with the parents and the confusion brought on by love for the parents, as well, brings guilt. From guilt comes the fear of serious retribution.

Kinds of Guilt

It is important for you to understand that there are two kinds of guilt: a *negative, neurotic guilt that can cause serious emotional problems,* and a *healthy guilt that is one of the greatest motivators for positive change!*

The cases just described are examples of the destructive power of unconscious, neurotic guilt. None of those children actually sat down and thought, *I am a rotten child because I can't please my parents!* These children simply felt rotten due to the attitude of worry or displeasure they sensed from the parents.

Without help or change, such children usually grow up to put themselves in a double bind. An insurance salesman once told me, "When I'm out trying to sell insurance, I feel I should be at home teaching my son to swim and play baseball. But when I'm at home with my son, I worry because I should be out selling insurance." What a predicament! He always feels at least a little bit guilty.

Real Guilt. This is an emotion I knew one time, and it taught me a lifelong lesson. When I was only six, it was the fad in our rural school to play paper dolls. It was in the heart of the depression, and no one had money to buy paper dolls or their clothes, so the older girls made their own. Some girls had boxes full of gorgeous paper fashions for their dolls. I was the youngest child in school and definitely was *not* an artist, so I had very few clothes for my paper doll (which I had cut out of a magazine).

One day I decided life was certainly unfair. Thelma had a whole shoe box full of doll clothes, and I had only six outfits. She would never miss just one! I broke the wise rule that no child should be in the schoolroom alone. During playtime, I sneaked in, hurriedly picked a purple evening dress, and slipped it into my pocket.

That paper dress became a hot coal in my pocket. No one knew I had taken it, but I knew it—and *I* knew I had no right to it. My usually healthy appetite was gone, and I could hardly swallow supper. All evening I was silently miserable. Finally, I knew what I had to do. The next morning I privately returned a somewhat crumpled paper evening dress to its proper owner. Perhaps I was cowardly for not verbally confessing my sin, but I was so shy that seems, even now, impossible.

Lesson Learned. Certainly the lesson I learned was this: *nothing is worth having at the cost of such immense inner agony.* No more guilt for me! Stealing has never been a temptation for me again. The real guilt for robbing a person of a real article was my motivator to stop stealing.

Distinguishing Types of Guilt. In a well-meant attempt to help people overcome the anxiety of guilt, our world today has made a big mistake. Counselors of all kinds often fail to distinguish good guilt from neurotic guilt. They have helped people to justify their wrongdoings or to harden their consciences, so they no longer see the wrong. This technique certainly alleviates guilt, but it has created a large number of people who have too little regard for others, or even for their own integrity.

With yourselves, parents, and your children, be careful to cultivate a sensitive conscience. Distinguish between real guilt that comes from doing wrong to another, or being less than one's best—and false, destructive guilt. False guilt dissolves in the light of accurate information and general honesty.

Causes of Guilt

The examples above make the causes of guilt quite clear, but let me list them:

1. *Constant disapproval and criticism by well-meaning parents* can cause a child to feel guilty for troubling them. Children who love their parents want very much to please them, and when they fail in this, they feel unworthy and bad.

2. *Continual blaming of a child for the parents' bad feelings.* This builds on the child's natural sense of omnipotence in a negative way. The blame may be extended to other children, and one child may be seen to be at fault for the problems of others. Such blame creates a power for wrong that causes extreme guilt, fear, and anger. This often results in serious emotional or even mental problems.

3. *Healthy guilt that motivates good changes comes from breaking known rules* or laws. Such lawbreaking results in harm to one's self or others—physically, socially, or emotionally. Remorse and guilt often prompt the "sinner" to stop

such destructive acts, and result in his being a better person and helping to form a better society—in his own small world.

Helping the Guilty Child

Since guilt almost always involves the whole family, you parents must be involved in its resolution. Following are some steps you will need to take in order to make and keep your family guilt-free.

Understanding Good Guilt. Read and reread the definitions of real and false guilt, until you are sure you understand the difference.

Healthy guilt follows a logical sequence. It begins with breaking a rule or a law, thereby doing harm to one's own self or someone else. There is a sense of remorse, sadness, or shame that comes with the awareness of having committed the wrong. This painful feeling should prompt the child to confess or apologize and make right the wrong as much as possible. As soon as I returned the stolen paper-doll dress, I felt immense relief.

Next, there needs to be a decision to avoid doing this wrong again. Then there should be the forgiving of one's self, by the other person and by God. This process will quickly prompt healing and restoring of love between people.

Dealing With False Guilt. Most false guilt comes from misunderstandings between you as parents and your child. You need, therefore, to reverse that and come to a deep awareness of the pain that you are unknowingly inflicting on each other.

There is a fine line between good training and discipline and a rigid, critical attitude. If you see your child acting defeated, or even defiant, it almost certainly means you have shown too much disapproval and criticism and too little pride. Perhaps he or she really can't do as much as you expect. Check that out. Or perhaps, in your efforts to help him improve in his abilities, you have pushed him too hard. Is your vocabulary full of *buts?* If you often say, "That's okay, Sally, but why didn't you do that earlier?" then you may be mixing your approval with chronic disapproval and the child will feel the criticism, not the *okay*.

Perhaps, like Carl's mother, you discipline your children by blaming them for your feelings or problems. They will quickly pick up a lifelong burden of guilt and carry a sense of responsibility for everyone they meet.

Helping Your Child Overcome False Guilt. If you realize you have helped your child into a predicament involving false guilt, I suggest you take these steps:

Explain the true facts, including the admission of your mistakes as discussed above. Think these through carefully and don't be either too hard or too easy on yourself.

Make it clear to your child that he or she is not a bad child. Even the shame, anger, and other painful feelings he or she experiences are based on misunderstandings and mistakes. Few parents, indeed, do understand how much their children want to please them, and out of this, they make the mistake of nagging, criticizing, and blaming.

Encourage your child to talk out his feelings of shame, anger, or fear and listen carefully. At this point, if your child does talk about the hurts he feels, you may become defensive and get into an argument. Above all else, don't let yourself slip into that trap! Wait until the child finishes, and honestly let him know how sad you are that you have hurt him so much. If there is some warmth between you, you may then explain your motives, which are almost always right. Wanting a child to grow up being reliable and a hard worker are fine desires. Knowing that can help your child understand you.

When the understanding between you and your child is quite clear, you will find forgiveness to be almost automatic, but usually *it's a good idea to seek and offer forgiveness directly.*

Now you are ready for a plan and a promise: to *avoid such destructiveness in the future.* Include your entire family in this plan, because you will need each other to help make it work. It will benefit all of you! The details of this plan will need to be your own, but should include these component parts:

1. *Some reminder to yourselves that will enable you to stop your unsuccessful or painful methods of discipline.*
2. *The development of clear, firm, and loving ways to train and discipline your children.*
3. *The cultivation of a positive, encouraging attitude.*

4. *Some understanding of and cooperation with the plan by your children.*

If you are a family to whom prayer is familiar, *a short prayer may complete the forgiving by the heavenly Father, and pin down your contract for change.*

Dealing With Mixed Feelings

When a guilt-ridden child becomes angry, he is likely to lose touch with the sense of guilt and even his love, and only recognize the anger. He intuitively will act out his anger in a blind attempt to get even for the injustice he feels. Such an angry child really doesn't want to do well, lest the parents feel they have won a battle. By doing well, a child may sense that he is making his parents look good to others, and since he is aware of more pain than love by now, he really doesn't want them to look good. So he is stuck in negative, power-struggling behavior.

Admit Your Mistakes. That fact reveals why a confession of some fault, at least, by you parents will stop the vicious cycle. By agreeing with the child's belief that you mistakenly have thought you were always right (and he was always wrong), he no longer needs to fight. You are joining him in his knowledge that sometimes you, too, are wrong. Can you imagine the relief that must bring to him? Most children caught in such a web take some time to believe the new facts, but just stay with it. He wants to believe!

Fear Mixed With Guilt. This requires a little different approach. First, of course, make sure both you and your child know whether he is really guilty, or is laboring under false guilt. Recognizing false guilt can, in itself, free your child from the fear of imagined punishment.

Usually, however, there is a long process of helping a truly frightened, guilt-ridden child out of his habits of painful feeling and misbehaving. Often such a child has physical tics or other behavioral habits that are infinitely annoying. Most parents have great difficulty in stopping their angry lectures at these unpleasant behaviors. You can be sure your anger will convey your disapproval, and your child's guilt and fear will worsen—and so will those annoying behaviors.

If you want your child to stop acting out her or his fear, *you simply must stop acting angry.* In my experience, the most helpful way to curtail your anger is to imagine a picture of the scared little boy or girl inside your child. Most parents instinctively reach out in loving protection to a scared child. Follow that instinct and comfort your child. Stop pressuring him or her, and simply love that child. As soon as the love is believable and consistent, go through the steps in the section just above.

Develop a New Program

In getting rid of the old, critical atmosphere about your home, you will find you must replace it with something better. In fact, I recommend that you do not stop your old ways *until* you have such a better plan ready to go. Familiar ways, though not always the best, are at least an accustomed life-style. Good changes need to be made slowly, so you all can find your way into them, and so they will last.

Replace guilt, fear, and anger with confidence. Begin with yourselves and tell each other, Mom and Dad, how proud you are of your courage and wisdom in making such an important change for your family. Extend this goodwill to your children. Concentrate on every *positive* thing about them and talk about these things clearly and simply—but honestly.

Never bring up the past. Old sins and mistakes can only bring with their memory the defeat and guilt they caused! Your child, unfortunately, will not be likely to forget those grim times. He doesn't need you to remind him.

Avoid labeling and blaming. Yes, even parents call their children names that carry bad images. And children commonly do this to each other. Stop such practices!

Tell someone else about the good deeds or qualities you are beginning to see. Such compliments help you believe in the reality of the change, and perhaps your child will overhear you telling it. This can help him to believe in the good side of himself!

Dealing With Incidents Involving Guilt

There are many children who are chronically troubled by guilt. But at a practical level, there are many misdeeds that involve momentary guilt. Dealing with that wisely can also be a challenge.

Our grandson loved to play with our old hand-operated adding machine. We had allowed that under our observation, and knew he couldn't break it or hurt himself. One day, however, I came upon him in the hallway outside my husband's study. He had pulled the heavy machine off the shelf and into the hall, and was busily rolling out the tape all over the floor. My footsteps startled him, and my frown of disapproval bounced off a tiny face that knew at once he was in trouble!

How I wish I'd had the patience and wisdom as a mother that I have accumulated as a grandmother. I sat down beside Andy and firmly explained that he knew it was okay to push the keys and turn the handle, but *not* to lift the machine and certainly not to take off the tape. I insisted that he help me reroll the long ribbons of unwound tape. He rolled as I untwisted, and together we fixed the mess! Andy repeatedly asked, "Grandma, why are you making me do this? It's too hard!" And I repeatedly explained, "You have to learn to fix up the messes you make. And I know that's hard!"

When we were all done and the tape was fastened back in place, I picked Andy up and hugged him. Very quietly I said, "Andy, that was a very big job for a little boy. It was hard. But you did it, and that helped me. I want you to know I'm very proud of you for staying with me and helping finish the job." His brown eyes smiled with my gray ones, and we were close friends. There was no further problem with the adding machine. What started with fear and guilt resulted in a lesson learned and a more loving relationship. That's what should become of all daily events.

When a child has misbehaved, he or she needs to be punished in order to relieve the natural, good guilt. Such punishments need to be carefully, wisely selected. For Andy, rewinding the tape was punishment enough. Sometimes your look of disapproval may teach the child, "Never again!" With other children more may be needed. Sending a child to his room, sitting him firmly in a chair for several minutes, restricting his privileges for a time—all may serve to relieve his guilt, as well as teaching him to change his behavior.

When children are older, earning money to pay for a broken or lost toy, or losing an allowance, can help them learn to make restitution and hence relieve their guilt. This sort of reparation also teaches a child a good sense of responsibility.

Be sure to make the cause, the kind, and the end of the punishment *clear*. And when it is all over, be sure you both know you really love each other. There is no need or room for ongoing guilt in your family.

Irreparable Harm

Rarely, I have shared with a family some irreparable damage done by a child. One boy, mentioned earlier, in a fit of anger broke a priceless vase his mother treasured. A jealous brother crawled into his baby brother's crib and pounded on him until he broke his tiny leg. A boy playing with his father's gun accidentally shot and killed his sister.

Such events, fortunately, are rare. But they do occur, and with them come great guilt and grief. The vase, though a *thing,* was irreplaceable. The infant's leg finally mended, but the sister could never be replaced.

In such instances, *the grace of forgiveness is imperative.* Simply help the child to get beyond the crisis to the deep feelings he experiences. Review the stages of grief, and help him and yourself through those. In your forgiving, the child can experience self-forgiving and a pattern for knowing of God's ultimate forgiving and healing.

When anger or jealousy prompts such an act, teach your child to control the anger. Even a young child can learn to express anger constructively. (*See* the section on Anger in the beginning of this chapter.)

Even in the worst of circumstances, the cornerstones of love, understanding, forgiving, and new beginnings keep hope alive!

JEALOUSY

Jealousy is a major destructive factor in our day, as it has been throughout history. Whether historic or current, global or personal, nearly every life has been touched by jealousy in some way.

Earlier I described my dismay and shock at the birth of my baby sister. That initial shock quickly developed into full-blown jealousy. She was much prettier than I, with her sparkling brown eyes and auburn, curly hair. She had the attentions I had once enjoyed, and in return I had to give up my freedom in order to entertain her. I resented that. No doubt about it! I was *jealous*.

Components of Jealousy

Jealousy is a complicated emotion, actually composed of several feelings. In my experience, it always rests on the fear or belief that one is somehow not really a good enough person—just *not okay!* Or, at least one *believes* he is not as good as the person of whom he is jealous. I knew my sister was prettier than I. I feared she was more loved or wanted than I.

Another ingredient of jealousy, then, is *uncertainty*. If I had known my sister was more important or loved, I might have grieved over my lost position and recovered. But I remained quietly unsure, vaguely hoping I still had some significance!

Also woven into this tangled tapestry we call jealousy is *suspicion*. Doubts about everyone's feelings for one's self as well as the object of one's jealousy constantly plague the jealous person.

Furthermore, there is a feeling of resentment that can ripen into anger and even hatred in many situations. The jealous rage between family members or lovers can actually result in murder. In fact, in the first recorded murder—of Abel by his brother, Cain—jealousy was the cause.

Factors Leading to Jealousy

Child's Private Comparison of Himself With Others. Most jealous children are sensitive and perceptive. They see the good points in others, and may even exaggerate them. All too often, they compare themselves unfavorably. They do not see their own assets clearly, since most jealous children are quite insecure. Even their good qualities do not seem valuable, due to their feeling that their looks, behaviors, or achievements simply do not measure up.

Parents' Value System (Or That of Other Relatives). All parents have dreams for their children. They long for an athletic son or a brilliant daughter. If it happens that such a child is born to them and fulfills their dreams, everyone is proud and happy.

More often than not, however, that dream is unfulfilled, or worse yet, one child fits the dream but another does not. When the latter occurs, the parents' unconscious pride in the child who fulfills their dream is obvious to the child who does not. The parents' values are part of that dream. They honestly love both children, but one has more of their approval than the other. Very often the one who feels left out will become jealous of the other.

Grandparents or other relatives and teachers may also take this role with children. They may hold up one child as an example to the other, unknowingly fanning the flames of jealousy.

Peer Approval. One child in a family may be successful in social areas, while another is not. Hearing cheers for a brother or sister may create pride in a less-popular child, but all too often it prompts jealousy.

Jealousy of Material Things. Perhaps this is more accurately called *covetousness,* but for our purposes, it is so much like jealousy, we will discuss it here. Possessions, and the status they confer on children, are often the source of painful feelings of inadequacy and jealousy. Children whose families cannot afford name-brand clothes, expensive games, or elegant homes, may actually become depressed over those differences, as well as jealous.

Helping a Jealous Child

Become aware of partiality (if any). How many times in the last week have you complimented each of your children? If you find that one child has a definite edge over the others, you had better sit back and think about why that is. I have actually heard parents say, "Well, Sally never does anything worth complimenting!" At once, you may be certain, Sally (or whoever it is at your house) does not fit your personal values. I have never seen a child who couldn't be praised for *something.* So take

your disapproving eyes off that child and use them to explore
that child's achievements and good points.

Find each child's assets. By seeing only Sammy's large nose,
you may overlook his gorgeous brown hair. In your annoyance
at Debbie's daydreaming, you may never have noticed how kind
she is to her playmates. Look keenly and objectively at each
child. Think about his or her strengths. Listen to others' opinions. You may be surprised that a teacher or baby-sitter
has great regard for the child with whom you have serious
problems.

Ceremoniously apologize. When you become quite convinced
and can clearly see where you have misjudged a child, sit down
and talk with him. Describe the tension and unhappy feelings
between you. (Putting feelings into words makes them clearer
and easier to deal with.) At this point, it is necessary that you
talk only of *your* fault in this situation. Your child has a part,
too, but he will work that out after you make some changes. Let
your child know how sorry you are at unknowingly putting him
down or devaluing and hurting him.

*Make it clear to this child that you love him as much as his
brother or sister, but that unconsciously they fulfilled your old
dreams exceptionally well.* Explaining *unconscious* to him is
not easy, but it will help him to understand himself better if you
try. (The unconscious part of us causes us to feel and act in
some ways that we don't really think about. They are like habits
that we do automatically, and they come from early childhood.
We have habits of feeling, wishing, and acting, just as we have
habits of talking and walking in certain characteristic ways.)

Such an explanation can help your child understand why you
seemed to favor another child, and will enable him to forgive
you and believe again in your love and his worth. Learning to
feel good about himself will be the greatest possible influence in
eliminating your child's jealousy.

Set up a plan for change. With your child's help work out a
plan for avoiding the habits that have allowed him to feel less
worthy than his siblings and friends. He will have some ideas
about that, so listen to them. Give yourself a reminder to prevent the natural tendency to slip into old habits. A note on the
refrigerator or bathroom mirror will help you remember to
compliment your child, rather than to criticize or ignore him.
Such positive feedback can reverse his jealousy.

Discipline everyone fairly. Many times the favored child seems to behave so that he rarely needs to be punished. Sometimes that is due to his being sneaky and not getting caught! Sometimes he is just an adaptable, compliant child who truly stays out of trouble.

At any rate, discipline each child privately and be careful that he or she really deserves it. Follow the rules for good discipline carefully, and the feeling that one always "gets it" and the other never does is likely to disappear. The rules of good discipline are these:

1. *Make your expectations and rules clear and fair, so each child understands and can follow them.*
2. *Include the children in setting up and changing these rules. (Parents have final veto power!)*
3. *Make the rewards or discipline fair and clear from the outset.*
4. *Consistently follow through in enforcing the plan—do this ceremoniously and privately.*

Help your jealous child to become self-confident. A confident child knows he is good at something; he is able to make and keep friends; he expects the best of himself and others, and is secure enough to feel good (rather than jealous) about the success of others.

Helping your jealous child to replace that damaging emotion with warmth and confidence, then, demands several things:

1. *He needs to master social skills in order to share activities and make friends. Teach him how to play tennis, swim, skate, or ski—depending on where you live and what activities are affordable.*
2. *He needs to develop empathy—the ability to know something about how others feel, so he can avoid hurting them, and can become kind and supportive.*
3. *He needs to learn to balance talking about his interests with listening to others' concerns. You will need to help him overcome his suspicions and fears about others, if he is to do this successfully.*
4. *He will need some play equipment and a willingness to*

share it. This need not be an expensive bike or video game. A kite or homemade toys may be more fun than expensive equipment.

5.   *Teach your child real values. If your child is jealous of others' material possessions, you may need to teach him how to create toys and fun. Appreciating and caring for the things he has can give your child a healthy sense of pride. Best of all, make the relationship in your family so loving, and your shared experiences so rewarding, that your child will have no room in his heart for jealousy.*

Giving up his old protection of resentment, suspicion, and negative attitudes will take time. Don't expect your jealous child to change at once. You will need to be patient and reassuring when neither he nor you really feels like it. You must be tenacious, positive, and *committed to success.* You can have it.

There may come times when you will need to remain firm about stopping the old jealousy habit. It is always helpful if you see your child's problems as due in part to old habits. Any habit change comes about haltingly, with frequent backslidings at first. These can reinforce the new habit rather than bring discouragement. Each time one slips into old ways, he can compare them with the new and better ones, and thus be even more encouraged to stick with it.

Whatever it takes, help your jealous child to give up that troublesome way of life. His whole future will be brighter and even more successful if he does so. As you help your child, I hope you will find a new contentment with who *you* are, and what *you* have. You and your child can grow together!

OVERSENSITIVITY

Probably everyone has friends who worry them because they are so sensitive. The least comment or happening can put them in tears for days, and they see everything as hostile or frightening.

Such habits begin in childhood. By recognizing the forerunners early, you can prevent a life of sadness for a child and frustration for her friends.

Example of an Oversensitive Child

Molly is an example of the supersensitive child. She was seven when I knew her, and in the second grade. She was tall and had attractive blue eyes and blond hair. She was neatly dressed but in much fluffier, more dressy styles than the other girls. She was bright, but after each problem she worked and each paragraph she read, she demanded her teacher's approval. Molly could figure out very little for herself. She was afraid of the rough games on even a well-supervised playground, and avoided joining in, thanks to notes from her mother asking that she be excused. Molly walked with the tiny steps of a pre-schooler and talked like a younger child.

Any correction from her teacher caused tears to spring up in Molly's baby-blue eyes. And a cross word or rough touch from any other child sent her scurrying to the teacher for protection. The teacher, with twenty-five other children, was worn-out with the demands of this one sensitive youngster. Molly was un-happy and to the other children she was at once a nuisance and a source of amazement.

As we studied Molly's family, we learned that she was the youngest child and her mother enjoyed her immensely—so much, in fact, that she unconsciously was overprotecting her. Keeping her emotionally and socially "little" met her mother's needs for closeness, but was destroying Molly's maturing process.

Molly demonstrates most of the signs of the overly sensitive child. Such children in general cry easily at the slightest hurt—real or imagined, physical or emotional. They act like much younger children normally do, and have failed to acquire even the ordinary, necessary calluses of life. They are unwilling to risk failure or even mistakes, and do not tolerate pain of any sort. These children subtly manage to get their way by pouting or withdrawing their love, realizing that their often-doting parents depend on that love. Because other children do not know how to relate to them, they are rejected by their peers and tend to clutch on to adults or older children. Usually they find some-one who needs to be needed, and these people become their friends.

The processes of growing up modify these traits somewhat,

but many of them carry over into adulthood, creating problems in jobs, marriages, and in parenting.

Causes of Oversensitivity

Parental Overprotection. Almost uniformly, such an outsized sensitivity is due to parental overprotection in an unusually adaptive child. My experience is that many of these children have suffered serious illnesses early in life, and the threat of losing them makes parents anxious and overprotective. These parents simply do not overcome that earlier fear. Sometimes the cause is an older child who has been ill, or may even have died. The parents seems unable to overcome the fear that such a tragedy could happen again.

Parents Who Reparent Themselves. Rarely, I have known parents who were abused as children to go to the opposite extreme with their own children. By pampering and overprotecting them, they seem to reparent themselves in some unconscious way.

Example of Sensitive Parent. Yet another factor in the development of an overly sensitive child is the example of a sensitive parent. When Mother or Dad cries easily, the child learns to do so, too. Some parents cry over a television program, or may weep at their children's mischief. In trying to reassure such parents, children may copy their behaviors.

Helping a Sensitive Child

By the very nature of the causes of sensitivity in children, the cure is difficult. *That difficulty lies in the deep needs of the parents.* As is so often the case, then, you parents must take the first steps to change this problem.

Take a look at your child. Compare her with other children and see if she (or he) is as happy or productive as her capabilities suggest. You will need courage to face this inspection honestly. It is tempting to make excuses or to rationalize away the existence of a problem, but once you admit the unhappiness and "differentness" of your child, you will be motivated to help her change!

Take a look at yourselves. What old needs could you unconsciously be meeting by keeping your child dependent through his sensitivities? Perhaps you haven't realized that you are carrying over old fears and placing them on this child in a different set of circumstances. Are you too little in control of your *own* sensitive feelings? In the freedom our society offers to be open and honest with feelings, perhaps you have unwittingly gone to an extreme. Could you be worrying your child with your extra sensitivity?

Don't hesitate to ask for help. You are very likely to need an outside opinion to help you to evaluate and cure this problem. Most parents are so close to their sensitive child that they truly cannot see the issue clearly. I recommend a family counselor for this kind of problem, because he is trained to understand those intricate interweavings of generations of time and emotions. With such help, you will find, I trust, an even closer relationship with your child than before, because it will be based on greater strength and understanding and less on needs.

There are steps you can take on your own.

Let Your Child Grow Up. Decide to let your child grow up and become independent. There is a natural tendency to do so in almost all children, unless that is somehow inhibited. Once you have made up your mind to begin letting go, the rest is easier. I suggest you look for other sources for meeting your needs. Try volunteering with handicapped children or an elderly person. Your need to nurture and protect your child can be met by enriching some other people's lives.

Control Your Feelings. If you are a "feeling spiller," work at controlling those feelings a bit more. Now don't go all the way to the other extreme and hide them, but just ease back a little bit. Both you and your child may be more comfortable. And do learn to laugh as easily as you cry. Humor in life is so important in balancing things.

Gradually stop the overprotection you have lavished on your child. Ask a teacher or dependable friend to guide or encourage you in this significant step. Going too fast may scare both of you, but going too slow wastes the precious happy time of normal childhood.

Give Your Child a Chance to Grow Up. Look for signs of mature behavior in your child and praise him or her for those. Let him know that you really want him to grow up, and that you will be allowing him to do so more and more. Think of some specific steps your child needs to take alone. For example, require him to do homework without your help. Start assigning jobs around the house. Begin letting your child make some of her own decisions. If they are not the wisest, don't worry. She has to learn by mistakes—and that will be hard for you to accept, because you have a long-standing habit of protecting her. But learning and growing are really what life is about.

Lessen the Comforting. Watch carefully for your tendency to seize upon any opportunity to comfort your child when she is upset. Our youngest child was easy to comfort, and I must admit I did enjoy the closeness I felt as I tried to help her through the vicissitudes of childhood. But I began to realize the comforting had gone on long enough. One day she came home from school, dramatically distressed over the trials of her day. I sat beside her as she lay on the sofa, spent with her hardships! Suddenly she said, "Mother, I think I've come to enjoy feeling bad!" It was a healthy turning point, as we both recognized together that the sensitivity had to go. She had to face her life and struggle through on her own. It has been exciting to see her do exactly that.

The too-sensitive child is in for some hard times. Work carefully to toughen your child just enough so he or she can cope well with a difficult world, but allow enough sensitivity to keep him tender and caring.

SADNESS

Sometimes in my working with troubled families I feel that the whole world must be sad. My husband, a family doctor, sees people with physical ailments rather than emotional ills, however, and he often reminds me that I work only with emotionally troubled people. In that, I find hope and comfort, but there certainly are too many children who look sad. I see them in the aisles of grocery stores, in shopping centers, and even in churches—children whose eyes are lonely and who seem to cry out for love and comfort.

Example of a Sad Child

Vicki was just that kind of sad little girl of six. She had been happy once, a long time ago. Her mother and dad were proud of her first teeth, and Mommy sometimes showed her a picture of herself as a baby with two pearly teeth shining through her smile. They had been excited about her first steps, and they had pictures of that, too. Home movies she had seen showed a chubby, wobbly little girl, barely making it from Mother's hands to Daddy's.

Vicki could not remember when she started to feel sad, but she did realize that Mommy and Daddy started to look mad and argued a lot. She knew Daddy didn't come home for dinner very often, and Mommy cried a lot. They were a little happier when her baby brother was born, but Vicki wasn't. No one had time for her anyway, and now he took the little time they ever did have.

She worried about her parents. Her friend's parents had gotten a divorce. What if her parents did that? Where would she go? And who would pay those bills her parents argued about? Why didn't Daddy ever smile anymore, and why didn't he hug Mommy or her?

Vicki is not a fantasy. She is a real little girl with a very different name but only a slightly different story. In many schools, over 50 percent of the children's parents have been divorced and are either struggling alone or heroically trying to put two strange families together.

In many more families, marital strife, alcoholism, or abuse create stress and anxiety far beyond the capability of a child's coping. These are the huge sadnesses of an ever-growing multitude of children.

Now let's talk about the daily small sadnesses of children who do not yet know those big, hopeless tragedies.

Symptoms of a Sad Child

The sad child, early on in the course of sadness, really looks sad. The eyes are downcast, and the corners of the mouth and the shoulders droop. He cries easily—usually a whimpering cry that lacks energy. He spends time alone, rocking, rhythmically sucking his thumb, and looking doleful. These signs may be

visible in babies only a few months old. They improve temporarily when the child is old enough to explore and entertain
himself, but in neglected children there is little if any improvement.

Older children may disguise their sadness as boredom. Such
children look and act irritable or angry. No activity interests
them, and they tend to lose themselves in TV, books, or music.
Sometimes they try to fill their gnawing emptiness with food.
And sooner or later many children, even grade-schoolers, discover the escape from sadness through drugs or alcohol.

Occasionally, a child may explode out of this sadness and
boredom with anger. Such angry outbursts make him feel powerful and relieve the hoplessness for a time. Continued anger
may get him enough attention to keep him acting out those un-
bearably sad, helpless feelings in this disguised fashion.

It is the anger that separates the aggressive, sad child from
the withdrawn, passively waiting child. The child who reaches
out for comfort, or even for punishment of pranks, is usually
better off than the quiet waiter. Too often busy teachers and
parents overlook the withdrawn child, allowing his sadness to
grow into despair.

Causes of Sadness

Usually sadness in children is the result of a loss. The mini-
sadnesses are almost a daily occurrence in the lives of children.
Broken toys, cessation of playtime, failure to win a game, the
loss of Mommy's or Daddy's time and attention when they are
busy or talking on the telephone—these are examples of daily
sadnesses little (and bigger) children endure. When there are
more losses and sad times than happy ones, children become
chronically sad or depressed.

Some disappointments, however, can be a healthy means of
helping children mature. The postponement of present pleasure
for future good is a major sign of maturity, and children, as well
as adults, must learn it. Giving a child sympathetic understanding, however, as he endures the constant flow of bigger and
smaller disappointments, can support him in enduring and
overcoming them without permanent sadness.

*Failing to forgive a child after he has misbehaved and been
punished is also likely to result in sadness.* Many parents be-

lieve they must withhold their love after discipline in order to make the child take it seriously. Until they give up in despair, however, children really crave their parents' approval, and the reassurance of parents' love when a child temporarily faces disapproval is vital.

More major sadness comes with the loss of a parent through divorce or death. A child in such a situation faces extreme helplessness; even despair may come over a child during such a time. Often the adults who are around the child in such a loss are immersed in their own grief, and they may overlook the sadness in the child.

The loss of healthy parental interaction with each other and with the child (as in the case of Vicki) *will certainly create a climate of sadness.* To feel secure, children need both parents to demonstrate affection and congeniality.

Prolonged and severe disapproval of or criticalness with a child will also produce sadness. This may quickly be covered by indifference or resentment, but every child needs regular praise and pride to feel happy and worthwhile.

Helping a Sad Child

We will discuss helping children with the major sadness of divorce later on. Let's think about helping a sad child day by day in a way that will prevent serious depression later on.

Explore your own attitudes. Parents, you do set the mood for your family, especially when they are young. Are you negative, critical, or downhearted? If so, start to help your child by learning to think, act, and feel positively. Take greater charge of your emotions and discipline yourselves to become pleasant, at least, if not really happy!

Keep personal stress under control. Even the most jovial people encounter times of stress that rob them of their joy. By understanding your stress, make decisions about it, and restore your good feelings as soon as possible. Explain to your family something about your problems and their ultimate solutions. This will enable them to give you understanding and support, prevent their worry at knowing too little, and help all of you focus on the better times ahead. Accepting the limits of certain kinds of stress may present a real challenge. Financial and health problems are examples of such stress, but learning to live within the restrictions of such problems can be an example to your family.

Are you unconsciously fostering your child's sadness? Due to a sad childhood of your own, you may be too sympathetic with your child. Don't encourage self-pity and prolong his sadness unnecessarily.

Comforting a sad child may make you feel warm and close, and you may unwittingly encourage his sadness to give you a reason to cuddle and comfort him. Avoid that, but don't reject real needs. When a child seeks comfort several times a day, it may be a sign that both of you enjoy that ritual too much!

Are your demands and discipline too severe? If your child's sadness has reached the point of giving up trying to please you or gain your attention, and he is becoming depressed, do consider this possibility. Don't become permissive, on the other hand, because children need parental authority, but authority merges imperceptibly into tyranny, and that is too severe. If you are unsure about your discipline and expectations, please ask a counselor. A visit or two may save you and your child a great deal of heartache!

Restore or introduce laughter. Life does seem to become heavy without your even realizing it. How long has it been since you and your family laughed together?

On a vacation trip many years ago, I realized that I was sitting in one motel room, feeling bored, while our children were enjoying gales of laughter in the next room. I quickly joined them and found out again how to laugh. I hadn't realized that laughter could be so elusive. Look for the humor in life's struggles, and you will find your mood and the atmosphere of the entire family will be changed.

Comfort your child's pain and sadness without encouraging it. Teach him to overcome or accept the hard realities of life. And in overcoming these, remind him to find and keep laughter. It is impossible to stay sad when one finds the fun in life.

10
Physical Problems

Hardly anyone totally escapes the trouble of some physical handicap. Either within an extended family or that of a close friend, there is, sooner or later, that accident or birth defect that inflicts the agony of a permanent handicap.

To help you understand the problems of those many handicapped people, I will describe them categorically under several main headings.

CONGENITAL HANDICAPS

Such a problem is present at birth. It may or may not be hereditary.

Orthopedic (Bone) Defects

These are numerous and range in severity from those that are severely handicapping, such as missing parts of the body, to completely correctable ones, such as clubfeet.

Neurological Defects

Like bone problems, neurological problems may be present at birth, and range from being extremely limiting to barely noticeable. Cerebral palsy, epilepsy, various kinds of progressive muscular deteriorative illnesses (due to nerve damage), and mental retardation are examples of congenital neurological defects. Sometimes these do not show up for some months or years, but the basic handicap dates to birth or before.

Endocrine System Defects

These are rare, but serious in their handicapping effect. A defect of the thyroid gland at birth causes *cretinism,* a disease that in some ways resembles Down's syndrome but can be quite successfully treated if it is diagnosed early. *Cystic fibrosis,* a uniformly fatal disease of most of the glands in the body, is present at birth. *Turner's syndrome* is a disease affecting several systems of the body but involves the absense of ovaries in a baby girl.

Diabetes is a common disease due to the failure of the pancreas (a very important organ that secretes many digestive enzymes) to put out insulin. The pancreas also is defective in the case of cystic fibrosis.

The Urinary (Renal) System

The child may be afflicted by the congenital absence or deformity of the kidneys, the tubes leading from the kidneys to the bladder or the tube going outside the body from the urinary bladder, or the bladder itself.

The Cardiovascular System

The heart and blood vessels may be so severely deformed that a baby cannot live. Many heart defects, however, can now be corrected surgically, and some are so mild, they cause no symptoms early in life and can only be diagnosed by medical tests.

The Lungs and Respiratory System

This can be affected by cystic fibrosis, a congenital disease. There may be various other birth defects, such as the narrowing or blocking of various parts of the finely branching tubes that carry air to the lungs. A fairly rare deformity is a tracheoesophageal fistula—an abnormal opening between the windpipe and the tube that leads from the throat to the stomach. It allows food and fluids from the stomach to flow into the lungs, causing severe choking, or even death. Fortunately, it can usually be found early and surgically corrected. Hyaline membrane disease is not a true birth defect, but it does affect the lungs of some infants soon after birth.

The Sensory System

These organs may also be affected by birth defects. Congenital blindness or deafness are still far too common. Fortunately, a number of years ago we discovered that viral infections, especially German (three-day) measles, could cause these defects, and by vaccinating children early in life, we can eliminate one common cause of birth defects of sight and hearing.

The Gastrointestinal System

This also can be affected by birth defects. The openings into and out of the stomach may be too large or too small, respectively. There may be narrowing or blockage of almost any area of the intestinal tract that would cause severe vomiting and failure to gain weight. On the other hand, a defect in the nerves supplying the large bowel, called Hirschsprung's disease, causes the colon to enlarge and makes it very difficult for a baby to have a bowel movement.

Defects of the Skin and Hair

These are common, but rarely serious. Birthmarks are the best-known example of congenital problems of the skin. These range from large freckles to bright red or purple discolorations that are sadly disfiguring.

HEREDITARY BIRTH DEFECTS

While any defect present at birth is *congenital,* many of these are *not hereditary. Handicaps that are transmitted from parent to child due to defects in the genes or chromosomes are hereditary.* They may be passed on to future generations. *Hemophilia* is a fairly common example of such a handicap. It is the inability of the blood to clot properly, so that even minor injuries may result in a child's bleeding severely. This defect is carried by the chromosomes of a mother, but affects only her sons. Some families seem to have a predisposition to *diabetes* and *cancer,* and many of the very crippling neurological birth defects are hereditary.

Some hereditary diseases do not become apparent for months or years. *Epilepsy* is found in many generations of certain families, but it may not become evident until a child has a high fever, or reaches a period of stress in life.

HANDICAPS DUE TO ILLNESS

Helen Keller became blind and deaf as a result of "brain fever," and was handicapped for most of her long life. *High fevers, dehydration, encephalitis,* and sometimes *meningitis* can cause serious handicaps to the nervous and sensory systems. *Polio,* once so dreaded throughout the world, left many of its victims condemned to wheelchairs for life.

HANDICAPS DUE TO TRAUMA

Every day emergency rooms receive the torn or mangled bodies of accident victims. Many of these are due to the avoidable carelessness of drunken drivers or simply unthinking people. Whether due to irresponsibility or to unavoidable situations, the results may be equally devastating.

Microscopic Surgery

Surgeons can perform miraculous feats of reattaching severed blood vessels, nerves, and muscles. Many recoveries are now possible from accidents that once would have left their victims hopeless cripples.

Helps for the Handicapped

Despite modern medical advances, however, many accidents do leave their tragic marks on people who are confined to wheelchairs, beds, or crutches. Artificial limbs can, with great effort, replace some of the functions of lost arms and legs. Mechanical engineers have invented devices that give a remarkable degree of independence to even severely handicapped people. Tubes that transmit weak puffs of air from a patient's mouth to electrical motors, move motorized wheelchairs or household equipment.

Laws require streets and public buildings to have special ramps, parking, and facilities to accommodate handicapped people. Only recently, however, I became acquainted with an intelligent and courageous lady who has lived in a wheelchair for many years. She told me that even the most posh of hotels, advertising their ability to provide for the handicapped, fall far short of actually meeting the needs.

PHYSICAL HANDICAPS RELATED TO EMOTIONAL PROBLEMS

These are much more common than one might think. People who worry a great deal, and who do not know how to recognize or express their needs and feelings, develop a great variety of physical symptoms.

Ulcers and Colitis

In adults, stomach ulcers and some cases of ulcerative colitis are commonly associated with worry and hidden anger. One of the most troublesome problems I used to encounter as a pediatrician was the complaint of stomachaches by children. All the best tests available usually revealed no physical abnormality, but the pain was there. Always, these children were worriers, and the stress of their young lives, I am convinced, produced the pain they experienced.

Nervous Tics

Nervous, anxious children develop tics of many kinds. These tics are sudden movements of the eyes, face, neck, arms, or any part of the body. They are precipitated originally by a particularly scary experience, but they become habitual when a situation even faintly like that one arises. These mannerisms are extremely annoying, and often give rise to additional stress due to parents' scolding and reminders to stop them. Since they are born of stress, more pressures invariably make them worse.

Children with tics need great calmness and peace around them. All possible pressure should be removed, and they should have unlimited amounts of unconditional love.

Obesity

Another of the physical effects of emotional distress is *obesity*. Certainly there are some physical causes for this serious problem, too, but they are relatively rare. Poor functioning of the thyroid gland is known to result in greater weight gains. Other glands in the endocrine system also may rarely influence obesity.

An Extreme Example. By far the most common problems that result in overweight children, however, are *emotional*. David was an extreme example of this. He was an only child, and hence was the focus of attention from his parents, grandparents, and several uncles and aunts. They believed that chubby babies are healthy babies, so they fed him well. David enjoyed both the food and the attention, and early on, he associated the two.

Later, David realized that food was the center of his family's social life. Large tables of food were present at all family gatherings, and food became symbolic of fun and celebrations.

After he started school, David's earlier chubbiness began causing problems for him. He could not run as fast, or do the climbing and other playtime activities that the other children did. He began to feel alone and sad. When he talked about his loneliness, his parents would offer him cookies and milk. After all, didn't every child need a little snack after school? But David's snacks became evening-long gorging bouts, as he learned that food can be a comfort in sadness.

Finally, David's loving parents did recognize that his weight was out of control. They had a physician examine him and prescribe a special diet. David, however, had used food for too long to meet his emotional needs, and he refused to give it up. He learned to sneak into the kitchen at night and eat his fill. To outwit his parents, and even the doctor, made David feel powerful, and so it was he learned that food was a weapon to use in rebelling against adults.

You can see that food served so many purposes in David's life that it became a monster. Tragically, in his case, the obesity became so great that his heart could not keep up with the demands of his circulation, and David actually died as a result of obesity.

Failure by Parents. While the severity of David's weight problem was extreme, the emotional factors in its development are extremely common. There are many children who suffer name calling by peers and their own inner embarrassment at being different because of being fat. In almost all cases, their parents fail to recognize the emotional factors in their obesity. They either excuse it, or set up a rigid regimen for dieting that only adds anger and rebellion to already existing problems.

LIFE-THREATENING HANDICAPS

A friend of mine is a pediatrician. In examining a beautiful child of six months, he felt a large, firm mass in the abdomen. His experience told him this was a dangerous sign, and the following examinations confirmed his fears. It was a Wilms tumor—a cancerous tumor of the child's kidney. She had been born with this tumor, though it was too small to be discovered then. Surgery did save that child's life, but cures for cancer cannot always be effected.

Cancers and Other Killers

Leukemia (cancer of the blood), bone cancers, and other malignant tumors do occur in children, as they do in adults. No one knows why this dread affliction claims the health and life of a child, but it is so.

Other illnesses that involve a high degree of fatality in children are *hemophilia* (described briefly above), *heart disease* (usually congenital, rarely infectious), and *cystic fibrosis.* The greatest killer of children and adolescents, however, is *accidents.*

Accidents—Greatest Killer of Children

One of the saddest experiences of my professional life was the death of a beautiful three-year-old girl. She had auburn curls and snappy brown eyes, but her curious nature led her to sample a glass full of orange-colored liquid. It was not juice from oranges, however, but an extremely toxic chemical. Despite heroic measures administered lovingly over a period of several weeks, the child died from the effects of that chemical.

There are many kinds of accidents, but they have one thing in common: they can be fatal!

EFFECTS OF PHYSICAL HANDICAPS

The limitations of the handicaps themselves, are apparent and frustrating enough; but there are also other effects, and they enmesh themselves with these to create a monstrous problem for both child and parents.

Being Different

While I value immensely the unique individuality of each child, I also am aware that children need to be like one another. Every child with an apparent physical handicap will automatically be different from his peers.

Role of Parents

Such a variation from the usual will, as soon as a child recognizes it, bring to him the grief and frustration of his helplessness in this situation. These emotions are reflected in the parents. *How parents accept the handicap and react to it will largely influence the child's response.* If they are bitter and resentful, the child is likely to be angry or self-pitying. When parents find courage to face these limits with creativity and optimism, sooner or later the child will learn to make the best of it, too.

Enforced Limitations

All handicaps include some limits not required of the average child. One of the trademarks of a healthy, mature person is the ability to recognize and bow to the inevitable. Now it is equally important that one not submit to that which can and should be changed. It takes great wisdom to know the difference.

Seeking Professional Help

The parents of any handicapped child need expert help to determine the limitations of that particular problem. Find the best professional help possible, and get all the consultation you need.

But once you hear the verdict and have it verified, be wise enough to accept it and courageous enough to face it. Within those limits, use all the creative energy you can muster to encourage, discipline, and support your child to make the most he can of the resources he has.

Certain Death

Facing limitations is one thing; but living with the inevitability of an early death is another! I have shared with parents in such prolonged grief. The parents of a child with cystic fibrosis went through the despair of recurrent bouts of pneumonia. Slowly their child improved and resumed her normal activity. In fact, she seemed so much better that they began to hope a miracle had cured her.

Inevitably, the crisis recurred, and then again, the improvement. Living on this emotional roller coaster cannot help but take its toll. Those parents went through times when the anger of their grief process seemed overwhelming. They were short-tempered with each other and with their children. At other times, their sadness was paramount, and the mood of the family was depressed. Throughout better times and worse, they all knew that one day the ever-returning bouts of pneumonia would claim their victim. That child would die. Certainly, only superhuman strength and courage could help a family through years of such sustained anxiety and grief.

HELPING A HANDICAPPED CHILD

Parents First!

At the risk of sounding like a promoter of the "Me First" philosophy, let me emphasize this: you cannot help your handicapped child until *you* get help! By this I mean that you must get enough information to understand the possibilities as well as the limitations of your child. You must work through the denial, anger, and sadness of your own grief. *And you must formulate an overall life plan for your handicapped child.*

Get help from one another, from your friends and relatives, from your faith in God, and from professional people. Very few families can make it alone through the prolonged or recurring bouts of trouble from a handicap.

Formulate a Plan

Whether your child's handicap is congenital or accidental, temporary or permanent, you will deal with it better if you make a plan. Let me remind you to get all the information you can, *first*. Be certain it is as accurate and complete as possible, yet keep an open mind about new facts as they may unfold.

Then sit down together as parents, and discuss all of the implications of the problem. Now don't do this just once, but talk again and again, until there are no more ideas or feelings left to describe. In such conversations, I hope you will find your grief being drained off, your lives more closely bonded to one another, and a wise approach to the future mapped out.

When you have made all the decisions you can, you are likely to feel less powerless, and therefore less hopeless and depressed. Having a plan gives you and your child something to work with.

Understand Your Child's Needs

Loving Acceptance. There are major physical needs that are unique to each handicapped child, but a common pitfall, in my experience, is that of failing to understand that child's *personal needs*. Loving acceptance, exactly as he is, must come first. The handicap may have exploded some magnificent dreams you had for that child. Do let them go, but begin to formulate some new and possible dreams!

Importance of Discipline. I cannot emphasize enough your child's need for good, consistent discipline! Handicapped children have many procedures to endure in the process of diagnosing their problems and prescribing treatment. It is absolutely necessary that your child learn obedience, respect, and cooperation. Be firm, consistent, fair, and loving. Follow through unerringly. You and your child will be glad you did. And so will the medical people who must try to help you.

Laughter Essential. The next need I want you to understand is the need for laughter. Do not get so absorbed in the working out of your plans that you forget how to laugh. There are funny things that happen nearly every day! In the heaviness of living with a handicapped child, it is easy to overlook the humor in daily happenings. Do not allow that in your family! Recall the fun in your day and share it with your family. Help each one learn to laugh at himself, and practice that yourself. Avoid laughing *at* anyone, but laughing *with* someone or inviting him to laugh with you can tide you through some very tough days.

Be Consistent. Do be consistent in your life by learning to recognize your temptation to fall into moods, and avoiding them. Careful self-discipline and control can help you to transcend the tendency to act too much the way you may *feel* at times. If your feelings are very negative, find a way to turn them around. Negativism is contagious—an emotional infection you cannot afford to transmit! But when you must be stern and set limits for your children, do so in a similar fashion every day.

Consistency means that in a given set of circumstances, you react in reasonably the same manner every time that situation recurs.

Be Loving. Don't forget to show and express your love for one another as a family. No one ever feels loved too much. Find a way to be loved yourselves, parents. Keep your love for each other and the healthy love for yourselves activated. Staying loving will assure being loved.

Ask for Help

For many years, I practiced a habit of being strong. In order to prove how strong I was, I took care of my needs and those of my family, my patients and *their* families, my friends and *their* families, and finally there came a day when I had to admit that I was tired. I had to face the fact that I was not always strong. I, too, had needs and weaknesses. I learned that it was perfectly all right for others to take care of some of their own needs (and even to look after me now and then!).

Recognize Your Own Limitations. In case that lesson sounds naive or simple, I know a great many people who have not learned it. Just as I did, they, too, go about trying to be strong all the time, and end up frustrated and fatigued. Especially is this true of the parents of handicapped children. There is a constant need for great strength to cope with the endless problems they must face. If they do not exercise great caution, they will fail to recognize their own need for help.

If you are such a parent, be aware that you can ask for help, and then overcome all of your reasons for refusing to ask. Most such reasons are actually excuses for trying to prove to yourself that you are stronger than you honestly feel.

How to Ask for Help. Your next question, then, is undoubtedly, "Well, whom shall I ask? Does anyone really care?" First, ask your own friends and families, but be careful to ask for *the amount of time* and the *kind of help* they can provide. In fact, I suggest that you make a list of the sorts of help you need, and allow them to check off what they would like to do. Once a month, taking the child for therapy or a doctor's visit can relieve you a bit. Sitting with a child one evening, so you can be free, is like creating an oasis in a desert for weary parents.

Other Available Resources. Other resources also are available. One heroic group of parents of severely handicapped children organized a monthly meeting. They arranged for speakers to inform them of all kinds of practical needs, from allowable income-tax deductions to future placements, should their children outlive them.

These same resourceful parents set up a plan for child care among themselves. It was not much harder to care for two handicapped children than one, since they were equipped and experienced. Such expert care gave the parents occasional entire weekends to be free with real peace of mind. Look about you. You, too, even in smaller communities, can find some other parents with whom to share.

Help From Older Children. Many mothers overlook a great source of help that is relatively inexpensive and extremely useful: asking for child care from older children or teenagers, even while the parents are there. Having such help costs very little, and can give you a chance to get your work done without the endless frustration of interruptions for the needs of your child. You may even get a rest time, with the assurance that you can be called if the sitter really needs you. Or perhaps you would most enjoy having your hired help do dishes or dusting while you spend uninterrupted time with your child.

Help From Other Sources. Finally, don't overlook the large national foundations such as March of Dimes, Easter Seal Society for Handicapped Children and Adults, and many other worthy groups. They have printed materials and lists of helpful individuals or groups in many locations throughout the country. For your needs or for your special child, ask your family doctor, look in your telephone directory, or call your county child-welfare office. You need not, by the way, need financial assistance to call on the usually wonderful people in your local welfare offices.

AVOIDANCE OF PHYSICAL HANDICAPS

Prevention

Due to the developments of medical science, the cultural climate of our times, and legal rulings, it is possible to diagnose some physical handicaps before birth. Such discoveries involve the legal option of an abortion. This option will be easy for many to choose, impossible for many others, and extremely difficult for many more.

I have listened to deeply sincere and intensely feeling people debate this issue many times, and I have entered into those debates. You may read and hear about them almost daily in the media. By all means, listen with an open mind and think carefully about all sides and aspects of the issue. It is my strong personal belief that abortion, deliberately planned, is the taking of a life. If you happen to have more liberal views, please consider the following issues.

Abortion Considerations

A basic philosophy that life should be easy. Our entire culture promotes ease and convenience as top values in life. In my experience, this belief is absolutely wrong. While I use convenience foods and enjoy being warm and well fed, I do not pursue these as having high priorities in my list of values. In fact, I discipline myself to do difficult things every day, and deliberately choose to challenge myself in promoting personal strength. Such strength of character comes from confronting and overcoming difficulties, not avoiding them!

A belief that you do not have to accept anything you don't want. Scientific advances have taken place with such acceleration that, unwittingly, we have come to feel we are omnipotent. We now have many choices we once never dreamed possible. It is tempting, then, to extend those choices to the most fundamental issues—those of life and death. When our legal system assumes the responsibility of defining life and permitting it to be extinguished by legalizing abortions, we, as citizens, need to exercise great caution. Legality does not necessarily define *morality*. The temptation to be all-powerful, and the opportunity to extend one's power legally, can deceive us. In today's world, each of us must determine our own sense of right and wrong and choose to submit to a higher power, trusting Him for wisdom and courage to face and surmount hardships.

The greatest strength lies not in the ability to choose to avoid hardships but in learning to cope. Recently I watched a track meet. All sorts of competitions were under way, and I was absorbed in the amazing feats of strength. The hurdles race especially caught my attention. The competitors ran a few paces and then jumped a hurdle, ran again and jumped again, until a tall young man finished. I felt the frustration of such a mixed challenge. It took, he later told me, intense concentration as well as extensive practice and training to win that event. One set of muscles effected the running, another the jumping, and he had to have a superb sense of timing to switch from one action to the other.

In bearing and raising a handicapped child, you will learn similar superb skills. Part of your life will be spent pacing yourself (and possibly other children) through the normal routines of life; but there is the ever-recurring hurdle to be overcome with that handicapped youngster.

You can legally avoid this in some cases, but you will miss a chance to develop super skills and growth in your character. Being truly strong is a great asset in a troubled and challenging world.

Institutional Placement

There is the possibility that a handicapped child may reach the point at which you can no longer manage him or her at home. If that happens, you will need to consider institutional care for that child.

Different Parental Responses. I have experienced both extremes in considering this painful decision. One father insisted that his baby girl, severely deformed and retarded by Down's syndrome, be placed directly from the hospital after birth in an institution. He never wanted to see her or remember his disappointment in the limits of her handicap.

Another set of parents with a child who was to drain them financially and emotionally for many years, with no hope of improvement, refused to consider placement. They deprived several normal children in their family of love and attention through their heroic sacrifices for this one.

Another family, very loving and sincere, had a severely retarded child. The grandparents refused to accept the diagnosis and tried to think of ways the parents could make her overcome the delayed walking, talking, and other developmental handicaps she faced. The young parents knew they could do no more, but they struggled with doubts and wanted desperately to have the support and approval of their parents.

When their child reached three years of age, the parents could no longer manage her care. She became violent and was big enough to break things and physically too large to confine. They could find no alternative to placing her in an institution that could care for her for life. The grandparents never forgave them, and added to their grief the prolonged condemnation of their painful decision.

Placement Guidelines. There are some guidelines that can help you to know if and when your handicapped child may require placement.

Is your child's handicap of such a nature that special training and attention will improve his functioning now, or potentially, in the future? Many handicapped people can learn to do jobs that will enable them to be partially or entirely self-supporting. Explore such possibilities as optimistically as possible. There are special schools and centers around the United States that may offer your child a chance.

At the other extreme, *is your child's mental and physical handicap such that, sooner or later, you will not physically be able to care for him or her?* You will need to plan far ahead, since competent care centers are not as available as they should be. A friend of mine actually looked around the country until she found a city that offered the very best care possible for her particular daughter. She and her family moved there in order to be near this child when she required institutional placement.

Special savings or public assistance will often be needed to pay for such expensive training or care. Start early to work on financial resources for a severely handicapped child.

Is your handicapped child's care robbing your other children of the resources they need in order to grow and develop? On one hand, helping to care for a handicapped brother or sister can be marvelous character building for children. On the other hand, such an experience can result in their feeling rejected and relatively unimportant. Keep a careful eye on the needs and feelings of your unhandicapped children. If possible, work through their hurts and needs with them; but if that special child's needs are so great that you can't meet both theirs and his, you may need to consider placement.

(*Such placement,* by the way, *need not be total or permanent.* You may have your child at home for periods of time and, as conditions change, you may be able to take him back home later on. The development, for example, of electronic devices for people who are almost totally paralyzed can enable them to be almost independent.)

Is the handicap of such a nature that he or she does not know you and cannot feel your loving care? Are you martyrishly sacrificing your time and energy, for example, on a person who has such severe brain damage that he is beyond conscious function? I realize that is hard to answer because people may sense your presence without being able to respond. Expert medical tests, however, can help you know if such is the case. Institutional placement, when it is available, may be far better for your child. You can then be free to find a job and help support him, be free to work with your other children, and be helpful to parents of other handicapped children.

Avoid Useless Martyrdom. While caring for a handicapped child usually is pure heroism it can, in rare cases, become useless martyrdom. If you are giving all you have and no one is the better for it, consider this possibility and avoid or stop it!

Public or Private Institutions for Your Child

Where can you place your child? There are two categories you must consider in planning for possible institutional care or training of your child: *private* or *public.*

Private Institutions. These are usually funded by the payment for the actual cost of a child's care. This will include nurses, physicians, therapists, and special educators, as well as substitute parents or care givers, cooks, housekeeping, and maintenance staff. This care is obviously costly, and will range upward from five thousand dollars a month, depending on the care your child's needs demand.

Public Institutions. These are provided by your own tax dollars through your local and state governments. In many states, these institutions are well funded and expertly run. That is not, however, always so. Due to the fallibility of human nature, and the whims of politics, money may be diverted to highways rather than rehabilitation. Due to the inevitable rules and regulations of public agencies, many professional people find it stifling, and even unbearable, to work in such situations. These highly creative people often work in freer, more rewarding settings.

How to Choose the Best Place. Be sure that you explore any place in which you may place your child. Like my friend, you may choose to move in order to find the very best place. Look for the following qualities:

1. *A warm, loving attitude expressed by the way staff treat one another, as well as the manner in which they touch and communicate with children.*
2. *See how clean and pleasant the environment is. The colors, textures, and cleanliness of a child's environment help make it happy or grim.*
3. *Find out if there is a plan for regular evaluation of your child's condition, and a treatment program to help him discover and develop his strengths.*
4. *Ask for the kinds of specialists who head up various departments and what their training and experience*

have been. Are they interested in research and willing to try new techniques and develop their own new ideas?

5. *On the other hand, you will want to be sure that your child is not used in trying out risky ideas that could conceivably hurt him or her.*

6. *Look for a sense of honesty and openness with you. If, in any way, you sense the staff have something to hide, be careful. Don't fall into the possibility of being paranoid, but there are some undesirable practices, for example, in the way children are disciplined. You need to be sure that your child will not be neglected or abused.*

7. *Does this place believe in looking for and promoting as much self-help and independence as possible? It is easier to simply take care of any handicapped person than to explore and develop ways by which he or she can eventually be responsible for himself, or even helpful and productive in the community.*

8. *You will probably look for a place that evidences some interest in you as parents.*

Will the place you are considering allow you to be a part of the treatment team? Do they communicate freely with you and keep you aware of your child's condition? You need to remain involved in your child's care. (You usually will need to ask for information, but any agency owes you the courtesy of specific information by competent staff.)

Keep in Contact With Your Child. If you must place your child in an institution, set up a plan for regular contact. I am appalled at the number of children (and adults) in institutions, whom no one ever visits or writes. Out of sight, it seems, is indeed out of mind. Your child's condition, of course, will influence the frequency of your visits and whether or not you can take him home sometimes. Letters, cards, telephone calls, or visits, also, will be determined by your child's awareness of and response to these. The staff should let you know how meaningful these are to your child. But even if your child cannot appreciate your efforts, you will know you have sent him your love. This can only be good for you as well as for your child.

Hope for Financially Troubled Parents. There are, unfortunately, many families with handicapped children who cannot afford to move, and who do not have the money for a private placement. You are left no choice except a public institution, and that may leave much to be desired. Let me give you, too, some hope.

By getting acquainted with other parents whose children also must be in such an institution, perhaps you can do more than you dreamed. Together you can raise some money and gain permission to fix up the area in which your child must live. Colorful wall hangings, toys or other equipment, flowers, and many ideas for improving their environment can be provided by caring parents. Encouragement and help for the often overworked staff can change the morale of an entire place. Serving as a volunteer can help you and your family to feel involved with your child, and may start a spreading movement that can uplift all institutions for handicapped people.

Use your creative gifts and develop the greatest optimism of which you are capable. You can help your child, even when he requires institutional care.

THE HYPERACTIVE CHILD

Hyperactivity has come to be a household diagnosis. Most children, however, who are *called* hyperactive are not truly that. The genuinely hyperactive child is best described as "driven." He is a wall climber, rarely still for even five minutes, constantly moving, making noises, and into everything. Even sleep may be interrupted and brief. It is hard to believe the energy such a child consumes—and puts out. It is difficult or impossible to cuddle, play games, watch television, or read with a truly hyperactive child.

Such a driven child needs to be seen by a pediatrician, a neurologist, and a child psychiatrist. Sometimes this is a sign of *severe allergies, slight brain damage,* or *infantile autism.* If none of those is diagnosed, you may be quite sure your child will outgrow this, but you will not be as sure that you will live through it!

Causes of Hyperactivity

Brain Damage. If there is brain damage in a hyperactive child, it is of a type that is difficult to diagnose, and probably brain damage as a cause is quite rare.

Allergic Factors. These are also hard to diagnose or to rule out, for that matter. A special diet that eliminates the coloring matter to make foods attractive, additives that prevent spoiling, many carbohydrates, and certain fruits has been widely recommended. This is called the *Feingold Diet.* In the experience of some people it is a miracle worker, while others have had no improvement. Perhaps this difference is due to the fact that some hyperactivity is due to biochemical factors in food and some is not. Be sure to try this diet if you like. It cannot hurt your child, and may help. (Let me warn you that it takes quite a lot of time and work, so be prepared for that.) Most parents who find it helpful declare that it is worth all the effort!

If you believe your child has an allergy, have your doctor check that out, and follow any recommendations he makes. It is certainly possible for a variety of allergies to exist, with varying manifestations. These allergies can make a child so miserable that he becomes nervous and hyperactive as a result.

Sensitive Nervous System. Some children are born with extra-sensitive nervous systems. They see, hear, taste, smell, and feel much more sharply than other children do. It is possible that these children also react emotionally in a more explosive fashion and are more active physically.

Lack of Communicative Ability. We know that children who cannot hear or speak are frustrated by their inability to communicate. Helen Keller is a classic example of a child whose wild behavior changed rapidly when she began to learn how to communicate. Perhaps some bright young children are frustrated by their lack of words to say what they want to say. And certainly they must be checked for *hearing problems.*

Form of Manic-Depressiveness. There are some significant studies going on that suggest children may have a mild form of manic-depressive illness. Some of them improve on lithium, a very successful medication for such a problem. A doctor especially trained in child psychiatry can help you find out if this may be your child's problem.

Depressed Child. Sometimes a grief-stricken or depressed child may cover his tender feelings with wild activity. I have seen children act this way after a death or a divorce.

Need for Firmer Guidance. Evidence is building that strongly implies the need of a hyperactive child for firmer and more consistent guidance from parents. In an effort to show respect and consideration for "children's rights," parents may give children illogical choices, and then disapprove of their decisions. An example of this is the experience I observed in which a young mother gently asked her two-year-old, "Susan, wouldn't it be nice if you put away your toys and took a nap now?" Susan, not thinking it at all nice, angrily threw the toys over the room, and then ran about the house to avoid the nap.

Childhood Autism. This, fortunately, is rare, but it may also be a cause of hyperactivity. It is described in this book in chapter 11, "Psychological Problems," under The Psychotic Child.

Treatment of Hyperactivity

Complete Medical Evaluation. This is absolutely necessary. Many doctors recommend a trial on certain medications. If your child's problem is severe, I recommend you try it at least long enough to see if it helps. If so, use it long enough to help your child form new habits. Then try him without it, if your doctor is willing. Many people are unnecessarily fearful of medication due to overuse by some doctors and patients alike. You need not be one of those abusers, but if you have a truly hyperactive child, you will be anxious to find something to calm your driven child, and to allow you enough rest to enjoy him!

Allergy Tests. Have any possible allergies tested by your child's doctor or an allergy specialist. The results of those tests will tell you whether you need to put your child on a special diet or have other allergy treatments. Don't hesitate to try the Feingold Diet on your own. It helps some children.

Handling All Hyperactive Children

Be firm, gentle, and very sure in your training and discipline. If you are indecisive or inconsistent in your rules and consequences, your child is bound to feel anxious and act out that anxiety in hyperactive behavior. If you don't feel very sure, act it anyway, while you are learning to be confident.

Tell your child exactly what you want him to do and make him do it, if it is important. The soft approach, "John, don't you want to go to bed now? Mother wants you to," just won't work with a hyper child. John usually doesn't want to stop playing, even though he wants to please Mother. How can he decide that? Don't give him such choices. "John, in five minutes, the timer will go off. That's your bedtime signal, so be ready for your snack and story" (or whatever your bedtime ritual is). He can feel safe and secure in your better judgment and healthy authority. If there are realistic choices, limit them, and help him learn to choose.

Keep the environment calm for a hyperactive child. Rock him slowly, sing and speak softly, have lower lights and softer music. Even the colors in his room should be subdued, if you have a choice, and any decorations and pictures should be pleasant.

Limit and carefully supervise television for the hyperactive child. Violence, loud noises, and the sudden scene changes of television can add to his nervousness.

If you have a truly hyperactive or "driven" child, get professional help. In addition, line up a collection of relatives and friends who will give you an hour's relief now and then. It will save your sanity and won't hurt the child.

Be sure to arrange the sharing of responsibility for a hyperative child by both parents. Sometimes one will be able to quiet a child more than the other. The more quiet moments such a child finds, the sooner he will settle down and stop the hyperactivity.

There are a few hyperactive children who may not improve. Generally these are limited to autistic or other psychotic or brain-damaged categories. You may have to consider temporary or even permanent placement for such a child, in a special institution. (*See* the section on Institutional Placement earlier in this chapter for some suggestions, if this should ever be necessary.)

Most of these children do improve. If you can survive the first few years, take hope. You will be able to handle anything if you have helped your hyperactive child to become normal!

(Portions of the section on The Hyperactive Child have been adapted from chapter 17, "Solving Their Behavioral Problems," in *The Complete Book of Baby and Child Care for Christian Parents* by Grace H. Ketterman, M.D. and Herbert L. Ketterman, M.D., Copyright © 1982, published by Fleming H. Revell Company.)

11
Psychological Problems

THE PSYCHOTIC CHILD

Schizophrenia

Danny, age nine, was having trouble at home, in his neighborhood, and in school. He was unable to sit still at school, but at home, his mother couldn't uproot him from his seat in front of the television set. The neighbors found it impossible to understand the quiet boy who did strange things such as stopping in the middle of a sentence to stare off into space.

When I talked with Danny, he confided several important facts to me. He admitted that it was hard to sit still in school, because he often saw strange scenes before his eyes—scary visions of green monsters rising up out of mud pits. He felt they were after him, but by moving around, he could erase them for a while. Television nearly always stopped them because it was exciting.

I also learned that Danny's mother and dad didn't get along well, and that they were harder on Danny after one of their fights. Danny's dad was really his stepfather, and he often wondered where his own dad was and felt that things would be better if he were there. His big brother seemed to get along fine, but Danny knew he smoked pot and took drugs. He often wondered why he was the bad guy, while his brother could get by with almost anything.

Danny told me that he often imagined scenes from outer space in order to escape his fears. He could forget his parents' arguments and their abuse of him in these imaginings. The problem was, sometimes even this escape became a waking nightmare, when those monster scenes came against his will!

Danny was intelligent and his senses were sharp. He could hear the faintest sounds and his vision was unusually keen. His skin was sensitive to the slightest touch and, in fact, Danny did not like to be touched at all. He was awkward and stumbled over his own shadow, almost. So he had trouble competing in the games and sports of the other children.

Danny is a fictitious name for a real person, and he actually displayed the symptoms I have described. He is typical of childhood schizophrenia, and far more often than we would like, doctors must tell anxious parents that their child is schizophrenic.

Symptoms of Schizophrenia

Most schizophrenic children manifest several of the following signs and symptoms:

They have highly developed physical senses. Like Danny, their vision and hearing are sharp, and they have a highly developed sense of smell and touch. They are uneasy with bright lights and loud sounds, and seem afraid or irritated when touched. Likewise they fear the unseen and dread the approach of night.

Usually, schizophrenic children do not seem to enjoy being held or cuddled, even as infants. I have held a number of such little children on my lap, and I sense a "lightness" and stiffness that is hard to describe. They feel as if they are little birds, perched and ready to fly away.

Often they seem to lack a sense of their own bodies' boundaries and the borders that separate them from the outside world. They are described as not being sure of "What's me? And what is not me?"

One of the most distressing symptoms of a schizophrenic child is that of hallucinating. That is a technical word for the vivid scenes of monsters and muck that so terrorized Danny. Sometimes such children hear voices calling their names, laughing at them, or taunting them. Seeing and hearing things that others do not experience can be most alarming!

Kirk's Inner World. Kirk is also a schizophrenic boy, and he described to me in vivid detail the inner world in which he lives.

He is afraid all of the time, so as he goes to school or plays ball, he constantly thinks on two levels. On the surface, he acts pretty much like everyone else. He makes average grades, acts like one of the gang, and does, mostly, what is expected of him. Underneath, however, he is always alert to possible perils and is devising intricate maneuvers to use in protecting himself against the dangerous world he perceives. This crippling habit is extremely common in schizophrenic children, though it may be experienced and described in different ways.

Some schizophrenics have great difficulty with language. They speak in a twisted, garbled way that is difficult to understand. Usually what they say is logical, once one knows them and how they think. They learn, as they grow older, to speak in terms of their imaginings or hallucinations. The borders between what is real and not real become blurred for a schizophrenic, not only physically but psychologically as well.

Children who suffer from schizophrenia do not tolerate changes. Even when life is very much the same day after day, they have difficulty. But when there is a major change, such as a family move, a new teacher, or new furniture or decoration in their home, they become uneasy. If you want to surprise a schizophrenic child, you will almost certainly be disappointed by his reaction. He will not like it, and will act afraid or angry. His world needs to slow down and stay simple, unvarying, and stable, if he is to learn to feel safe. (For treatment of schizophrenia and other psychoses, see section later in this chapter, "Helping a Psychotic Child.")

Autism

When he was a year and a half old, Lonnie's mother brought him to me for a pediatric checkup. He had been an unusually healthy baby, so I had not seen him for some time. His mother was worried about his behavior, however, and suspected that he might be deaf. Sometimes he would seem to listen as she read to him, but at other times she would look directly at him, say something to him, and he would totally ignore her. He was starting to have tantrums, and even at eighteen months, these were so severe that his mother could hardly keep him from hurting himself or her. He would not talk, no matter how hard she tried to teach him. She was worried about the possibility of Lonnie's being mentally retarded.

Physically and even neurologically, I could find nothing wrong with Lonnie. He was strong and very hard to examine due to his constant resistance against every move I tried to make. I could understand his mother's frustration and fatigue, because she found him equally resistive every day.

Because I was baffled and deeply concerned, I sent Lonnie and his mother to a large medical center nearby for further tests. After a lengthy evaluation there, we all had to face the tragic fact: Lonnie was an autistic child.

Little Known About Autism. Now the sad part of this diagnosis is that even today, after much study and effort, we know very little about autism. While the seeming deafness and failure to speak along with other developmental lags indicate serious neurological or brain damage, we cannot in any way find proof of such damage by available tests. Even in the few cases where death has intervened, autopsy studies of the most careful kind have not revealed any chemical or tissue damage to the brain or nervous system.

Symptoms of Autism

The autistic child is characterized by failure to speak, extremely resistive behaviors, frequent, severe temper tantrums, and inability to function in normal childhood situations such as school, playing with children, or living peacefully within the family. He is unable to sit still for stories or television, and seems to be driven by a great restlessness. *Medication helps moderately, but does not cure such a child.*

Institutional treatment is almost always needed for an autistic child. A rigidly structured environment, extreme firmness, and a strong behavior-modification program seem to have the greatest potential for helping. Due to the intense energy drain such treatment creates, few families can provide adequate care. At least for periods of time (and sometimes permanently), institutional care and training are advisable or necessary.

Tourette's Syndrome

Carl worried his neighbors. He would sneak up behind them while they were gardening or walking, and scare them. Sometimes he would push or hit them, but they were most troubled by his crawling about making noises like a dog or cat. Carl was ten and should know better, they thought.

Symptoms

After a thorough evaluation, we discovered that Carl had a disease known as Tourette's syndrome. In many ways it resembles schizophrenia. But in addition, a child with this illness has the recurring habit of making various animallike sounds.

Perfectly normal children go through stages as they grow in which they make many bizarre sounds. Little boys, for example, love to mimic the sounds of cars or motorcycles, as they play with their toys. Perhaps children afflicted by Tourette's begin their sounds just as innocently, but they become habitual, seemingly beyond their control.

They also evidence various jerking motions of their bodies. A grimace of the mouth or eyes, or a jerk of an arm or foot recurs with some intensity. As with the noises, these movements seem to be beyond the control of the victim.

Treatment of Tourette's

Again, I must admit, medical science has no helpful or certain explanation of this affliction. We do, however, at least have specific medications that help control those mannerisms, and enable the child to function in a more normal fashion.

We believe Tourette's is a variation of schizophrenia that is evidenced by these physical signs as well as some of the emotional and psychological symptoms of schizophrenia.

Manic-Depressive Illness in Children

Rare in Children? The textbooks and diagnostic manuals do not discuss this illness as even occurring in childhood. A colleague of mine, however, believes that in some form it may be identified in youngsters. He is doing careful studies, and feels that he can identify some cases in childhood that later on will burst into bloom as manic-depressive illness in adults. Medical research is so slow and tedious that it will take some years before he can show definite proof of his suspicions.

Symptoms

The few signs we do know that are suggestive of this illness include extreme, uncontrollable rages followed by genuine, deep remorse. Usually there is a sleep disturbance. And often there is a cycle of great activity, alternating with times of relative peace.

There is almost always a family history of manic-depressive illness. This affliction, in its full-blown, adult form, is characterized by alternating periods of intense activity and deep depression. During one or both extremes, the victim often believes he or she is some other person—an apostle, a world hero or tyrant, or any extremely famous person. Such patients may, like a schizophrenic, hear voices and see things in a state of hallucinating.

Treatment of the Manic-Depressive

One of the greatest medical discoveries of recent years is that of the drugs (legal, of course!) with which we now help the victims of mental illness. Lithium is such a medicine. It is a simple chemical, and the body needs only small amounts of it. But the manic-depressive patient seems to need more of it, and for unknown reasons, does not get enough in a normal diet. By taking carefully controlled amounts of lithium, such patients can almost totally control the extremes of their moods and activities and live normal lives.

If you know of such a family history and suspect you see signs developing in your child, get him to a child psychiatrist, and ask for help in diagnosing and hopefully treating this problem.

Causes of Childhood Psychoses

To be very frank with you, no one knows for sure what causes autism, childhood schizophrenia, or any other psychological problem in children. Through the years, many theories and studies have given us helpful ideas. Unfortunately, so far that's all they are—ideas.

Physical Factors. At one time, all mental and emotional illness was mysteriously categorized as being demonic, hereditary, or just plain meanness. We do know now that some of the major factors in the cause of such difficulties are physical.

Furthermore, we are learning much more about stress and its impact on the body through the nervous and endocrine systems, and the biochemical changes these cause. Certainly psychotic children endure stress of the worst kind. They experience intense feelings and reactions, but they are often unable to verbalize them, and thus cannot find comfort or reassurance.

Research Projects. Several years ago, researchers used the technique of filtering the blood of a severely schizophrenic patient through a renal dialysis setup. This equipment is lifesaving for people whose kidneys do not function well, and removes certain poisons from their blood. The research team took the material that was removed from the blood of this psychotic person and injected it into a volunteer member of their group.

The person from whom that substance was removed improved dramatically for some months, and the one in whom it was injected became severely schizophrenic for some time. What a courageous person it was, of course, to volunteer for that experiment! Unfortunately, the ability to continue such efforts to discover the cause and develop a cure for psychoses is hampered by several facts. First, it costs a great deal; second, there are too few people who are willing to dedicate their lives to the research; and third, there are a great many people who suspect all doctors and researchers of making "guinea pigs" out of people!

Other Physical Aspects of Mental Illness. Other facts that help us know there are physical aspects of mental illness are these:
People who accept and use responsibly the medications that have been discovered, improve so much that they can live relatively normal lives. When they refuse or abuse those medicines, most of the time they worsen and must return to a hospital.

A scientific specialty area has arisen that explores and promotes what is called "orthomolecular" theory of medicine. They believe it is the submicroscopic and biochemical factors that influence the functioning of the brain and nervous system. They recommend huge amounts of certain vitamins and focus carefully on the trace minerals and proper dietary components. They claim remarkable improvements in their patients. Since there are certain risks in overdosing vitamins, other doctors are afraid of this philosophy.

Psychological and Emotional Factors—The Double Bind. Less than fifteen years ago, it was taught that a major cause of stress in psychotic children was the "double bind," in which their parents unwittingly placed them. Eventually, the child would learn to set up his own double bind, and hence he lived in constant fear of serious disapproval. He even felt such disapproval of himself that he could not tolerate his specific real world and escaped into the fantasy world of his psychosis.

The double bind is illustrated by this case history. Donna grew up with a mother who seemed to believe she was a good mom only when she could find fault. Donna remembers trying especially hard to set the table in a way that would please her mother. After months of heroic efforts and constant failure, she finally placed every item on the table in precisely the right place. Her little face glowed with pride as her mother said, "Donna, that's exactly right." But her joy was short-lived, for her mother promptly and angrily added, "Now why didn't you do it right before?"

Those four basic emotional needs of children (unconditional love, approval and praise, consistency, and enjoyment) are rarely met for the psychotic child.

Even when a child of this kind of negative parent finally gains his or her praise, he finds it mixed with the poison of disapproval. Psychotic children almost never feel unconditionally loved or approved of. They experience little joy, and the only one of the basic needs that is met is that of consistency. Unfortunately, that consistency is often destructive.

As studies revealed biological factors to be more important as a cause of psychoses, people began to discard the double-bind theory. It was painful to see parents face the fact that they, unwittingly, had helped cause their child's distressing condition. Many parents, furthermore, would not accept this information, and refused to make the needed changes in their attitudes and habits.

Frankly, I feel strongly that the best chance we have for helping a psychotic child lies in understanding both physical and emotional factors. It makes very good sense that too much parental anger and disapproval, coupled with too little love and laughter, in a highly sensitive child, can help create the stress that triggers the physical reaction.

Loneliness. This is certainly another emotional factor in psychoses. Psychotic children realize their differentness and withdraw, helping to create a vicious cycle of seeming to be increasingly different, and hence more rejected by peers who feel uneasy around "different" people. The more they reject him, of course, the more strange he feels, and the more he withdraws. Obviously good treatment demands gently but insistently breaking into the psychotic child's private, lonely world.

Trouble in Communicating. A casual contact with a companion on a recent plane trip taught me a vital lesson. My friend shared this story about her twenty-month-old son. He was her third child, and had been a very happy and contented boy until only a few months before. Almost overnight, he had turned into a whining, even screaming, monster. She and her husband tried everything in their considerable repertoire of parenting skills, with no improvement.

One day she became aware that this child was trying to say something to her. It sounded like, "Ma, waa!" She assumed he wanted water and gave him some. He promptly and emphatically threw it on the floor, and said again, "Ma, waa!" This time she put him in the bathtub, thinking he wanted to play in the water. Still no peace, only anger. Her husband finally said, "Honey, could he be saying, 'Mama, watch'?" She spoke to her frustrated child, assuring him she was watching, and he showed her a simple attempt at turning a somersault he had observed his brother doing. For the next several days, she related, they had no more angry, destructive behaviors from that child. He could communicate.

Certainly a psychotic child needs help in order to be able to communicate.

Poor Level of Trust. All of the facts, physical sentivity, emotional disappointments, and the complex stress factors these create, make the world of the psychotic child one that is full of fear. Since he cannot communicate well at best, and since he has such a lack of trust, he feels trapped in the center of a nightmare.

One young woman with whom I worked for a period of time was especially sensitive to the hurts of others. She wept as she heard or read of a child's abuse or an adult's robbery. Wars were unthinkable to her. One day, as we talked about her loving, sensitive heart that lived in a cruel world, she said, "Doctor Grace, teach me to care, but not to care!" Her plea is printed indelibly in my memory. It was her schizophrenic way of asking for relief from her fearful world of too much response to so much pain!

Helping a Psychotic Child

Guidelines to Follow. Whatever the precise diagnosis, these are some guidelines that will help you to manage the difficult problems of a psychotic child.

Seek expert help. If you suspect your child is autistic or schizophrenic, do not delay. Seek a qualified child psychiatrist. Being a medical doctor as well as having additional training in mental illnesses, such a doctor can evaluate and treat this severe problem better than almost anyone else.

Very likely he will ask for consultation with a neurologist, perhaps a pediatrician, and very likely, a psychologist. Such an evaluation, while complete, will be costly. Do your best to arrange for those costs, because each consultant will add vital information to help you understand and cope with this problem. In most states, there are clinics and large medical centers where costs are less prohibitive. Do not be afraid to tell your doctor that you may need some financial assistance.

Once the tests are complete, you may expect a detailed report, explaining them and what their results imply for you and your child. The doctor should then give you the best recommendations he or she can offer. Be sure to ask all the questions you need or want to know. Understanding can help you to make the essential decisions you will face later on.

Plan on a lifetime of care. While there will be extended periods of time that your child may seem quite well, there are likely to be recurrent bouts when he is agonizingly worse. It is wise, therefore, to plan on some medical supervision throughout his life. I find that many young people, especially, resist this idea.

Naturally, they want to run their own lives without pills and free from the advice and help of a doctor.

In fact, I find many parents, as well as children, who blindly and stubbornly resist the use of medication. Realizing the heartache of addiction and drug abuse, I can well understand such fears; but in the case of a truly psychotic child, the refusal to allow medication will seriously impair his improvement and will teach the child an attitude of defiance that is sure to keep him sicker than he needs to be.

Perhaps it will help to understand that mental illness is much like diabetes and heart disease. Those who are afflicted with these illnesses need daily medication and regular medical checkups. With increased stress, they need more medication and more intensive supervision. But when life goes smoothly, they may do with much less.

It is exactly so with a psychotic child. When life is moving along well (and you parents have much to do with that!), he may need little, if any, medication and may need to see his doctor only now and then. But when changes are imminent and the stress accumulates, he will need the support of medication and the trusted psychiatrist. You must set the example and teach him the signs of impending stress and how to cope with it.

Follow usual psychiatric treatment. Your doctor will recommend regular weekly visits with your child for several months, at least. These visits may be spent doing play therapy, talking about the child's daily activities, and rarely about feelings. Most psychotic children become anxious and confused when they start thinking about unreal things and tend to escape into their fantasy worlds.

Through the use of dolls and other toys, psychotic children will often play out their fears and worries, and so relieve the tensions within them. Focusing on real-life situations can help a child learn how to act and get along with friends, so he is less likely to need the scary world of his hallucinations as an escape.

Your child's doctor will probably see you on some regular basis, also, though some doctors have associates who will give you the insight and guidance you need. You will need to have a trusting and open relationship with your doctor. He will need your information regarding family changes, and you will need his guidance and encouragement.

*Medication. Be certain that you explain your fears about med-
ications,* but seek your doctor's recommendations with an open
mind. He will know the difference between mind-altering, potentially addictive medications, and those that can help restore
to your child a more normal life. If you cannot trust this doctor,
talk with others, including your family physician. All well-in-
formed doctors are likely to agree on some combination of the
tried and tested medicines.

*Be certain that you understand any possible side-effects of
medication.* Some people are likely to evidence an allergic reaction to any medication, so find out what to look for, and report
that promptly to your doctor if it occurs.

*Avoid letting your child adjust his own dosage, and don't try
that on your own!* A phone call to your doctor's office will
usually be all it takes to get his guidance on dosage adjustments.

*If, by any chance, your child shows signs of becoming
suicidally depressed, be extra careful to keep all medications
safely locked away.* Be sure to report any such fears to your
doctor, and keep any dangerous items away from the child.

As you and your child work together with his doctor through
the months and years that you both will need help, I hope you
develop a trust and love that will enhance your own lives as well
as your child's.

Some Special Guidance for Parents of a Psychotic Child

Out of many years' experience with severely troubled children, I have gleaned some ideas and techniques that I hope will
be of value to you parents of a psychotic child.

Guidelines

Be careful to keep his special world as "soft" as possible. In
decorating his room, for example, use cheerful colors in soft
tones. Look for prints or designs in curtains, wallpaper, pictures,
and bedspreads that are real and peaceful. I suggest that you
avoid abstract designs or unreal characters such as superpeople
or extraterrestrial figures. Find or create designs of real plants,
flowers, birds, nonfrightening animals, or pets that especially
would interest your child. Let him tell you what he would like in

his room, but even if he wants some bizarre creatures, gently and firmly refuse that. Children do, by the way, seek an identity with the very monsters they fear. By becoming familiar with them, I suspect, a child may struggle to overcome his fears.

Keep sound and light levels lower than you may like. Such excess stimulation as loud sounds and very bright lights can create tension in a psychotic child. Now don't turn your home into a morgue! Just watch it and be moderate.

Keep your child's time schedule and daily routine as structured and consistent as possible. He will not tolerate change well, and sudden changes are unbearable. So when you know there will need to be a change at a given time, tell that special child well ahead of time, and then remind him as the time approaches. Even in changes that are planned, each day, give him forewarning. A reminder that dinner time is coming can help him shift gears and be ready with less fussing. When he does accept an unexpected change with reasonably good grace, give him some honest praise. It takes real effort for a psychotic child to change old habits.

Keep him or her involved in doing productive tasks that are challenging but have a foreseeable end. Schizophrenic children have a tendency to form a fixation on one thing and have trouble leaving it. One child focused on chess, another on jigsaw puzzles, but it was very hard to interest either in anything else. Try to prevent some of that fixation by introducing a small variety of projects that may earn him some pride and praise for his efforts.

Encourage your child to learn some physical skills well. I believe that swinging, circular motion, swaying, jumping, and skipping will stimulate certain centers in the brain. And such stimulation often improves the child's balance, coordination, and perhaps helps him separate himself from his environment better. Doing such activities with your child, just for fun, can bond you to each other, increasing his sense of trust along with his neuromuscular development. Do avoid, however, making these heavy work sessions. Don't quit too soon, but don't expect perfection. It is especially important to keep balance in your child's life.

When your doctor feels your child is ready, try to bring a special friend or two into your youngster's life. Choose this person carefully. He needs to be calm and understanding, and he especially needs that beautiful gift of accepting your child as he is, quietly expecting him to do the normal things.

Be with the children in such social interactions to guide and supervise until you and the children feel safe.

Since few schizophrenic children tolerate physical touch, you may, without realizing it, omit this very vital element from your child's life. A social worker I once knew took a schizophrenic child to live with her for a while. Bit by bit, she checked out this girl's reactions to touches on various parts of her body. She remained totally unresponsive, until my friend tickled her gently on her feet. The girl broke into a giggle. So every night my friend tucked the child in bed with a happy tickle of her toes. Very gradually, she added a stroke of her forehead, a touch of the hand, and finally a kiss on her cheeks. The child slowly began to trust the touching and enjoyed my friend's careful affection.

Develop and maintain a firm, deliberate manner that is loving and gentle. Allow a psychotic child only a few choices at a time, and then only when you feel he can choose wisely. Go back to the handling of a two-year-old and start over because that is often the stage at which a psychotic child has some trouble with his development. By starting over, you can offer him and yourself a chance to do it better this time. When you must take a stand opposing your child, be strong, kind, and consistent. Don't set up such a standoff, however, unless you are prepared with help to see it through.

Keep hoping. Progress in a psychotic child is extremely slow, and the backslidings happen so fast and discouragingly. Don't give up! A little bit at a time is better than none. So hang in there!

Hospital Care

There are sure to be times when you or your doctor will realize that your child needs care beyond that which you can give. There are various reasons for that sort of crisis, and you may not always know why it has built up; but you will recognize that you or your child cannot, at this time, handle each other, and that you could even be damaging each other. *Please do not feel that you have failed or that your child is going away forever.*

Hospitals are for crisis times, and your child will be sent home as soon as both of you are ready. Again, it is the balance that is important. Don't give up too soon, but don't hold out so long that you risk harm. It is at such times that you will be especially grateful for your doctor's support and advice.

Psychotic people can learn to live successfully and productively in this world. Help your child to join the ranks of those who do!

THE NEUROTIC CHILD

Actually, the new medical diagnostic manual does not list neuroses for children. By this term, I refer to the seriously troubled children who are not out of touch with reality, hence are not psychotic, but certainly are unhappy people.

A neurosis is the habit of trying harder and harder to recapture a good feeling or experience that was once enjoyed, with only minimal success. The neurotic person does this habitually and unconsciously, putting out increasing effort, usually with less and less results.

Case History. Kim is typical of such a problem. She had been especially close to her daddy, but he and her mother were divorced when Kim was only three. He had been the parent who disciplined her, and at times he was harsh, but after a punishment he would hold Kim and explain the whole episode. He would then hug her, and often they would play for a while.

After he was gone, Kim expected the same routine from her mother, and, later, from her stepfather. But Mother could never create the same feelings with Kim, and she disciplined her from a distance by sending her to her room or lecturing. It was not comfortable for her mother to hold Kim, or to get down and play with her on the floor like Daddy did.

Kim tried harder and harder to get close to someone! She misbehaved in increasingly serious ways, and finally began to hit her mother and even her teachers. She desperately needed someone to hold her, to restore the warm closeness she had known with her dad.

Signs of a Neurotic Child

Actually, many of the troubled-child categories in this book would be defined as *neurotic*. Since this book is meant to be practical more than scientific, let me describe the symptoms of a neurotic or "nervous" child.

Emotional Symptoms. The nervous child looks unhappy. When I sit in a classroom full of children, I carefully observe their faces. Most of them usually are intent and studious, but several look up at times and their faces reflect worry or sadness. Others, refusing to work at all, look defiant or angry. The face of a child is almost always an accurate map of his emotions. Sadness, anxiety, and anger all etch their signs very early in the faces of their victims. Observe your child when he or she is unaware of your watching. What you see is at least a part of what he feels.

Physical Signs. When a child feels upset long enough, and with sufficient severity, he will almost certainly develop some physical habits that relieve or express that tension. Excessive thumb sucking or masturbating are examples of such habits. As a baby, those physical activities brought a pleasurable sensation to his body. As an older child, it is likely that a sensitive child, lonely or worried, may seek to recover that feeling. Unfortunately, it is impossible to return to earlier times, so the feeling is not as satisfying as the child remembered. It does, however, feel a little bit good. Furthermore, it draws pretty intense attention from adults, so the habit seems to be worth continuing.

Other physical signs of a nervous child may be the return to bed-wetting or soiling that are discussed in chapter 8. Disturbances of eating or sleeping habits are also common in neurotic children. They may overeat, refuse to eat, or make themselves vomit. They may sleep constantly, be unable to sleep, or have nightmares. But such problems almost always plague the nervous child.

One of the most annoying of physical responses to nervous tension in a child is the appearance of a *tic.* Tics are usually sudden in onset. They are seemingly involuntary, and they vary in the part of the body they affect. They involve strong, spasmodic motions of the muscles controlling a certain area of the body. Blinking of both eyes or winking of one are common. Twitching of the mouth, jerking of the neck, and nervous coughing are all examples of tics. Parents, in my experience, find these so annoying that they simply cannot control their inner urge to scold or nag a child about them. By such an attitude, they are adding to the tension that created the tic, and it inevitably becomes worse.

Social Signs. A neurotic child is likely to interact socially in one of three broadly categorized patterns.

The rebellious, angry child. Many times the angry child is actually testing out the adults in his life to see if they care, or are strong enough to manage him. The child whom I observed in kindergarten is an example of this. She angrily defied her teacher to make her mind, but actually it was quite possible to help her join the children at story time. All I had to do was take her firmly by the hand and lead her!

With older children, however, their testing out may become very aggressive. They are quick to lash out with fists or feet, and can hurt the one they see as an opponent rather badly.

Perhaps more frustrating than the openly rebellious child is the *stubbornly passive one.* The child who sits all day rather than pick up his toys, clean his room, or finish his schoolwork, is hard to combat. By his quiet resistance, he has learned to disarm his parents. After all, he thinks he's not doing anything bad. Parents of such a child usually learn to nag and scold, but they rarely discipline him as effectively as they might his more aggressive counterpart.

People pleasers. Children, usually sensitive and intelligent ones, quickly learn what they must do to get along with their parents and other adults. Their efforts to please are rewarded by some love and approval, but these are inconsistent, so the children also fear rejection and anger.

Such children are not really secure in their parents' love, but they learn how to earn more approval and sense a bit more love and warmth than the rebellious child.

This child always wants to run your errands; at school he washes the blackboard, or will dust the floor—almost anything to gain some attention from an adult. He never believes that what he does is okay unless someone else approves it. He needs continual encouragement and reassurance from others.

Basically, he is insecure, but he has found a way to get some positive feedback. He tries harder and harder, however, to get good feelings, with less and less success. This is the pattern of a neurotic child, with conditional rather than unconditional love, and too little approval to build a healthy sense of self-esteem.

Worried, frightened child. Some children are conscientious and loving, but they are overwhelmed with burdens. They worry about their parents or grandparents. They are troubled about their grades or their failure in sports. They have nightmares and become afraid of many things. Usually such anxious children also fear that they are guilty of all sorts of real or imagined misdeeds. They worry about being punished for their badness.

Sometimes a worried or frightened child covers his vulnerable feelings with anger and aggressive acts. It may be difficult to distinguish such a child from the basically rebellious child— but watch his behavior and his facial expression. He will look anxious and usually has elaborate plans and precautions to protect himself.

Helping a Neurotic Child

Blind Spots. Obviously, to help a troubled child demands that you as parents recognize the existence of a problem. While that sounds simple, it indeed is the hardest step of all in correcting any difficulty. Troubled children are rarely created by deliberately cruel or mean parents. They develop silently, gradually, out of parents' daily efforts to be the best they can be, but even good parents have problems and blind spots. When these are of a serious type, a troubled child may result. It is by those blind spots, caused by the forgotten forces that began in the parents' own childhoods, that problems arise. And because blind spots are, indeed, *blind,* parents cannot see them, and therefore, they cannot correct the problems.

The encouraging fact, however, is this: *blind spots can be cured!* If you are a parent, take courage, because that very courage can overcome your fear of the pain of facing your failures. And by facing them, you can change and correct them. There is great hope for you and your child!

Look for the causes of the tension in your neurotic child. These may be many, but here are some of the common, primary stressors of childhood.

Painful Relationships. Whether this pain involves you parents, friends, or teachers, look for the thorns in your child's emotional life that are due to this factor. Usually the child is not safe in the certainty that he is loved and wanted.

Impossible Expectations. Feeling unable to do anything that really pleased my mother marred my childhood. I now know she wanted me to become responsible, but then I could feel only my pain at her disapproval. Be careful, then, that you do not duplicate her mistake. Have realistic expectations of your children, and keep them positive. Stick with those youngsters until they measure up to their very best, and then give them your whole-hearted praise—with no *buts* or *if onlys!*

Inconsistent or Harsh Discipline. Remember that discipline means "teaching." What does your discipline teach your children? It may be that you are making them learn fear of your unruly temper or confusion from manipulation or wishy-washy inconsistency. They need to know that you care enough about them to be firm, to follow through, and to do so in a way that clearly says, "I care so much, I will give and tolerate only the very best!"

Find your child's assets and strengths, and help him or her develop those to their very best. It is easy to see one's goal in parenting to be that of correcting all of the problems and shoring up all the weaknesses in the child. This is actually only a minor part of being a good parent, and it will, in fact, take care of itself—if you latch on to the assets and build them.

Develop Interests. Expose your child to as many activities and areas of interest as possible. Observe her reaction to those experiences and provide more of those that make her vibrant with joy. When I was only seven, my father took time out of his long day's work to take me and my sister to hear the U.S. Marine Corps Band. It was a rare opportunity for our small town to enjoy the stirring music of an excellent band, and the auditorium was so crowded that we had to stand. My father perched me on his shoulders for as long as he could, so that I could see the colorful uniforms as well as hear that exciting music. I loved it, am still grateful for his extra efforts, and thrill to band music even now.

It takes such sacrificial efforts to find and encourage a child's interests. It is so well worthwhile! Whether it is an interest like mine in hearing and enjoying great music, or the even more difficult but rewarding feat of performing or creating in some way, help your child find and develop that ability.

Develop an understanding heart. One of the bright spots in many troubled times with my mother is an illustration of the value to a child of empathy and compassion. I loved to play with my older brother's typewriter, and whenever I thought I could get by with it, I pretended to be a secretary typing elegantly! It was quite clear, however, to my mother, that I could jam the keys, and we did not have the money for unnecessary repairs. One rainy evening, I was pecking away at those fascinating keys, when Mother came into the room. I froze in midstrike, awaiting the lecture I really deserved. Instead, she quietly commented, "Gracie, I know it's fun to play with that typewriter. But your brother needs it, and we can't risk having it accidentally broken." I loved her for that gentle empathy. In fact, I decided to give up the fun that could have resulted in disaster.

You, too, can learn this kind of understanding. Children need that for their wishes and activities as well as their troubled feelings. Try wishing with your child when she wants an impossible thing. It will make the pain of the denial quite bearable to know that you understand about and share the yearning.

Understanding the Worrier. If your child is a worrier, let him know you understand that concern. The chances are, he learned that habit of worrying from you, so you really will empathize with him! Teach him to talk about those concerns, and as he talks, lead him to an awareness of the choices he has regarding the subject of the worry; help him reach a decision from those options, and observe the relief he will manifest. Defining one's concerns makes them possible to solve, and choosing solutions will cure the anxiety. Of course you must help put that decision into effect and see it through.

I can assure you that in teaching such a method to your child, you will help yourself as well. The same steps can eliminate most worry from any life!

Establish your rightful parental authority. Much childhood anger and anxiety are related to what the child sees as parental weakness. If you have not provided the strength of consistently being in charge of your family and attending to their needs, you will want to do so. If you do not know how to do this, read books, talk to friends, observe other parents, or seek a family counselor to teach you; but do so as soon as possible.

The most secure, self-confident, and productive children, according to excellent research, are those whose parents take charge. Without being tyrants, they are the final authority. They allow a great deal of pushing and arguing in order to develop initiative in their children, but they know when to step in, call a halt to further discussion, and settle the issue. Almost never do I see a truly troubled child from such a family.

Helping a neurotic child is tough. It is a long, tedious process. But it can be done, and it is infinitely easier than trying to help a dyed-in-the-wool adult neurotic. Prevent the need for that by working through the problems now!

THE GIFTED CHILD

You may think it is foolish to include a discussion about gifted children in a book on troubled children, but perhaps that's because you have not experienced some of the sadness of many gifted children.

Gene is a gifted child. His IQ is well above average, and he shows flashes of brilliance in creative abilities in his classroom. His parents are aware of his rare qualities and waver between feeling somewhat in awe of him, and being irritated because he is so inconsistent in his achievements. Furthermore, they often disagree about their discipline and expectations of him. Gene wonders, he admits, if they are thinking about a divorce. He wants to be a regular kid sometimes, but at other times the great curiosity within him cries out for expression. He doesn't feel like the regular kids feel. Gene is so confused and full of anxiety that he has great difficulty sitting still and finishing any task.

The Bored Child. A good friend of mine (who is a physician) tells me that when he was in elementary school, his teacher thought he was retarded. Actually he was so bored that he simply didn't bother to fill in his workbooks or turn in any assignments. He knew that he understood the material, so why should he bother to write it down? When he finally had a teacher who really challenged him, he learned to study and did exceedingly well.

Problems of the Gifted Child

The conflicting feelings and ideas create confusion. A gifted child usually does not understand why others learn more slowly than he. If he is impatient with them, they will come to resent him. It is likely that children will be jealous of a child to whom learning comes easily, and who wins all the spelling contests.

As in the case of Gene, a bright child is quick to detect problems between his parents or any other people. He is a child, yet may feel like a wiser person than the adults in his life. Such awareness may be accompanied by a great deal of insecurity or even fear.

A sense of being different may isolate a gifted child much as it can a handicapped child. One gifted child I know often yearns to discuss precociously wise ideas and fascinating experiences—but there is no one whom she feels understands her or cares to listen. In fact, for a long time she believed she was stupid because people often laughed at her or seemed totally indifferent to her ideas.

A gifted child, like my friend, may be bored, and out of boredom, become irritable or rude. Such a child often has only a vague sense of why he is bored but can't clearly express it, so he finds no relief or understanding of the problem. Occasionally I have seen gifted children who were a bit lazy, simply unmotivated to achieve, but frustrated by their failures. One boy said, "I just wish my dad would give me a kick and make me do my homework!" He really was craving attention from his dad.

There may be social problems due to a child's intellectual giftedness. She may be placed in a grade that is ahead of her peers. Socially, she may belong to her own age group, but intellectually, she would be wasting her time at that grade level. This situation may cause real conflicts for the child, friends, and family.

Reasons for Giftedness

By now, I hope you parents have come to realize that having a gifted child is not altogether a joyful situation. This, too, has its problems. Nevertheless, I know most families would be proud and happy to have such a precocious child. Just what are the forces that mold such a youngster?

Heredity. While several factors influence giftedness, none of them could be effective unless the innate mental and neurological foundations were there to build upon. Special talents in art, music, and physical agility are almost always traceable to some ancestors. Just how such abilities are etched into the genes and chromosomes that determine an individual's ultimate identity, we do not yet know—but there they must be.

Early Stimulation. Second only to the inherited abilities of a child is the kind and amount of early sensory stimulation he receives. Actually, the first three months are the prime time to give a baby lots of cuddling, touching, smiling, and even exposure to various colors and sounds. Apparently, such stimulations of a baby's nerve fibers that carry sensations to the brain cause that brain to develop to its very best, while it is most easily influenced.

If your child is older than three months, however, do begin now teaching her to enjoy as many experiences of a pleasant kind as possible. Tickling, stroking, tossing, and blowing on her neck, are examples of happy kinds of touch. Singing, whistling, talking, and playing happy music can stimulate the child's sense of hearing. Pleasant colors, a mobile over her crib, bright pictures and books, when your child is old enough, can prompt visual development; various textures, temperatures, tastes, and odors will have their effect on the senses of taste, smell, and touch.

Provide such stimulation on a regular basis and in an organized fashion, and you may rest assured you will have offered your child the best start you can.

Constancy. All children need constancy. It is this quality of a reasonable sameness to life that creates a sense of security for any child. The greater that security is, the freer will a child be to focus his interest on learning and developing whatever special talents he has, whether he is especially gifted or not.

Self-Confidence. Healthy parental authority in training and discipline has been shown to be a major factor in building self-confidence. And self-confidence is extremely important in a gifted child, if she is to feel free to explore and take risks in learning experiences.

Recognizing Emotions. Freedom from chronic anger, fear, and anxiety is essential to all learning. These vulnerable emotions are marked inhibitors of all progress of children. Teaching children to recognize these feelings, talk them out, and overcome them, then, becomes extremely important in giving any child his opportunity for optimal development.

Sense of Responsibility. The gradual, consistent release of a child to her own responsibility is also necessary if you wish to create a healthy and gifted child. Any overprotectiveness tells a child that she really is not capable of taking care of herself. Mom and Dad must do it for her. Now do provide appropriate care for each child, but look around and see if you are going too far as compared with other good parents. To teach responsibility, give your child the chance to make as many of her own decisions as she is capable of making. Do not rescue her from the natural consequences of any irresponsibility, and be sure that your own discipline is consistent and fair.

Taking Pride in Child's Achievements. Be interested in and proud of your child's activities and achievements. The earlier in life you can start, the better, but do so now. Attend as many of his special events as possible. Post his pictures and writings where the entire family will see them. Call the grandparents whenever possible and tell them of your children's achievements. Remind them, if you must, to compliment the children when they can do so honestly. Help your family to enjoy one another's successes and celebrate them in some special way.

Be especially aware that children's successes need to be *theirs* and not yours, parents! It is easy to fall, unknowingly, into being proud of yourselves, rather than of your children. Of course, you must recognize that good and successful children reflect excellent parenting in most cases, but allow the credit he deserves to fall on your child. It will motivate him to even greater accomplishments.

Be an Example. Model for your children the joy of exploring, the thrill of discoveries, and the permission to risk failures for the sake of growing. My father, though unable to attend school for very long, was an avid reader. He shared the discoveries of his learning and personal thoughts, as well, with his family. He encouraged each of us to grow as far as we could.

Teach Your Own Philosophy. Teach your child your philosophy of life. I hope you have formulated some ideas of how you see yourself fitting into life as a whole. Teaching children about their ancestors, and helping them discover a sense of pride in belonging to the past as well as the future and the present, will give them a sense of significance and security.

None of these ideas alone can guarantee for you a gifted child. Nevertheless, I trust you will agree that they represent sound practices in child rearing. They will, all together, give each child the best possible chance to become all he can be! And who could ask for more?

Helping a Gifted Child

The reasons for giftedness offer you a great many ideas about helping your child to reach his or her maximum potential. But if your gifted child is troubled by the problems described earlier in this chapter, here are some suggestions for help.

Keep your mind open to the fact that this child may have problems as well as strengths. If you are a person who had to struggle your way through school, it may seem to you that being exceptionally bright is all anyone should ask! But learning easily is only one aspect of your child's life. If you will observe your child as a whole person, you may find some painful areas that need help.

Help your child to feel normal. It is easy for parents to slip into an unconscious worship or awe of a gifted child, and certainly teachers become excited when they discover such a student. Avoid that by thinking about *all* of your child—not just his brain. Keep your child from the conceit that so readily antagonizes other children and creates the climate of jealousy.

Avoid bragging about your child while you are giving him the compliments he earns and deserves. The latter are helpful, but bragging can give a child too great a sense of his importance. Do not compare your gifted child with others who are not so well endowed. This will add to his sense of differentness that can create serious social problems.

Discipline and train your gifted child just as you do your other children. Correcting any child helps him to develop a balanced sense of who he is—a person with strength and weakness, a person who is cared about, one who can improve. Such correction, of course, must be balanced by the praise and compliments that mirror his strengths.

Teach your child a special sense of responsibility. "To whom much is given, of him much shall be required." Whatever your child's gifts, he owes the world his very best use of those talents. Whether those abilities are great or small, and no matter if your child's personal world is very little, that philosophy holds true. Help your child recognize that, and work to improve the area in which he lives.

Teach your child to recognize the special abilities of others. If he sees that each child has some special creativity and ability, he will not need to feel different or isolated. Perhaps you will be able to teach your child to help his friends to succeed and enjoy *their* achievements as well as his own.

Accept your child *unconditionally,* teach him sound principles for living (as well as learning), comfort him when he is sad, rejoice with him when he is happy. You and your gifted child can enjoy life together.

THE LEARNING-DISABLED CHILD

A Case History

Bobby's parents were both well educated, professional people. He was their oldest child, and from early childhood evidenced the honesty and remarkable degree of responsibility that often characterizes a firstborn child. He took school very seriously, even in kindergarten, tried hard to get along with his teachers and classmates, and studied hard. But somehow the letters became jumbled, and even the simplest words did not sound to him as they seemed to sound to the others.

As his best buddy reached the top reading group, Bobby was struggling through the first workbook. When his sister started school, Bobby was in the second grade. She whizzed through the alphabet with ease, reminding Bobby of his laborious efforts. Year by year, he felt just a bit more distance between himself and his classmates. His parents went from frustration and lectures to worry and concern about Bobby's school problems.

The school people assured Bobby and his parents that he was just a bit slower in learning, but they were confident he would plod his way on as far as he chose to go in school.

Finally Bobby's parents took him from the overcrowded, busy school district, and placed him in a private school. There it was finally discovered that Bobby had a severe case of dyslexia. He couldn't read, so none of his classes was an experience of success for him. As he failed more and more, he grew increasingly discouraged. Seeing his sister's success and his parents' worry convinced Bobby that he was hopelessly retarded.

In a school with small classes, much individual help, and an explanation for his problems, Bobby flourished. He overcame the dyslexia, went on through college, and recently finished a postgraduate degree.

Learning Disabilities

Dyslexia. There are many children in schools today who have handicaps in specific areas of learning. For many this problem is limited to reading and is called *dyslexia.* In others, it is related to mathematics, and for still others, it is spelling that seemingly defeats them. In some cases, the reading and spelling problem is associated with a reversal of letter shapes. When *b* means *d* to a child, *bad* becomes *dab* or vice versa. We can all agree that such confusion would make it difficult to master spelling and writing as well as reading.

Neurological Factors. Not only is there a problem with mastering the sounds and shapes of letters but there also are neurological factors that enter into the learning process. As the eye sees a letter or word, it sends a message to the visual center of the brain, which then connects with the cortex (or outer layer) of the brain. Apparently it is there that the original object or word seen by the eye is decoded into something we have seen or heard before, or that seems new. People who study learning problems believe that perhaps some short circuit takes place in these complex nerve tracts that interferes with the recognition of words or, in similar ways, with sounds through the nerve tracts that interpret sounds.

Overcoming Disabilities. While researchers are still studying the reasons for learning disabilities, educators are working hard to find ways to overcome them. Many schools have teachers who are specially trained and gifted in teaching such children to read, write, spell, and master arithmetic. If you believe your child has a special problem with learning, ask for him to be tested and placed with someone who can help him master his disabilities.

Outgrowing Their Disabilities. Even with a minimum amount of specialized help, many people seem to outgrow their learning disabilities. Usually by the seventh or eighth grade, these young people begin to tally up enough successes in school to believe in themselves, and once they begin to do well, they can't be stopped.

Lack of Concentration. Whatever obscure neurological or bio-chemical factors there may be, there are some practical issues involved in learning difficulties. When a child worries too much, when he has only partial information about family concerns, and when he has too few successes on which to build, he will have trouble with concentrating. It's hard to deal with multiplication tables when you're worried about your parents' reaction to your grade card, or you know your grandpa has had a heart attack. I see many children who are so preoccupied with television or exciting plans for special future events, that they are unable to focus on mundane topics like the Civil War or the people in Latin America.

While it takes specially trained teachers to help a child learn proper letter and word formations, you as parents can help with the emotional blocks to learning. Let me suggest these steps for your consideration:

Consider and write down all the things about which your child could be worrying. Do this with your spouse or a person who knows your child well. Then ask your child about any worries he may have, and add them to your list. Don't forget that he, like Bobby, may be worried about his tough times in school. Strangely, children often try to protect their own parents, so your child may not want to reveal his concerns. Don't press him to do so now, if he seems reluctant, because you will no doubt discover most of those by yourselves.

Take one or two of these issues each day and discuss them with your child. As much as possible, get the child to talk about them and about his feelings regarding these problems. If he feels like crying more than talking, be grateful, and let him cry out his grief and worry until the tears are over. Comfort and reassure him.

Give him whatever information you can that will clear up those worries and really put them to rest. You may need to talk with a teacher or school counselor to get some facts that will reassure your child regarding his learning difficulties. Take your child with you to such a conference as you check out the availability of tests or tutoring to help him in school.

Do not exaggerate or minimize your child's concern or feelings. Regardless of how simple they seem to you, they are real to her. Just practice listening to your child, and encourage her to be more open with you about all of her worries. Let her feel your strength and wisdom, and assure her that together you and she can handle any difficulty. Now you must, of course, find the courage and strength that will help you to stop worrying. Your child will know how you feel, so don't try to fool her!

Both you and your child may talk with the heavenly Father about any and all concerns and leave them with Him, if you are a parent who believes in prayer.

Be available to each child every day for the purpose of keeping that child's mind free of stored-up worries. If he doesn't come to you, go to him, and ask if he needs to talk. Please avoid nagging, but simply be open and available. Do whatever you must to keep your own minds free from anxiety.

Seek professional guidance if you feel confused or overanxious about your child's problems. Many school counselors, as well as other mental health professionals, can give you reassurance and practical suggestions that will help both you and your child. *Avoid worrying,* because unfortunately, rather than helping him, that will only convince him that he is a terrible problem. He already suspects that. There is a big difference in *having* a problem for which you will eventually find the answer, and *being* a problem for which there are no apparent solutions. Help your child discover the areas in which he is successful, and let him know your honest pride in him. Don't overdo that, however, or he will think you are covering up your worry and pity.

Try to leave the teaching of your child to his teacher. If she asks you to help with some exercises or homework, do so, but avoid nagging. With the best intentions in the world, some parents keep a child plugging away at homework so much that he simply rebels. My sister, who taught elementary school for over forty years, found that children did better in school when their evenings included some times of fun and warmth within the family.

Occasionally, tutors may help a child with a specific learning disability, and can prevent the tension that usually builds up when parents try to help such a child with homework. But again, keep enough free time for your child to relax and be a child. Almost always, children outgrow learning problems. If you don't allow those to be compounded by personality disorders or rebelling, he will compensate for them and forge ahead when he is ready. But he cannot return later and recapture the essence of childhood itself. Be sure your child develops socially and physically as well as intellectually.

I strongly recommend that learning-disabled children explore a wide range of other interests. Often real talent is overlooked in mechanics, art, music, or acrobatics, while the child's energies are focused on the academic areas. To repeat: a great deal of experience is showing us that many children simply must *outgrow* their disabilities.

Now don't think I'm telling you to ignore schoolwork! *Seek expert help in school, and work with the advice that system gives you.* But help your child understand that his other interests and abilities are also important. Find ways to develop those, and as your child tastes success in any area of life, his confidence will grow. Success generates success. I never knew a child who could not succeed at something! Help your child to succeed!

THE SUICIDAL CHILD

Accidents are the leading cause of death among teenagers in America. Second only to accidents is *death by suicide*—and suicide is creeping into younger age groups. A ten-year-old child told me recently that he and his brother have a plan set. If and when, in their opinion, life becomes much worse than it is now, they will go out riding on a family motorcycle and never return. They have already experimented with the accident they plan, and are prepared to make it fatal when the time comes.

How tragic that children could find life so unbearable that they do not want to live! And how frightening that they have so much power and so little protection that they can actually cause their own death.

Right to Die?

At a recent seminar on death that I attended, I was amazed to learn that some leaders in the mental-health field believe that people have the right to die if they wish. There were major debates about whether anyone has the right to stop efforts to commit suicide.

Certainly studies indicate that if anyone is truly determined to take his own life, no one can stop him. But studies also show that most younger people, especially, do not *want* to die. They want to be noticed and heard; they want to escape from unhappiness and boredom. And they discover that a suicide threat or attempt accomplishes that quickly and effectively—but very few want to die. Potentially suicidal children need *understanding, protection,* and a *healthy way out of the sadness* in their lives.

Signs of Suicidal Possibility

There are several well-known and recognizable signs of possible suicide that every parent needs to know. Be careful that you do not overreact and unwittingly implant the idea of suicide in your child's mind; but by all means, *do not assume that suicide happens only to someone else's child.*

Here are some serious indicators that you can rely upon to help you evaluate your child if he seems to be seriously suicidal. These may develop in a variety of combinations, but if you see several of them in some intensity over a period of time, I urge you to seek a counselor to evaluate your child.

Changes in Physical Behaviors. These changes will last for two to three weeks without significant alleviation, if they are to be considered serious.

1. Unexplained changes in eating habits

A child who has had a healthy appetite, and who abruptly loses that without physical illness, needs attention. On the other hand, a child who is a picky eater but suddenly begins eating constantly (unless he is going into a growth spurt) may well be trying to comfort himself while being seriously depressed.

2. Changes in sleep habits

Children who have repeated nightmares or bad dreams need to be able to talk about those dreams and find comfort. A child who has unusual difficulty falling asleep or awakens frequently, or one who sleeps excessively (over nine or ten hours a night), very likely is undergoing stress. Such stresses may add up to an unbearable burden. Be sure to check out your child's stress level before it reaches the danger level.

3. A change in activity level

A child who has ordinarily been quiet may go into unusual activity, clowning or doing a variety of projects. On the other hand, a child who normally is active and playful may withdraw and stop sports or any activity. Either change, if it lasts several weeks, needs to be investigated. If emotional stress is responsible, be sure to ask for help.

4. Accident proneness

A suicidal child will often be involved in a series of mishaps. These may in themselves be a cry for help; but they *may be,* even unconsciously, an accelerating descent into the ultimate accident of suicide.

Changes in Social Behaviors. Such changes, as with those that are physical in nature, need to be reasonably lengthy in order to be of concern.

1. Appearance

It is not the actual mode of dress or grooming that is significant, but the abrupt, sustained difference that needs noticing. A child who has carefully groomed herself and always worn clean socks and underwear may suddenly lose interest in the neat appearance that was normal before; or a child who was careless and happily disheveled may turn into a primping perfectionist. Unless this can be clearly accounted for by early puberty, you had better find out why this change is happening now.

2.   Change in social interactions

Related to the changes in physical activity, there is often a sudden difference in a suicidal child's social activities. A shy, withdrawn child may fling herself into social activities, probably in an attempt to escape her depression; or a socially busy child may suddenly withdraw into a moody loneliness, unable to share the happiness of others.

3.   Change in behaviors

One boy who tried seriously to take his life, preceded the attempt by a period of minor legal infractions. He stole small items, annoyed his neighbors, and clowned around at school. He didn't care about living anyway, so "anything for a joke" became his motto. The excitement temporarily made him less depressed, and the punishments relieved his guilt feelings.

4.   Giving away possessions

A child who is planning suicide is likely to give away his most treasured possessions. He may include notes that hint darkly about his no longer needing them. He may leave a will, bequeathing items to particular people. When a child sees no tomorrow, all treasures become meaningless.

Changes in Emotions. A child who has been peaceful and happy may become irritable and moody as a sign of possible suicide. Perhaps the most deceptive of all signs of a suicidal child is the one who has been moody and impatient, but suddenly seems tranquil and happy. Such a person apparently acquires some peace of mind by deciding to take his life. The previous conflict is over, the way out has been determined, and the person's mind is finally at rest. This is rarely experienced in children, but I have seen such a state in adolescents.

Changes in School Adjustments. A child who is seriously contemplating suicide sees no reason to work at anything. His schoolwork, therefore, is quite likely to deteriorate. Once in a while, I have seen seriously depressed youngsters put out a sudden spurt of effort to try to succeed in school. When this did not readily produce success, however, they became more depressed than ever.

Loss of Future Plans. In evaluating troubled children, I have learned to listen carefully for their concepts of the future. One young lady was quite sad and wept copiously as I listened to her loneliness, failures, and hardships. Within five minutes, however, she was telling about a party she was attending the next week. Her tears were forgotten as she described her dress for the event.

Such a future, immediate or remote, is not part of the thinking of a suicidal child. One young boy with whom I worked insisted that he looked forward to absolutely nothing. As I watched the hardness of his jaws and the sadness in his eyes, I knew I had evidence of seriously suicidal potential. For him, any tomorrow was only more of a miserable today.

Causes of Suicide

There are three major emotions that are present in variable degrees in all suicidal people. These are *anger, helplessness,* and *sadness.*

Anger. Almost always the angry component seeks vengeance against those people who have made life so unbearable. Ironically, the victim knows those people really care because his thoughts are these: *When I'm dead, you'll be sorry you treated me so badly!* The person who takes his life truly has the last word in any persistent battle!

Helplessness. This is a strong component in suicides of young people. They can do nothing about the problems they face, or the people who create them, but they *can* escape. The sense of helplessness is carried over into adult suicides as an unconscious sense of the weakness of childhood that was unbearable.

Sadness. The sadness of suicidal depression is heavy, and becomes a pain that is almost unbearable. Due to the helpless feelings, the victim often cannot understand the cause of the sadness, and certainly can do nothing to ease the pain. There is simply an overwhelming sense of futility.

Guilt and fear. In addition to the anger, sadness, and helplessness, there are often some additional emotions of guilt and fear. The guilt may be real or imagined. And the fear may also be based on prior severe punishments or only the sense of deserved discipline. Nevertheless, they may add enough strength to the depression to tip the scales in favor of the potentially fatal decision.

It is bad enough to feel such a burden of negative emotions. As long as one only feels hopeless, then, logic, caring, and more accurate information can stop the suicidal intention and reverse it. But when the depressed person adds to those feelings the intellectual conviction that things *are,* in fact, *hopeless,* then we have a serious risk, indeed.

The events in life that produce such emotional and intellectual despair are varied and yet similar.

Unmet emotional needs. The sadness emanates from loneliness and a sense of being unimportant and unloved. There is also a sense of worthlessness and failure. In children, let me remind you, there are those fundamental needs for love and approval. The suicidal child feels that neither is met.

Within the limits of what he knows, *every child seeks out love, attention, acceptance, and some sense of significance.* When all that he knows to do fails to prompt the supplying of those needs, he will be convinced of his helplessness to do anything more to achieve a response. And, indeed, he is helpless against the overwhelming odds of adult powers, so he gives up.

It is this very fact that prompts his anger and motivates his suicidal vengefulness. *When I'm gone, you'll miss me! Then you will cry as I do!*

Family history and examples. One girl I worked with made her first suicidal attempt one week after her father's suicide. Many times, in looking through the suicidal patient's family history, it is replete with suicides. The child of ten who had a suicide pact with his brother had lost two close relatives and a grandparent to suicide. There seem to be subtle messages from parents in some families, conveying the belief that life is not worth living, or that someone is so bad he or she does not deserve to live.

Such messages become focused in the minds of many a child. Since the world tends, for children, to revolve about them, they take such messages and personalize them. Essentially they hear, "Life is not for you. You may as well die!"

Contagion. By no means do all suicide victims receive such information or have such examples in their families. It is especially common in youngsters, however, that they bond themselves closely to a friend. If that friend takes his or her life, the child may follow suit. Especially is this true in young love affairs. Suicide pacts can be formed that result in double deaths. Be extra cautious, therefore, if a friend of your child has tried to take his life.

Preventing Suicide

Suicidal gestures or attempts, fortunately, are often unsuccessful and recovery is certainly possible, so let us discuss how you parents can prevent such a tragedy in your family.

Evaluate your philosophy of life. Ask your spouse or a trusted friend how he or she sees and hears your beliefs about life and death. You may be unaware of your pessimistic outlook on the world. Think about your own family history. Find out if there were many relatives who suffered from depression, and see if there were any who committed suicide.

Think through how such negativism may have affected you. You can probably recall conversations from your childhood that conveyed gloom or despair. A chronically sad face on your mother or father could have been enough to teach you that life is grim.

Open your mind to new information. There are many books on positive thinking and attitudes. Read some of them. Get acquainted with someone who has developed positive attitudes. Listen and learn from that person. Practice looking for the loving, positive approach to life situations, whether you feel it or not. Positive thinking begins with *discipline,* not with feelings. As you practice the cultivation of creative, optimistic attitudes toward life, you will be surprised to find the feelings coming along later on. You cannot give your child a hope that you do not experience.

Review your child's needs. It is easy to take for granted that our children are getting their needs met. The more stress builds up for you parents, the more you may forget to assess the unmet needs of the children. If your child evidences any of the symptoms above, sit down and think about his needs for *unconditional love, pride, approval, consistency, and enjoyment.* Is he or she getting enough of those qualities daily? If not, work at putting them there!

Observe your child's life-style. Review the signs just listed of potential suicide in your child. If three or more of those signs have been evident for as long as three weeks, you may have a child with serious depression and possible suicidal tendency. Do not put off seeking help. At least pay a visit to a qualified family counselor. Lay out the fears and facts as you see them, and encourage your child to speak up about his feelings as well.

You may very well save that child's life and prevent a lifetime of grief for yourself. Furthermore, you can enrich the life of your whole family and find happier, more successful ways of living.

Listen to your child. Talking out the anger and grief of life may not cure all ills, but it will at least give you a chance to understand what's going on, so you can conceivably help. Be sure that you talk *with* your child and not *to* him. That means you listen as well as talk! If your child is moody, give him some time to be alone, but gently intrude into his life. Listen to him, share your love and concern with him, and don't react to his grouchiness with your own anger. This will only push him further into despair.

Stay hopeful. Keep your concern loving and positive, and reassure your child that if he can't talk with you, and you can't help him enough, you will—together—find someone who can help both you and him.

A Word of Comfort

Perhaps, for some parents, these warning signs came too late. Maybe the prevention is no longer possible because your child became one of those suicide statistics. I have sat with parents for whom this was true, and some of them have been close personal friends.

Let me tell you that there is no use blaming yourselves. Even if you have made foolish mistakes, remember, so does every parent! Your child's death was his choice, and the mistakes that helped allow it to happen were shared by many others.

Review the process of grief and work your way through the painful maze. Learn all you can from this heartache, so that death will not have been in vain. Then use the wisdom you will gain to help other parents of other depressed children.

Surely in death, as in life, you can trust the mercy and love of the heavenly Father with your child, and for your own healing and growth.

12
Social Problems

There are many social and cultural influences in every community that affect our children. In turn, children and their "rights" are having a major impact on society. Laws that protect our children from abuse and neglect were long overdue. Despite those laws, however, such abuse and neglect are increasing in most communities.

A BRIEF LOOK AT OUR SOCIETY

Schools are troubled about children who seem unmotivated or who suffer from learning disabilities. Disrespect, rudeness, and serious behavioral disorders make special classrooms the necessary norm in many schools.

Family instability is of such proportions that some authorities feel families are a thing of the past. The pain of broken marriages and the loss of a parent is familiar to many families and the counselors who try to help them.

A wide variety of sexual issues trouble many thoughtful people today. The mores that historically defined masculinity and femininity have almost disappeared, and sexual identity is becoming an area of confusion for many older as well as younger people. The sexual activity that is so widespread (and almost frantic in its quality) is a sign of personal as well as social problems.

Several decades of unusual affluence have given families distorted values, afforded money for drug and chemical abuse, and perhaps, made pampered weaklings out of too many people.

253

How such spoiled people can cope with possible future hardships is a question we cannot answer.

Crime and its implications concerns everyone. Robberies and
rape are commonplace, and all large cities keep a regular census
of murders. Family and community violence are fearsome for
nearly everyone, especially in cities.

Obviously we cannot address such massive issues in this
book, but we can examine the major social problems of children,
their causes, the prevention, and cures that you as parents can
effect.

THE SOCIALLY
DYSFUNCTIONAL CHILD

Despite the crowding together of families in today's over-
populated world, many families experience great isolation from
others. Due to many social and personal factors, families withdraw into the privacy of their own apartments or houses, and
develop their own unique life-styles. Children from such families often do not know how to get along with their classmates.
Some of these children are shy and lonely, and others are aggressive or controlling.

One entire school area was terrorized by a group of such children. Several ten- and eleven-year-old boys and girls had found
an unwieldy power through bullying younger children. They
began to demand that everyone join their "club," and in order
to do so, required donations of liquor or pills from family sup-
plies. They added later the necessity of some minor crime such
as stealing or physically abusing another person.

Children in the neighborhood were beaten by these young
criminals just often enough for the thugs to avoid being caught,
but often enough to keep everyone terrorized. The local merchants dreaded the sight of them in stores, because they became
so skilled at shoplifting and getting away that they could not be
caught.

In school, obviously the atmosphere was hardly one where
learning even the basics could take place! The children were lit-
erally living out a hierarchy of destructive power. Each was so
busy spying on others or feeling fearful, he could not concentrate on studies.

Due to an inspired principal, counselor, and staff, I am happy

to report that within one year that school had been turned
around. Instead of terrorizing the community, each classroom
sought a project in their neighborhood that needed help—and
they offered that help. There is hope for change if people will
invest their energies in bringing that about!

Symptoms of the Socially Dysfunctional Child

The Bully. Such a child may be like this gang—*bullying, rebellious, disrespectful, and energetically troublesome.* Such children are noticed and demand attention. Worrisome as they are,
however, perhaps they are healthier than other kinds of socially
troubled children.

The Sneak. It is *the quiet, sneaky child*—this youngster may
"hit and run" without getting caught—who may become set in
bad habits. Such children become skilled at stealing, cheating,
lying, and psychologically abusing their peers. Because they
rarely get caught, it seems to them that "crime pays," and they
stay involved in their misbehaviors. All the while they are
learning to hold in contempt the adults who fail to even be
aware of their deceit.

The Isolated. And then there are *the isolated children,* whose
behavior is not aggressive but is so different from that of other
children that each is uncomfortable. Other children instinctively avoid discomfort, so the socially "different" child becomes even more isolated.

The most common behaviors of such children include rhyth-
mic body movements, such as *rocking or nodding the head* as
if in time with music; *stroking their bodies in various ways;*
compulsive thumb sucking; and *masturbatory movements.* At
times, an observer would believe such a child to be severely retarded, but that is usually not the case. These children have
learned to get too much of their comfort in life from their own
bodies, instead of external activities.

Those From "Good" Homes. These "isolated children" are the
exaggerated problems, extreme in their expression but not common in many areas. Much more common are the children from
so-called good homes, where children fail to learn the common

courtesies of life. There are unbelievably large numbers of children who are rude, demand to be first, and refuse to take turns or share. They seem ignorant of words such as *please, thank you,* or *excuse me. I'm sorry* is certainly a foreign language. They are unable to feel or show compassion for another's pain, and they evidence a lack of moral judgment. They, in fact, do not know how to tell right from wrong, and plunge headlong into getting what they want, without considering values. They are selfish and callous at remarkably early ages.

Causes of Social Dysfunctions

The Family. Socially maladjusted children come from families that are rich and poor, of all racial backgrounds. The factors that seem to be common to all of them are these:

Parents' example is one of either aggression and selfishness, or isolation and suspicion. One of the most socially troubled children I have tried to work with was a carbon copy of his father. This man was wealthy, but his success was based on taking advantage of others, not caring about the needs of his employees, and seeming totally selfish. His son took what he wanted, did as he pleased, and acted charming enough to get by.

Parents give too little time or energy to their families. Whether time and energy are devoted to the pursuit of material success, marital struggles, or making ends meet with a welfare check, is immaterial. The children suffer when they get too little care from parents. They must have *love*—protective, tough, and tender—to thrive and become socially responsible.

Failure of parents to establish values. By the lack of significant values, parents fail as models, but even more importantly, they do not teach these to their children. Without values, there are few rules. And without rules, children have no consistency, logic, or meaningful limits in their lives. A society that has for over two decades ridiculed the "Protestant work ethic" has offered nothing better.

Abuse and neglect of children by parents certainly influences social behaviors. No doubt this tragedy in today's society is a by-product of adult stress and inadequacy, but it is causing an explosion of problems for the future.

By the very nature of their problems, parents of socially troubled children usually rescue them from the discipline of other people. They need so badly to be right that they blame others for the problem behaviors of their children.

The Community. This includes institutions and individuals outside the home.

The Churches. They sometimes are unaware of community needs. Some churches do reach out and visit homes, but often such visits are primarily focused on increasing church attendance, rather than identifying and ministering to the simple daily needs of struggling families. In many instances, dysfunctional children cannot be controlled in Sunday school and become so disruptive they must be excluded.

The Merchants. Despite a ban on selling alcoholic beverages on Sunday, many young people insist on having them. To them, being under the legal age for purchasing such items is also irrelevant. Some grocery stores still demand proof of legal age and refuse to sell beer on Sunday, but recently I watched a group of teenagers at a local quick-food store. They walked out with quantities of beer without regard to their age *or* the day of the week. It appeared to me that some of them did not even pay for their items. The manager seemed to be blind to the whole scene. Such indifference (or hesitation to "cause trouble") gives even more power to young people who already have too much. They need to know their limits.

Fortunate indeed are the children who are caught and disciplined in their very first episode of stealing. The busy merchants who care enough to deal with these young culprits may prevent a life habit of stealing and disregard for others' property.

The Schools. When the U.S. Supreme Court ruling made prayer in schools illegal, a much more damaging restriction went into effect. Somehow, school staffs began to believe they could no longer teach values or morality. There is no law that forbids it, but several years ago I personally sat on a state committee involved with the education of young children. Several people tried very hard to introduce some curriculum goals involving simple morality for children. Those in authority flatly forbade even the use of the words; yet if the family is failing to teach values, and many children no longer enter a church, who will inform them of right and wrong, and define for them the difference?

The Media. Television and movies have been analyzed, studied, and selectively condemned without visible improvement! Parents, you can no longer depend on ratings, and you dare not close your eyes to the dangers. Think critically as you watch TV or read movie reviews. What is this program going to teach your child? A movie called *E. T.* is a charming fantasy of a creature abandoned by a spaceship from another planet. The story of the child who rescues and cares for him is delightful, but most of the adults are made to look foolish or mean. Certainly I can't deny that adults are often both! But in a world where respect for elders, especially parents, is so sadly lacking, I deplore exaggerating that idea.

Children's books and literature must be carefully screened by parents. Now I am not one who believes in book burnings (though that sometimes sounds like the easiest approach!). Read some, at least, of each book your little children read, and by all means, think about those you read to them! Many of these are meaningless nonsense, but some are promoting outright disrespect! One such book describes three bears—Mama, Papa, and Baby Bear. Papa gives a bicycle to the little bear, and then proceeds to show him how to ride it. Throughout the book, by pictures and words, Papa Bear is made to look bumbling and idiotic, while Baby and Mama are barely tolerant of his goofs. If a child whose father seems awkward or inept at times hears that story, consider what the child is being taught by such a book!

Television commercials for children commonly portray the child as the ultimate authority, knowing far more than mother about various brands of cereal or peanut butter! Do you want your children to believe they are wiser than you, parents? I can tell you, children who believe that are insecure!

The Neighborhood. Too often children win a con game with their parents. The phrases are so familiar I am surprised they still work, but they do. "Everyone's doing it!" "All the girls have X brand jeans." "All the guys have such and such shoes!" And because parents want their kids to fit in and to be like everyone else, they give in. There is a horrible waste of money and risking of values by parents who fall for that line. Parents, start communicating with each other in your neighborhood. You can change some bad practices through stopping unsupervised parties and refusing to waste money on famous-name clothes that will be outgrown too soon.

Every neighborhood is composed largely of families. Let your community be a model of positive, creative thinking and reaching out to support others in healthy family living.

Helping the Socially Dysfunctional Child

Role of Professionals. In areas where large numbers of families have known breakups, loneliness, and deprivation, major social changes are needed. Setting up supervised after-school play areas, guidance and teaching of parents, and providing for the basic material needs through jobs that will promote dignity and self-respect are some minimal essentials. Some especially troubled children might benefit (as would their parents) if the children lived temporarily in a foster home with frequent visits home. Institutional care can turn around the apparently destructive tendencies in some young lives. Though it seems sad to remove troubled children from their own homes, I have seen that doing so can enable parents to reestablish normal living, while the child is returning to emotional and social health. With such help, they can often be restored successfully as families.

Where even one parent realizes there is a problem with children, socially, much can be done.

Role of Parents. Of course, the first step is *recognizing the problem.* In order to face this issue honestly, you will need to accept the fact that you parents will need to make some major changes. You need to evaluate your attitudes and the beliefs by which you live. Are they satisfactory? Or perhaps you have never stopped to define your values, but just get through your days as best you can. *Change that now.*

Open your eyes (mentally) to see your child's attitudes and behaviors. Is he kind to his brother and sister, and does she help you when you need her? How does he act at school or when you take him to the store? If you don't like your answers to these questions, you can do many things to change them positively!

Sit down and talk about the bad behaviors and even worse feelings that are commonplace in your home. Explain your own part in this state, yet avoid blame or guilt. Then begin working on a plan for change. Different feelings and new information and awareness will be needed for any change, but a plan is necessary for the follow-through in forming a new set of habits around your house. And *you* probably have many old habits to break, so plan and then follow your plan. If you need guidance, go to a family counselor. He or she would love to help someone who already has a goal and some ideas! At any rate, get a friend or relative to support and encourage you and your children. You may all need to learn new ways of thinking, and certainly will need new habits of talking, acting, and treating others.

As you work with your children, I hope you will find a marvelous benefit for yourselves: that of the joy of real intimacy, compassion, and caring!

PROBLEMS OF THE ADOPTED CHILD

A great many adopted children have no more problems than biological children. They are proud that they were wanted, grateful for the love of a parent who made the tough choice to give her child the best chance in life, and love their adoptive family sincerely. This happy experience, however, is not always the case, and many adoptive children go through some rough times. Their adoptive parents also experience difficulties.

Causes of Problems

Search for Identity and "Roots." Many adopted children wonder who their birth parents are, what they look like, what they are good at, and how they lived when they were children. What are the people like who might have been their grandparents? When these children feel securely bonded to their adoptive parents, such questions are purely curiosity.

Adoptive Parents May Feel Threatened. When there are problems—even those that are normal for any family—an adopted child may wishfully think, *If only I had my* real *parents, they would understand!* When they state such thoughts aloud, adoptive parents are quite likely to feel deeply hurt! They have stayed up with earaches during long, sleepless nights, washed diapers, sacrificed for schooling, and so on! They believe they *are* the real parents, and may see that child as ungrateful.

Such hurting can become explosive and result in retaliation and perhaps in rebellion, or end up in a counselor's office.

Usually, simply understanding the child's feeling as a normal fantasy and helping him accept the facts of life can settle such anger promptly. Don't feel threatened by the accusations of your adopted child. Most children pass those out from time to time. Your adopted child simply uses different words!

Why Did My Birth Parents Give Me Away? Adopted children, like any children, may develop a poor sense of their worth. When an adoptive child does have an inferiority complex, he and his parents may become anxious about the cause of such a poor self-image. A child's search for that cause sooner or later may lead to the question "Why did they give me away?" *Perhaps,* he believes, *I was no good, even when I was born. I must have been a real nuisance!* And he can dig a deep ditch of despair for himself.

The answer to that, of course, lies in regularly explaining to an adopted child just how much those parents did love him or her. It takes a truly protective and mature love to place a baby where it can be secure. I have seen a parent selfishly keep a baby just to avoid the pain of giving it up, but she allowed the infant to suffer because she was totally unable to care for it.

Adoptive Parents May Feel Inadequate. For various reasons, people who are unable to conceive or bear children of their own may feel guilty—as if they had done wrong and are being punished. They may feel unmanly or unfeminine. The reasons for such feelings are deep-seated, but the emotions are very real and painful.

If such insecure parents end up with insecure adopted children, you can see how readily difficulties may erupt. So, parents, get counseling if you need to, but work out those feelings and fears of your own unworthiness, so you can offer a firm foundation for the building of your child's life.

Adoptive Parents May Have Shaky Marriages. It is a common fallacy that having children will make a troubled marriage secure. This is never more untrue than with the use of an adopted child for such a purpose. Sooner or later, this kind of unstable marriage is likely to crumble. The tragic result is the leaving of a vulnerable, helpless child with a single, often-traumatized parent, while the stronger one goes away to build a new life. Such children *do* suffer!

Mismatched Families. Social agencies go to an amazing amount of trouble to match, in detail, the traits of the biological parents with those of adoptive parents. The results are remarkable resemblances physically, mentally, and even in creative interests.

Private adoptions, and even black-market adoptions, are not unusual, however, and with these, everyone takes potluck. One highly intellectual family adopted a child of an unknown background. The child had an IQ that was barely normal, and shared none of their interests. The discrepancies were so intolerable to both child and parents that they finally had to place the child in a foster family. Now obviously these parents had some problems, for a baby of their own could have had an intelligence similar to that of the adopted child. Nevertheless, matching babies to families is a fine science, and I strongly recommend adoption through a qualified agency.

When and How Should We Tell Her? This question, though old, is always new. Society goes through cycles in answering it—and those answers range from the first birthday to *never!* It never works, from my experience, to be dishonest with children. Sooner or later they find out, and it is a blow to their trust in the parents when they do.

I recommend that you practice telling them as soon as you get them. If they are infants, they won't understand anyway, so you can perfect your telling before it is likely to cause any damaging misunderstandings. Listen to each other, if there are two of you, and talk about your explanation until you get it just right! Then review it only on birthdays, or whenever the child asks for it. Someday, I hope you'll find neither you nor the child needs to hear it anymore.

Medical History. It may be most important for your child to know certain medical information about his blood relatives. A history of diabetes, epilepsy, or other inheritable diseases can help your doctor in diagnosing and managing certain health problems. Qualified adoption agencies will provide such information to adoptive parents.

Help for the Adopted Child and Parents

Never be ashamed to admit that you need help of any kind. Needing each other and sharing one another's burdens is what keeps us human. Certainly when a problem is as intricate and as personally involved as that of adoptive parents and children, you may really have no other choice. Do use that help as soon as you recognize the need. Don't put it off, because you all deserve to get on with happy living.

Here are suggestions to help you and your adopted child.

Be proud and grateful to be adoptive parents. It took a great deal of time, energy, money, and most of all, *motivation,* to find and adopt a child. To make all that effort took very special people. Many biological parents rather stumble into parenthood, but you worked and planned for this event. So if you have tended to feel inadequate, you may give up that feeling. Enjoy your role!

Share as much as you can about the birth parents. Without identifying them, find out whatever you can about your child's other parents. Learn about their coloring and size, their interests, and medical histories—anything that would be helpful or of concern to your child someday. Store it away in your minds, or even in a journal. When your child starts to ask, or you feel like discussing it, do so! The more openly and comfortably you can talk about the other parents, the less threatening they will seem to you, and the less likely is your child to use them against you! Any negative information about those parents is best left untold, unless you are certain your child needs to hear it.

You are the real parents. Without discounting your child's birth parents, you need to acquire the deep knowledge that you are legally, emotionally, and in every sense, except birth, this child's *real parents.* This process is called "bonding," and it does not require giving birth to a child to be bonded with him. Rest in that fact, and teach it to your child from the day he enters your lives! Never forget this truth.

Understand the processes of grief. Your inability to bear your own child, and your child's loss of his biological parents, may well cause all of you some grief. You need not grieve forever, but do recognize that and finish the stages. Avoid staying angry or feeling sorry for yourselves. Reread the chapter on the grieving child, and *finish* that entire process if you haven't.

Help your child develop his own healthy identity. The more confident a child feels, the less likely he is to need anyone else's identity. You may help him or her avoid that compelling search for the natural parents' identity by formulating his own security.

An aptitude or interest survey by your own careful observations or some psychological tests will be useful. Without burdening the child, slowly help him to perfect his skills in these areas of special interest. Be extra careful to praise your child's accomplishments with specific feedback. He will need to know what is good about what he does in order to believe in himself.

Search for Child Given in Adoption

Several years ago, a friend came to me for advice about an associate of hers. This woman had borne a child and was unable to provide for her needs, so she gave her up to be adopted. She had seen a television program in which such a mother had been reunited with her young adult son. The drama of that program stayed with her, and finally she decided that she, too, would search for her lost child! Despite my strong advice against such a move, she pursued her search. Finally she found her daughter, now eighteen years of age and ready for college. She was bright, loved her family, and felt secure with them. She had long ago resolved her grief for her biological mother.

At first the daughter resisted even seeing this echo from her infancy, but due to the woman's insistence, she finally agreed to a meeting. Far from the happy event of television, theirs was a dismal time. The girl felt confused and wondered why she could not get excited or, in fact, experience any feeling for the stranger. She felt vaguely guilty for letting her down but was too honest to pretend. She did not need this person, could not think of any way to help her, and was grateful when she left.

In my experience, *such disappointments are far more common than are happy reunions.*

Whether or not to search for biological children (or parents) is becoming a common question. And since courts are making available the records that make possible the tracing of such a person, many people will be facing a decision that once was made for them.

Teach your adopted child to think carefully and make

decisions wisely. Share his feelings and let him know yours. As you grow in such intimacy and understanding, he will agree with you—you are both blessed to be an adoptive family!

THE TROUBLED CHILD OF DIVORCE

Divorce, directly or indirectly, now affects the majority of American homes. Many schools report at least half of their students live in families that have suffered the pain of broken marriages. I know of very few families in which some close relative has not suffered a divorce. This pain is especially difficult for children. They are part of both parents and usually love each one of them.

Typical Example

Pamela was only seven when her parents decided to settle a long period of marital trouble by getting a divorce. She was especially attached to her father, and she grieved inconsolably over his absence. Her brother didn't miss him as much, and began to ridicule her when she would cry out her longing for Daddy. Pam tried to persuade her parents to get along and stop the divorce. She then actually injured her leg in an attempt to coerce those divided parents into getting back together. None of her pleas or tricks, however, influenced her parents. Pam's helplessness, added to her sadness and anger, created a period of serious depression.

Emotional Reactions

Children of divorce experience a range of profound emotional reactions.

Fear. This is one of the first feelings to hit a child. He is afraid of losing his security in the absence of one parent. Perhaps the other may leave also, or maybe he will have to go away. A fear of being abandoned is almost instinctive. The falling apart of his family shatters a child's whole world.

Helplessness. This is one of the worst emotions we know. By its very nature, it entraps its victim. Certainly children like Pamela are powerless throughout the struggles that precede and are a part of any divorce.

Guilt. This is described by most of the children of divorce with whom I have worked. Early in life, children tend to feel omnipotent—the whole world revolves about them. Furthermore, many of the parents' disagreements focus on various problems involving their children. Whether parents realize it or not, very little that goes on in a family escapes children's awareness. It is to be expected, then, that children feel responsible for the divorce and experience intense guilt.

Confusion. This is easy to understand in divorce. Even the husband and wife who are involved have mixed feelings. Most divorcing couples I know stay strongly emotionally involved with each other, although this is a negative and destructive relationship. Being a step removed from their conflicts, a child will often sense the caring each spouse feels, and yet he sees them hurting each other. It really doesn't make sense! Children love both parents, yet they feel angry at them. Their own feelings are confused as well as the parents' feelings! A child's view of divorce is one of topsy-turvy bewilderment.

Grief. This emotion, with all its denial, anger, and deep sadness, is every child's legacy from a divorce. Too often there is no one to help the child get through his grief, because his parents are involved with their own pain.

Children act out these intense feelings in many ways but rarely express them directly. They have bad dreams and awaken with fears. They may regress to wetting or soiling if they are fairly close to toilet training. Many younger children become hyperactive and "naughty." This serves two purposes:

   1. *It focuses the parents' attention on the child instead of on each other's anger.*
   2. *It usually results in some punishment that helps relieve his guilt feelings.*

Children may withdraw and isolate themselves emotionally and physically in their sadness and anger. They may need some privacy, but sooner or later, they need even more to talk out their feelings.

Children of divorce often feel that they cannot express themselves to either parent about the other or about the entire situation. One seven-year-old boy was misbehaving in school, refusing to do his work, and was angry at home. He clearly said that he just needed to talk about missing his father, but when he mentioned his dad, Mother would cry or be irritated. The only means by which the child could express his feelings was by acting them out.

PRACTICAL PROBLEMS OF DIVORCE

Avoiding Divorce. Since divorce has such devastating effects on spouses and children alike, I urge parents to avoid it! By good professional counseling, many problems can be solved. Often a marriage can be strengthened by each spouse's remembering that commitment "for better, for worse"; learning to accept some of the "worseness"; and determining to grow personally, while waiting for the spouse to get better. Really working to understand each other's sometimes garbled communication system is essential as well. Your clergyman can often help by encouraging and supporting both of you in the tough times that even good marriages know.

Whatever it takes, make every possible effort to strengthen and fully heal your marriage if it is in trouble. No marriage is perfect, and being single has its own share of problems. But in most cases, the heartache of children who are crushed by the impact of divorce is the most far-reaching difficulty of all!

No matter how hard people try, however, divorces do take place. And when a marriage is in such serious trouble that it cannot be fixed, a divorce may be better for everyone. Since it looks as if divorce is here to stay for a while, you need to understand some of the issues at stake. You can help prevent or alleviate some of the worst problems affecting your child or the child of people you love. Here are some ideas that can help you.

Alleviating Problems of Divorce

Do not criticize each other to the child. In fact, each parent and family friends, as well, need to point out the good qualities of both parents. True enough, children may wonder why two such "good" people can't get along, and that is an opportunity to help them learn from your mistakes. Explain as well as you can why the divorce was necessary. You can do this honestly and without insulting anyone. Disagreements do not necessarily mean that either party is wrong or bad.

Do not use the child as a go-between. It is tempting for divorced parents, or other relatives, to be curious about the activities of the absent spouse. The child who spends time with each one can be the source of such information, but most children sense they are being used as informants and resent it. This is especially true when the information results in sadness, arguments, or anger for their separated parents.

If you must be divorced, get an emotional divorce even more quickly and completely than a legal one! Freeing yourself as a divorced parent from resentments, blame, and preoccupation with the whole situation, will solve many of the problems of your children, as well as your own. You may even become friends with your ex-spouse and work together constructively for your children. I have seen a number of divorced spouses forego their anger at each other in order to help their troubled children.

Avoid competition for your child's love and loyalty. Many divorced parents resort to buying the children's favor. Out of guilt or loneliness, the absent parent may make visits a party time, or load a child with gifts he neither needs nor wants. The other parent will usually react in anger and accuse the ex-spouse of spoiling the children. I have seen parents retaliate by trying to buy even bigger and better things.

Discipline. Another expression of competition is in the area of *discipline.* The question of strictness or permissiveness is difficult to answer at best. Divorced parents are especially susceptible to problems involving this issue. One parent inevitably feels he is the ogre, while the other gets to be an angel. Children quickly learn to take advantage of such situations to manipulate both parents to their selfish (and often destructive) advantage.

Avoid pitying the child. In marriage or divorce, many bad habits of parenting are prompted by pity. Feeling sorry for a child promotes pampering, teaches him self-pity with its paralyzing helplessness, and allows you to rescue him from healthy reality. Rescuing may make you feel wonderfully heroic, but rescuing children too much keeps them weak and dependent.

Be slow and cautious in reaching out for a new dating relationship. Both divorcing parents and their children experience grief. Prompt replacements of the absent spouse with a girl friend or boyfriend is a form of denial. It disturbs the grief process, and often is a form of retaliation against each other. Worst of all, it allows for a major decision that may lead to a new marriage—to be made in the worst of emotional circumstances.

Before Dating Again. Children, as well as divorced parents, need to take one step at a time. First, finish grieving. Next, reestablish your own peace of mind, your new life-style, and grow from the mistakes of the past. *Then* consider remarriage, if your religious beliefs permit. A child who has just lost a parent through divorce does not want to lose the other to a new spouse, and is likely to resent the new person from the start.

When you feel you are ready to start dating, talk it over with your children and a family friend. Counseling with your minister or other professional person is often a wise plan. Sorting through troubled emotions, broken hopes, and new problems is no small task. When grieving children are involved, the solutions may demand outside help.

Getting Through It. The following are some simple rules that will help you support your children through a divorce:

Parents, if you must separate, as mentioned before, *get an emotional divorce before a legal one.* Work through your hurts and anger until you reestablish peace within your own lives as well as between the two of you. If you can't get along together, at least learn to be courteous and kind, apart.

Be aware of your children's range of needs and feelings:

1. *Allow them to talk, cry, and express their anger. Comfort them until they have finished their grief.*
2. *Explain the reasons for the divorce without blaming or condemning each other.*
3. *Encourage the children to feel loving toward both of their parents and the relatives.*

Plan plenty of time for the child with both parents, and make that time as nearly like "normal" family living as possible.

Parents, *stay in charge*. Do not let a child threaten to go to the other parent when he is angry with one of you, or for his own selfish advantage. Avoiding such "Ping-Ponging" takes the efforts of both of you.

Help your child keep respect for both men and women. Avoid any implications that all men are mean, or all women are selfish, in order to give him or her the best chance to develop a healthy sexual identity.

Development of Healthy Sexuality in the Child of Divorce

At this time in our American culture, mothers are still given custody of the children in most cases, though men are beginning to be more involved with their children, and some are now gaining legal custody. In order to establish their own personal and sexual identity, children need both male and female role models.

Role Model Important. If you are a single parent and the absent spouse cannot fulfill this need, find such a role model for the children. Help them love, trust, and respect adults of both sexes as close friends. Grandparents, uncles, and aunts can often be such backup people. So can teachers or neighbors. Do not hesitate to ask an appropriate person for special help in clearly defined ways. No one person can do everything a child needs, but you can build a support system of several people who may supply most of those needs without being burdened.

Big Brothers Clubs. Men who are able and willing to give time and energy to little children seem especially hard to find. Encourage your church and school to use more men as teachers or youth leaders for young children. Try your local Big Brothers Club. They are wonderful men dedicated to this very service to little children, especially boys. In many cities, however, this group has had hundreds more requests than it has volunteers.

Teach Sexual Identity. Parents, your efforts will ultimately teach your children their sexual roles. Pay special attention to their dress, activities, and their concepts of manliness and femininity. Be proud of such qualities as they do develop, and let them feel your approval.

While divorce, like other losses, brings pain to you and your child, you can turn that pain into a strengthening experience—for yourself as well as your child. ". . . weeping may endure for a night, but joy cometh in the morning" (Psalms 30:5).

THE CHILD TROUBLED BY FULFILLING PARENTS' NEEDS

Typical Example

Steve was in the fifth grade when I first saw him, due to his disrupting the entire class. Despite superior intelligence and a handsome appearance, Steve was barely passing and had few friends. From watching him in class, and from the staff's description, I expected to see a typical bully, who bolstered his shaky ego by terrorizing the "less fortunate."

It was a surprise, therefore, when I saw Steve alone, to find that he was a remarkably bright and insightful child. Within five minutes, in fact, he was crying, and by his heroic efforts to stop, I knew it was not usual for him to cry. His only real friend was going to move away, and Steve was sad. As I talked quietly and listened to him, he revealed that he never cried around his parents. I learned that Steve believed they always wanted him to be happy. Any time he was worried, sad, or angry, they talked or joked him out of his real feelings into an often fake substitute for happiness.

Later on I learned that Steve's parents had been sad as children, and it was *their need to be always happy,* not Steve's, that they were trying to fulfill. They had worked so hard to make him happy, in fact, that he had become miserable. He understood what they wanted, and tried to please them, but was too honest to succeed at meeting either their needs or his own.

The Parents' Expectations. Some parents have exceptionally successful and happy memories of their early years. They may unconsciously seek to relive those days through their children. A mother who was Chief Cheerleader or Homecoming Queen may ever so lovingly strive to get her daughter to excel similarly—whether she wants to or not. And how many boys I have known who struggled mightily, but in vain, to fulfill Dad's dreams of being a great ball player!

Consciously or unconsciously, most parents have dreams for their children. Whether those involve fulfilling lost hopes or reliving exciting times from your own pasts—or any other dream—you need to be careful. Don't entirely give up your dreams, for they can become goals in life, but see to it that those dreams are honestly shared by your child. Find out if they are possible for her before you push her into a path that will be darkened by more dread and failure than it is lighted by joy.

Parents often have an extreme need to be perfect parents, and they can believe they have succeeded only if their children are perfect. And perfection—looking handsome, being successful in sports, making top grades and enjoying popularity—is simply too heavy a burden for most children to bear.

How much better eventually, if you observe your children closely; help them explore as many facets of life as they can; talk with teachers and others who know your children well; then guide them to focus in the area of life that is their unique specialty. There may be one such gifted facet or several, but once you both have found that, develop it. Firmly and patiently stick with the children, nudging them toward their goal. And by all means, be proud of both it and them!

Helping the Burdened Child

Almost always, in working with the parents of troubled children, I hear them say, "We only wanted Jim to be happy! What went wrong?" After pondering this familiar lament long and deeply, I am convinced that parents must stop being obsessively concerned about children's happiness!

Relieving the Burden. These are the steps to relieving a child burdened with fulfilling your hopes and dreams—whether they are for him or for yourselves!

Be honest with yourselves and each other about what it is you want for your children. If you have unconsciously burdened them with your own unfulfilled needs and ambitions, or you are unwittingly trying to relive your lives through them, stop doing so!

Talk with your children and observe their own feelings, needs, interests, and special skills. Whether you understand or share those is not as important as your approval and pride in your individual child's accomplishments.

Whatever it takes to encourage and provide help in the development of their special interests, try to arrange for that. Many times that requires lessons, tutoring, or equipment. Obviously such costs must be budgeted, but many children are willing to go without some things in order to have those they truly treasure. All of my family sacrificed to help me through the expensive years of my medical training. I know they were glad to do that, and so I was glad to work for my children's school and other interests. You need not give children whatever they want, but being willing to sacrifice some for their good is a parent's privilege.

Let each child be *himself.* Guide him in his explorations of himself and his world. Give him the freedom to choose, with help, what is right for him, and to pursue it to excellence. Accept his feelings and help him express them appropriately. Understand his needs and help him fulfill those. You will have set him free from the heavy load of carrying your needs as well as his own.

THE IRRITATING CHILD

There are some troubled children who do not fit any exact category, but cause problems to everyone around them. For lack of a better name, I am calling them the Irritating Children.

Typical Example

Joyce is such a child. She demands attention and time constantly. No doubt she also really needs this attention, but her demands are made so insistently that the needs are lost in her pushy way. She speaks in a whiny, irritating tone of voice that is a cross between sadness and anger. She seems aware exclusively of her wishes and lacks sensitivity to the pressures that are already exerted on her parents. She crowds in when her brother is involved with their parents, and torments him mercilessly. Joyce is a pessimist; she sees and expects the worst at all times.

It is significant that Joyce is the mirror of her grandmother. That woman has been difficult for Joyce's mother to understand, and seeing so much of her mother's personality in her child has often made it impossible to feel warmly toward Joyce.

The Development of an Irritating Child

The irritating child usually has a history of being quite *different right from birth*. She is frustrating because her needs seem to chronically flow at crosscurrents with her mother's. Her mother loves her exceptionally well, but feels that no matter how she tries, she cannot please this child or make her happy.

Many times this early frustration is *compounded by worry*. Perhaps she is brain-damaged. Could she have allergies? Out of such anxiety, there begins a series of medical visits that often bring comfort to the parents. They can finally believe this problem child is not their fault. It is easier to believe the cause is some rare nervous or biochemical factor than to feel they are bad parents. And there certainly are physical elements of stress that are involved. It is, however, a mistake to believe that the entire problem is physical, because the interpersonal issues, then, are likely to be ignored rather than resolved.

Sometimes there is misinterpretation of the child's behaviors. Recently a mother described the constant activity of her four-year-old daughter. She was always exploring, climbing, and making messes. This mother is a very neat, organized, and peace-loving person, and she could interpret the child's activities as being designed purposely to "get" her. Even when she knew better intellectually, her emotions still boiled up whenever Lori created her messes.

The angry reaction of her mother confused Lori, who only felt the compelling urge to explore and grow. She began to resent the anger, however, and then she would add to her inherent curiosity seeking a deliberate act to get back at Mom for hurting her feelings. Anger, of course, tends to generate more anger, so their special vicious cycle was established.

Parents feel guilty over their anger. Periodically, Lori's mother realized the truth: they were simply two very different people. Lori wasn't all bad, and the mother knew then that she had been too angry. At such times, she would be extrapatient and gentle, but just as Lori began to feel safe in this gentleness, her mother would have one bad mess too many and would explode again. Lori became an increasingly irritating child, acting out in real curiosity and sneaky anger her honest inner needs and feelings. Her whining and fussing became ways to solicit Mother's gentler attention, but Mother's inconsistency prompted Lori to test out her responses. This constant testing irritated Mother even more, increased Lori's nervousness, and kept their problem going.

Helping the Irritating Child

Try to be understanding. The irritating child has those same needs every other child has: _unconditional love, pride and approval, consistency, and congeniality._ This child, for all the reasons just listed, loses his parents' approval first. The light goes out in the eyes of any child who no longer senses his parents' pride, but feels disapproval instead. As the child looks angry or acts hurt and withdrawn, the parents often feel rejected and may, in turn, fail to demonstrate their love. Whenever they realize this failure, parents tend, as did Lori's, to try extra hard to be loving. But they can only sustain that effort for a short time, so the consistency also fails. Certainly there is little joy or laughter in such a family, so the fourth need is also unmet.

Just what is it that irritates you about this troublesome child? Very likely he has some of the traits you did not like about one of your parents or siblings, your spouse, or perhaps even about yourself. If so, you will unconsciously feel some of the hurt, angry emotions you experienced with that other person, and these feelings will pour out on your child. Simply knowing that can help you to relegate those emotions, at least, to their real source. You and your child are left then with only his current issues, rather than an accumulation of old problems as well.

Sometimes it helps to *write down* all the things your child does that irritate you. As you do that, take time to think through why he does them, and what, if anything, is really bad about them. More than likely you will find a depth of understanding that will enable you to truly forgive and love that child with a new consistency.

Separate your frustration from worry. Most irritating children need not worry you. They will come out of their frustrating stage as you learn to understand and forgive them, freeing up your loving again. When your worry is gone, your child can feel that he is not too sick or too bad, and the restoration of hope for himself will bring more joy into your lives.

Define your needs as you do for your child. It's very hard to stay loving with a child who seems to always be out to get you! By understanding your child's nature and needs, I hope you will find assurance that he really does not intend to hurt or frustrate you. He only has a high level of energy and a curiosity that demands exploring and doing things. When you can believe in your child's love, you will be getting more of your own affectional needs met, and things will go better yet.

Turn that energy into positive channels. Instead of allowing that annoying child to demand, whine, and test you out, *organize his time.* Get the help of an older child (borrow or hire one if you need to), and plan each day to keep the child busy. I suggest you share those activities that you can enjoy in honesty, and let someone else help in the things that are likely to tax your patience. Talk over all the events of the day at bedtime in a quiet, loving time. When you do revert to being angry, explain to your child that this anger is partly your problem and not a sign he is a bad child.

Explain the irritating mannerisms of your child. Many times, disapproval of an irritating child is so broad and all-inclusive that neither he nor you can really define what is so annoying. After you have made your list, above, categorize all the details into several basics that even a child can understand: *your whining voice; coming to me demanding something when I'm rushing to get dinner ready; refusing to let me hold you when I need your love.* These are some examples of irritating behaviors. Tell your child you are working to change your responses, and that you need him to help you by working at his side of things. *Then set up a plan with him.* For example, when he wants something, he is to catch you when you aren't in a big hurry, and you will try to take time out to listen. Include in that plan a reminder to both of you to change old habits and stop nagging.

Catch yourself and your child being good. To replace the old, irritating ways of acting and reacting, try to pat yourself on the back when you are patient, and by all means, praise your child when he acts appropriately instead of irritatingly. Honest pride in changes will motivate both you and your child to do better.

Be aware of avoiding negative attention. The irritating child, over a period of time, has learned to ask for and react to negative, angry responses from adults. As you begin to stick with gentle, loving, and firm ways of dealing with that child, he will have some problems believing those ways, and will tend to go back to his old ways. Be patient. In time the new habits will be just as natural as the old ones were, but they will be so much happier.

Summarizing

In summary, the irritating child is annoying to you because of his own ways, but also for what and whom they remind you of. Separate those habits from him as a person. He is irritating also because of the way you have learned to react to him and his ways. Change those. He is irritating to you partly because neither of you is getting your emotional needs met.

As you break down this problem into its smaller parts, you and your child can work out a plan to resume your basically loving, happy way of life.

THE LONELY/SHY CHILD

Recently, I observed a third-grade child on a public-school playground. His classmates were busy with a variety of games, noisily, happily competing to win. Only this one youngster was standing on the sidelines, alone. Sam's shoulders sagged, and his eyes yearningly followed the activities of the others. His loneliness, in stark contrast with the joy and excitement around him, was painful to watch! He appeared powerless and so vulnerable.

Typical Example

Elaine also was such a child. Few children lived in her neighborhood, and they were either too old or too young for her to enjoy. She did play some with the younger children, because they didn't try to boss her around like the older ones did. At school, she was rarely chosen on teams because she wasn't very good at sports. She did make excellent grades, but the other kids seemed to hate her for being smarter than they were. Once in a while, Elaine was invited to a birthday party or a Friday-night slumber party, but somehow she felt out of place or different. She simply never learned how to fit in.

But she wanted so much to be popular! If only once she could be the very center of attention in a happy way! Even at home Elaine felt out of tune with the family harmony. Her little sister did nothing wrong, and she (Elaine) did nothing right. She felt as if she were outside of her house on a cold evening, looking through the windows at a warm fire and seeing light and comfort, but was locked out. She could find no way in!

Symptoms of a Lonely Child

Elaine and Sam are very typical examples of lonely children. They were not happy being alone and deeply longed to be more accepted by other children, to feel comfortable with them. Elaine's parents' unconscious preference for her sister was not even known to her, but she vaguely sensed less approval from them, and felt inadequate. She was so accustomed to criticism that even by age eight, she had learned to disapprove of herself.

The lonely children of our world share these symptoms:

They usually feel sad and wistful, like Elaine, *feeling as if they are always locked outside, looking in,* or like Sam, yearning for fun! Their personal interests are not satisfying because they are social people and yearn for companionship.

Though they are not necessarily paranoid, they are sensitive and self-conscious. They feel awkward, and sense that others are critical of them, and generally disapproving. While this often is the attitude of their parents, these lonely kids learn to stand back, so others are uncomfortable with them, and step back, too, making an even wider gap between them.

They lack both the courage and the social skills that could enable them to cross over the distance that separates them from others. Sometimes they compensate, like Elaine in her studies, with other skills, so they often are seen as aloof or snobbish. This keeps even well-intentioned children from reaching out to them.

By accident or by observing others, a lonely child may learn that favors for others can make friends. Sometimes they are unaware that friends who are "bought" in this way do not last, and some are so desperate for companions that they don't care. Such children are easy prey to those who are ready to take advantage of them.

Clowning and bullying behaviors may cover up a lonely child. I know youngsters who will take a dare or do almost any mischief, just to be noticed. And an aggressive child (called a *bully* in slang) is almost always lonely and insecure.

Causes of Loneliness

Many lonely children have lacked playmates early in life, and simply never learned how to talk, play, and just be with others. It is hard for them to learn this skill, when suddenly they are placed in a classroom full of children. Sometimes parents unknowingly overprotect their children, teaching them to retreat from normal neighborhood squabbles to their home. These children fail to learn how to work through common playtime hassles.

Painful or frightening experiences with playmates may scare a sensitive child into withdrawing into loneliness. One extremely isolated girl described repeated episodes with her older brother. He was much bigger than she, and she felt in awe of him. When they went swimming, he thought it was fun to repeatedly push her under the water. He knew she was safe, but she was terrified. When she called out for help, she recalled her mother laughing. Obviously her mother felt it was all in fun, but the child was serious. Her helplessness became a habit, and she never did escape her fear and loneliness. To her, mother and brother both sided against her. She assumed everyone else would, too.

Disproportionate sensitivity and criticism are a common problem in lonely children. They are so alert to disapproval that even normal correction seems painful to them. If parents are harsh, or even emphatic, these children wince in emotional pain and withdraw into more loneliness. Their parents are often well meaning and may scold them even more for being so "babyish," thus multiplying the problem.

A lack of skills in sports or games is very likely to be part of the trouble of a lonely child. I know a grade-school boy who does not have a father, and has never learned to play ball. He is awkward, and trips when he tries to run. Though he pretends not to care about his lack of skill, it does isolate him from his peers, and certainly adds to his loneliness.

Some children are, in fact, very different from the rest. Gifted children may think and react quite differently from their peers. At the other extreme, children who are slow learners may not be able to keep up with their peers. A psychotic child, though rare, certainly sees himself and his world in distorted patterns.

Perhaps your child is lonely simply because there are no playmates in your neighborhood. There are, in fact, many areas that are short of children. "Only" children are not always lonely, but they certainly may be! Whatever the cause, the results are the same: constant pain and loneliness. These need to be removed from childhood.

Helping a Lonely Child

Tedious as the process is, it helps to think through the list of causes of trouble in children, because this enables one to focus sharply on helping them.

Begin at once to teach your lonely child to have fun. I suggest you start at home. Schedule some time to play and keep the playtime just for fun, not for developing skills. You will be doing that as well, but as certainly as you begin to focus on that, you will become critical, and *that* is what few lonely kids need! The play needs to be something that you, the parent, enjoy. You probably can't make fun out of an activity you abhor, even with the best intentions.

Watching funny TV programs together (if you can find any), telling comical events of the day, or good jokes you've heard, are other techniques for introducing some fun and social skills to your lonely child.

When you feel that your child is ready with some abilities to play and laugh with others, bring another child into his life. For some lonely children, in fact, that is all they need. Look about your neighborhood, among relatives and friends, until you spot a child who would be easy for yours to get along with. Usually a fairly outgoing child is good for starters, but try to find one who won't overwhelm your son or daughter. It may take some effort, but get them together regularly and be with them for a while. Lonely children often need coaching and encouragement to overcome their isolation. You can provide that, but be sure to avoid overprotecting him or her.

Enlarge the number of friends gradually, until your child takes off on his own. You may need to gently insist that he follows through with making plans and contacting these friends. A shy, lonely child rarely changes habits quickly. Make your child telephone a friend now and then to chat or to invite him to share an activity.

If you have an only child, you will need to be aware of the need to "import" friends. I strongly recommend that you include at least one friend regularly, if you are parents of a single child. This peer interaction can be a fine substitute for the healthy sharing and competing that a brother or sister would provide.

If you have fallen into unwittingly labeling your child, stop that practice as fast as you can. I now look back and realize that I spoke of each of our children at times as shy. They were not extrovertive, but given time to get acquainted, they were quite friendly. No doubt, I taught them to be more shy than they were by saying that about them! Please avoid my mistake!

Recently I tried an experiment with my grandson. He had begun to hide his face from strangers, and seemed to be developing a sense of shyness. I waited until I saw him smiling at someone in a group and quietly commented on how friendly that was. Before I realized it, he was smiling at many people and responded warmly to their comments.

Be careful to give your children only positive labels!

If you have been too critical and disapproving, break that habit. Continue to train and correct your child, but do it more gently and positively. "I know you can clean your room better than that!" spoken encouragingly is far more effective for a lonely child than, "Your room is always such a mess! It's no wonder no one wants to come and see you!"

Stop any bad habits your child may have developed as a result of his loneliness. If he is "buying" friends, clowning, or simply sitting back in self-pity, make it clear that these habits must go! Then from this list, or your own creative thinking, set up a plan to replace those patterns with good ones.

Teach your child to look for other lonely children and reach out to them. In helping someone else, one can find real satisfaction and can begin to develop a sense of worth and confidence.

Teach your child to be contentedly alone at times. Spending some time alone can prompt individual growth and creativity. Our oldest daughter used to play school by the hour. She used old workbooks, taught from them, and graded them with a flourish of red pencils. I attribute some of her academic skills to that creative play. As in all areas of life, it is the balance that is important—time alone and time with others is one of those balances.

A child who has been habitually lonely and sad may need a reminder of his choices. First, he need not stay sad. Even though he is alone, he can do something fun and feel good. But teach him some other choices as well. Remind him to call a friend, and help them plan an activity. Go for a walk with your child, or talk with him. Have a game or activity that you enjoy available at times. Help him change his own activities, or get him to plan some future event. You may think of many more. Just refuse to sit and do nothing, giving in to your own defeat or loneliness, and do not allow your child to do so.

Ask for Help. In making changes with a lonely child, please do not be reluctant to ask for help. If you don't take advantage of them, people will often be willing to help you. So be frank with teachers, neighbors, and relatives. Tell them you have a lonely, unhappy child, and ask them for specific assistance such as ideas, borrowed playmates, or just encouragement. Your child need not stay troubled by loneliness!

THE NOMADIC CHILD

The average American family moves some fourteen times during the span of that family's existence. Since many families move much less frequently than that, we know that other families move considerably more often!

Typical Example

Janie was such a nomadic child. When I knew her she was ten and in the fifth grade. She made good grades, but she was lonely and seemed totally disinterested in even trying to remedy that. She had attended six different schools, counting the one she was enrolled in that year.

Her father was in the armed forces and was unavoidably frequently moved. The family preferred to stay together, so they had no choice but to move with him. Janie had said *Good-bye* so many times that she no longer would let herself care about anyone. She vowed she would never say, "Good-bye!" again. With the last three moves, she had placed an increasingly tough shell about herself, so she could not feel the pain of leaving friends ever again!

As children like Janie grow up, they can develop such thick shells that they may even be unable to experience warm feelings for their own families. The calluses of the nomadic child extend throughout his life.

Causes of Nomadic Trends

Materialism. In order to get ahead in business, many wage earners fall into the temptation of going along with every new job offer the company makes. Many times, unfortunately, there is no choice except to lose a job entirely. In Janie's family, the discipline of the service left her dad no options. But sometimes the choice is there—and the plum of a promotion or salary increase often takes precedence over the welfare of the family. Please resist such temptations! The emotional and social health of your children is worth more than great wealth. It is the experience of many families that the extra costs of living, as they climb the corporate ladder, consume the increased income anyway.

One young girl with whom I worked for several months moved from an average-income area in her city to a more affluent community. She grieved over the loss of her old friends, and never quite made it into the circles of the somewhat snobbish young people in her new neighborhood. Her personal adjustment was shaky at best, and this move facilitated a serious emotional breakdown.

Corporate Control. For reasons of their own, large corporations plan to move certain levels of their management staff at periodic intervals. Those reasons are beyond the scope of this book, but they do not take into account the welfare of the families of those employees. In recent years, some of these companies have been able to modify their dictatorial policies on this issue.

Family Problems or Habits. I have known families who seem
unable to adjust peacefully in any community. Sooner or later,
they have quarrels with neighbors, misunderstandings with
school personnel, and a falling out with the church. The only
answer for such a family seems to be a move.

Discontent or general restlessness of mothers or fathers may
be another reason for moving. The excitement of finding and
fixing up a different house can focus that restlessness for a
while. Unfortunately, it usually returns, and still another move
may seem to be the answer.

Helping the Nomadic Child

Prevent the Moves! Children need stability and "sameness" in
order to be secure. Moving can't always be avoided, but keep it
to the barest minimum! Obviously, you parents must have jobs
in order to support your families, but when you have the choice,
make it wisely, and in the best interests of the entire family.

When You Must Move:
Face the grief at leaving your home and friends together.
Talk about your sad, angry, anxious feelings until they are
under control, and encourage your children to share their feelings, too. Remember the likelihood that children will cover
their sadness with anger, and don't let that fool you. Help them
express their sadness as well as the anger.

*When the emotions are under control, start explaining the
facts.* There's no use giving information when the family's feelings are too upset. They won't be able to hear you anyway, but
when they have settled down, explain the reasons for the move.
Make your children aware that you are choosing what seems
best for them (if you had a choice at all).

Gradually, begin to discuss the positive aspects of the move.
There is a certain adventure in exploring a new neighborhood
and different house, and even a new area of the country. Include
the children and their wishes in the plans and process of moving
as much as possible.

Be positive role models! Children tend to adopt their parents'
attitudes, so if you can find a sense of excitement in the antici-
pated move, the chances are good that your children will follow
your example. It may take them a longer time, but be patient.

Continue to offer comfort and understanding as long as it is needed. Grief tends to recur in cycles, and your children may act quite excited about the move one day, but the awareness of a lost friend may send them into the depths of despair the next. Remember that completing the grief process is the best healing you can find.

If you sense your child is detouring into self-pity, you may need to get firm. Do your best to distinguish between real grief and the maudlin search for sympathy. Explain the difference to your child, and let him know you will not give in to the "pity" routine.

Help each child to leave some memories of himself with his friends. A small gift of some toy they have enjoyed together, or a special book for the school library, can help your child feel that he will be remembered. It needs to make a difference that your family has lived in and related to your community. A memento can help your presence to be remembered!

Help each child plan to take some memories with him. Photographs, carefully mounted and labeled, can become lifelong treasures. Pressed leaves, a small rock or shell, or other priceless but free tokens from favorite spots can be bittersweet reminders of a special place and time.

Above all, moms, *don't* make moving time the occasion for dumping all of your children's special treasures! Cherished toys and books, even though broken or torn, will be comforting to them during the uncertainty of their changes.

Make plans for occasional contacts. A rare phone call, letters, or vacation plans can help you and your children through the painful process of cutting old ties. However, be careful to avoid promises that you are not likely to keep. After your move, feel free to talk about the old friends and experiences. Even though such talk may bring back sadness, that will pass with time, leaving mainly happy memories.

Benefits of Moves

Family Intimacy. There are some positive results of moving that may help both you and your nomadic family! I have seen many such families drawn into a loving intimacy with one another that many families never achieve. When friends are lost, the need for one another within the family increases. If you are aware of and responsive to that, you can help each of your children to relate more warmly to one another as well as to you, Mother and Dad.

New Friends. Such family warmth, however, will need to be balanced with a gentle nudging of your children to make new friends. As soon as you feel they can, begin to insist that they reach out to new acquaintances. And set the example for that!

Exploring the New. Spend as much time as possible with your family exploring your new community. Find more favorite walks, parks, or special-interest areas, and help your children to enjoy them as much as the old ones.

Moving time is certainly not all fun, but neither is it all sadness. When you must join the ranks of nomads, make it as high an adventure as you can!

PRECOCIOUS ADULTHOOD

Typical Examples

Marilyn had a set of parents who were really physically mature children. Her mother was a drug addict, her father an alcoholic. She recalls fixing cereal and milk for her mother for breakfast, because her hangovers prevented her from getting up. Her father thought it was cute to let Marilyn sip his beer, and laughed uproariously as she grimaced over a taste of his whiskey.

His laughter died, however, when he saw her in the hospital several years later, mangled in a car wreck that was due to her own drunken driving. Marilyn grew up at three, but she only grew up a little bit, and like other premature adults, she had such weak foundations that she crumbled with adult stress, and reverted to the childish habits of addiction.

Bill was worried about his girl friend. She was paying far too much attention to Mike. When he called her, she sometimes sounded cool, and once in a while she didn't want to talk at all. Bill was unable to eat as he usually did, and began having bad dreams. Bill was only eight, and his girl not quite that old. His parents were worried about his romance and its effects on him.

Sarah was nine and in a public school, but she wore platform shoes with heels and hose. Her dresses were styled like a teenager's. Sarah, like Bill, was preoccupied with the opposite sex, and became self-conscious about her appearance in order to attract their attention. Sarah was nine—going on nineteen.

Vickie was always with her parents. She was an only child, and they included her in their activities most of the time since her birth. She never learned baby talk, and always has talked and acted like an adult. In conversations, Vickie can hold her own with most people. Her parents' friends feel uneasy, however, because they are worried about her handling adult conversations. She is only ten.

In most cities and towns, there is a growing number of latch-key kids. They wear their house or apartment keys around their necks, let themselves in, and spend varying time periods alone before a parent returns. Usually they also get themselves off to school in the morning, and lock their own doors. These children, almost heroic in their efforts to avoid being a burden and even helping their parents, are prematurely old.

One such child is now an adult friend of mine. She is insecure, compulsive about things being done in the right way, and she has trouble trusting anyone else to take proper care of matters.

Causes of Growing Up Too Soon

The reasons for premature adulthood are varied, but the results are the same: young people with fears and unmet needs, building their lives on weak foundations.

Parents' Dependency Needs. Parents like Marilyn's are not uncommon. With the growing number of alcohol- and drug-dependent adults, the children are having to take over many responsibilities, or leave them uncared for. The tragic sequel to this drama is the condition of the next generation. When these children grow up and have kids, they are likely to find even more ways to have their children take care of them. They will try harder to cover up their sense of inadequacy in neurotic patterns of living.

Peer Pressure and Parental Abdication. When some children demand fashionable clothes and name-brand shoes, many others feel they must follow suit. As they dress alike, at ever earlier times, they also develop ways of acting and talking alike. When peer pressure says to grow up prematurely, and parents permit that, they are giving it their approval. Stopping that process is not easy for young children, but it becomes nearly impossible when they reach adolescence, with its built-in independence.

Parents are Unable to Play Little-Kid Games. Most parents try to join in their children's play, but far too often, they end up teaching their children how to be grown up. When parents have not had a congenial, wholesome childhood themselves, it is extremely difficult to know how to encourage their children to be age-appropriate.

Hurry Up and Grow Up! Parental pressures make them want their children to grow up and relieve certain stress. Single parents, especially, are susceptible to this temptation. The need for their children to be less dependent is understandable but nonetheless harmful to their children.

Influence of the Media. Television, movies, and magazines—all portray the power of children in our society. Commercials are highly geared to the whims of children, and the overt messages that they know better than their parents are numerous. Information about adult matters is available to curious children in a variety of ways. See to it, parents, that you are aware of such often-subtle messages, and clarify their errors for your children. Obviously, you will not want to insult him or insinuate that he knows nothing, but do not allow your child's security to be robbed in such a fashion. He needs you to be wiser and stronger than he, until he is ready for a solid, mature, adult status. When advertising of an adult nature is seen, explain to your youngsters that they need not be concerned with these matters until they are grown up.

Results of Growing Up Too Soon

An Irreversible Process. Once children have experienced the sophisticated adult life-style, even in a small way, it is nearly impossible to return to the carefree innocence of childhood. The compulsiveness born of too much, too early responsibility, is difficult to reverse.

When the advancement is marked by major-crisis events, the scars left are permanent. A girl of twelve came to live in the home for Unmarried Mothers where I worked. She had just completed the seventh grade, and the social worker who formulated her history asked her, "Maureen, when did you start dating?" Maureen looked at her worker in astonishment. "But Mrs. Jones, I'm too young to date!" True enough! And this child from a strict family *had never dated.* She became pregnant on a walk during the halftime break in a school ball game, but she could never go back and recapture the fun of dating as an early teenager. She had grown up too soon.

Personal Needs Unmet. Once a child has become independent (and growing up too soon includes that), it is unlikely that he will be able to resume being a dependent, obedient child.

Dependency. Due to a divorce and their mother's return to work, two preteenage friends of mine assumed the major duties of their household. For a number of months, they had a great deal of freedom to govern their own young lives, as well as carrying big responsibilities at home.

A change in their mother's work finally enabled her to be at home much more of the time in the evenings. Try as she would, she found it impossible to resume her earlier mother role. The children carried their load successfully, but they were totally unable to release it. A major segment of their childhood had been lost, and the best they could do was finish their grieving together and move on.

Creativity. The chance to explore childhood creativity is also hard to recapture. The vivid imagination and pretense of the preschool child is activated by the warm climate of security and parental examples, and permission for such activities. When this climate is spoiled by the coldness of early maturation, it may never be recaptured. Certainly it will be more limited than in the lives of children who are not so rushed.

Consider next, *burnout and belated rebellion*. A major need of school-age children is that of developing a sense of *responsibility*. To assume that duty too early and too largely, however, can create the "burnout" factor. When children have worked too hard, and learned the adult toughness of life too soon, they often weary of such burdens later on. In the lives of many adults, we see a belated phase of teenage rebellion, with a type of irresponsibility and misbehavior that hurts many lives.

Helping a Child Who Has Grown Up Too Soon

Become Aware. Most precocious adulthood happens unwittingly and gradually. It is born out of the pain of family stress and problems, so parents usually are unaware of its progress. Take a look at your children's faces and their daily lives. Are they going about their own affairs without your permission, or even your knowledge? I recently saw a thought-provoking automobile bumper sticker that asked: DO YOU KNOW WHERE YOUR CHILDREN ARE?

I worked with one family whose grade-school child frequently had to call about their neighborhood to locate her mother. All too often, she found her in a local tavern. Such role reversal, increasingly common in today's society, results in tragically premature adulthood for a child.

Observe Other Children and Talk With Other Parents. Knowing what to expect of family living in a world that has been out of balance for some decades is no easy matter. Take a look at other children in your neighborhood, at school, in local parks, or recreation areas. You will see all gradations of maturity in the children. Pick a style of functioning that seems to fit your philosophy of life and adapt it to your family. *Remember that children need some responsibility. They simply need to have that balanced with freedom and surrounded with protection.*

Discuss the Situation With Your Children. When you are clear about your errors, and have some ideas about making changes, sit down together and discuss the issue. Explain your mistakes in expecting too much responsibility, allowing too much freedom, and providing too little parenting. Encourage each child to voice the feelings and concerns they have harbored. Listen to them with your hearts as well as your ears, and comfort them, if you can, because of the grief from the loss of their childhood.

Make a Plan for Changes. While it is true that one cannot undo the process of precocious maturity, there are some things that can be salvaged. Be forewarned! Some of those will involve giving up certain freedoms, and your children will not appreciate that one bit! So dwell on the positive aspects first, and make the regressions that are possible balanced in their benefits and losses.

For example, plan days that will include meals that are lovingly prepared by you, conversations that share feelings and activities, and time to work and play together. Learn to laugh together during the course of your shared day. When it's time to put restrictions on the precocious freedoms, do so gradually and gently. Explain the dangers in their excess freedoms, and reassure them that they will gain those back as soon as they are really mature enough to avoid the risks that are involved.

Be careful to avoid the classic danger of the "pendulum swing." When one has hit an extreme on one hand, it is easy to go to the other extreme in attempting to undo the mistakes. I strongly urge you to inch your way slowly back to the middle, balanced area of life. You will avoid unnecessary struggles, and may totally prevent serious rebelliousness that can complicate this reversal process.

Expect This Process to Be Hard! By the very existence of this sort of trouble in a child, you illustrate the facts of problems in the family. Such problems make it difficult to correct the trouble, just as they made its development easy! Be prepared, therefore, to struggle through the remedy. Plan on its being a long, slow process, with errors on both sides of the elusive middle line. It is tenacity that will win this struggle.

Being a parent is tough at best. When you are dealing with a troubled child, it becomes nearly unbearable. What I hope for you parents is this: as you gently lead your youngsters back to a healthy childhood, may you recapture many of its joys yourselves!

THE TROUBLED CHILD IN SCHOOL

Parents and Teachers at Odds

There is no question about the facts of increasing difficulties within our schools. Behavioral problems are multiplied, disagreements between parents and faculty are added, tax support is subtracted, and discouragements are compounded.

Idealistic young teachers find themselves bewildered and disenchanted. The mass of fine, new information they want so much to teach is often rejected completely by apathetic or naughty youngsters.

Many experienced teachers who once could point with pride to their hardworking, highly achieving pupils, now feel they have failed. Their best efforts are insufficient to provide controls or motivation. They are puzzled and hurt by parents who complain, "Why isn't Danny learning? It's your job to teach him!"

Parents and teachers who so badly need to work as a united team often end up being adversaries. The parents themselves are often on opposing ends of a spectrum. All of them want the best for their children, but many believe in permissiveness and pampering, while others are convinced that children must have strict rules and firm discipline.

Common Problems of Schoolchildren

The problems of schoolchildren are many, and I have selected only the most common and worrisome ones for consideration.

Disrespect. Teachers and parents alike list this as a major handicapping problem. Many children show no respect for one another, for their teachers, or for property. Saddest of all, they have no real respect for themselves! One kindergarten child repeatedly said to his teacher, "I don't wanna color that picture, and you can't make me!" With some twenty other students to manage, he was right. *She couldn't make him!*

In some schools, defacement of property and outright destruction are common. Stealing is rampant, and fights may become dangerous. Sharp knives are not uncommonly found in the possession of children. There is a great lack of courtesy or a sense of compassion, but an abundance of bragging and bullying.

Inability to Concentrate. In evaluating several hundred school-age children having serious school problems, I have learned that most of them are preoccupied with worry. They are anxious about their failures, worried about relatives, and even concerned with possible nuclear warfare.

Schoolchildren receive a barrage of information from television, radio, and bits of conversation. They rarely have opportunities to learn enough facts to reassure themselves, and often the facts are indeed frightening in their implications. Such mammoth, current concerns make the memory work of history insignificant by comparison.

Many worried children cover up their inner anxieties with hyperactivity and mischief. By constantly getting into some sort of trouble, they can distract their own attention away from bigger problems.

Power Struggles. By the time they reach the third or fourth grades, many children have given up part of their rebelliousness and are learning. Some, however, continue to resist all effort at teaching them the need for obedience and cooperation, as well as academics.

Power struggles may be openly defiant, and many times these can be dealt with, even though it takes great energy and much time. In other situations, however, these battles are quiet and passive. Children simply won't do their tasks. No matter how hard teachers try or parents coax, the work is not done or turned in. I have known children to deliberately lose their homework or stuff it into their desks, rather than to give up their contests of will! Still more rebellion against authority is played out by pretending to be unable to understand or recall material.

Helplessness. Some children seem to come to school from an environment of overprotectiveness. They are unable to do almost any task on their own. When a teacher works with them individually, they can do a good job. But left to their own devices, they seem to freeze. They do nothing until the teacher nudges them and helps them again. They demand constant re-assurance and encouragement.

Aggression. In a well-meant attempt to motivate people and help individuals to feel important, our society has emphasized "assertiveness." For many children, this is blown up to become aggression. Such children fight frequently, attack other children, and are impudent and rude to their teachers. They are selfish and demand more than their share.

Often, aggression masks great fear and personal weakness. The world's worst tyrants have been such frightened, inwardly weak people, and that is no less true of classrooms than the world!

Extreme Competitiveness. Closely related to the problem of aggression is that of competition that is out-of-bounds. In any class there are several pupils who *must* be first in line and who *will* have an extra turn. Their hands are up to answer questions—even when they know they do not know the answers. Often their parents defend any threat to their child's intense need for winning and may argue against the teacher's judgments.

Poor Motivation. In addition to the resistive children who are power strugglers, there is a segment of any class who simply do not care. They have given up or have never really tried. Usually these children have arrived at school with a low opinion of themselves and their capabilities. They see the other children moving ahead, but they try so little that day by day they are increasingly left behind the class. They simply have no successes, and so they have no approval. I am confident that it takes success to generate success.

School Phobias. Karen was a beautiful, brown-eyed girl of nine. Those eyes, instead of glowing in childish exuberance, were sad and frightened. Karen simply could not think about schoolwork. Her mind was focused on the daily arguments her mom and dad had. She was angry at her mother, because she seemed so helpless, yet she felt very sorry for her when she cried. Many times Karen felt afraid of her father's angry voice and threatening appearance. Sometimes she could get them to stop fighting by pleading with them. And often she could comfort her mother's tears away. What really worried Karen was what might happen when she was away. Mother needed her, and if she were at home, she could help her world—shaky as it was—to stay glued together.

Karen dreaded leaving home, and finally panicked when it was time for school. She refused to go, and when her parents took her against her will, she tried crying. If her tears did not soften them, she developed headaches and stomachaches. Due to her great anxiety, these aches were quite real. She even found she could raise her temperature enough to get sent home. Karen was a child with school phobia—she seemed afraid of going to school, but actually she was terrified of what might happen at home without her there to know and stop it.

Children who suffer from school phobias usually add to their fear and worry a power struggle. They see the weakness in their parents, and almost intuitively they seek ways to make their parents be strong and caring. Certainly, they test the strength that is there to see how great or small it actually is. Children desperately need parents to be stronger than they are!

OTHER ACADEMIC CONCERNS

In addition to these behavioral symptoms of many school-children, there are valid concerns about the schools in the United States.

Declining Achievement Test Scores

Over a number of years, Scholastic Aptitude Test scores have declined. Colleges find freshmen entering their portals who are much less capable than in the past. With the overall increase in knowledge, this lag creates great concern among school staffs at all levels. For each child, the primary schools lay the foundations of learning. What is happening to cause the ongoing decrease in test scores? No one knows for certain, but each parent needs to make this a personal concern.

Very recently, the Scholastic Aptitude Tests have shown improvement. Some authorities at a recent conference on marijuana abuse sounded hopeful that schools are winning the struggle against that harmful drug. They believe the effects of marijuana (so long-acting and specifically inhibiting to learning processes) alone may have damaged those SAT scores for years. If its use is truly declining, as they believe it has since 1978, perhaps we will see solid improvement in academic achievement for our young people. Certainly, most school staffs are working hard to help our children to learn.

Curriculum Content

A large city high school lists well over two hundred subjects offered to its students. At the same time, there is a decline in academic excellence, and there is evidence that young people are not learning even the basics, even though schools are increasing the courses offered. We can only assume this is an effort to motivate students to learn by finding some topics that will intrigue them.

Such attempts filter down to the elementary schools, as well as junior and senior high schools. Trying to please and tease children, however, gives to them another segment of an already unwieldy aggregate of power. Children in our society do have a confusing balance of power and helplessness. If, in their weak world, adults seem even weaker (and by trying to please or placate them, that is how adults seem), then what a frightening state! Out of their fear, children muster some sort of strength, and with it they try to control their environment and test out the power of the adults.

Concentrating on the Basics. A number of school districts are trying to simplify their curricula. By focusing on a few basics, they hope to enable students to master them and develop real skill. Through skill comes confidence, and one may expect academic improvement. And that, in fact, is what many of these schools are finding! Behavior is improving and achievement scores are higher.

Homework—Yes or No?

Many thoughtful parents are worried about the lack of homework assignments by their school systems. Not only do children fail to bring work home but schools, in fact, have stopped asking it of their students.

On the other hand, equally well-meaning parents insist that childhood should be carefree and happy. They are convinced that homework would spoil this pleasant climate of childhood.

Both kinds of parents need to understand two facts: 1) a major task of school-age children is the *development of a sense of responsibility;* and 2) *happiness is the result of being productive.* Schoolchildren need some homework—but not too much—for these two life-shaping reasons, as well as to help them master the facts and skills of school tasks.

Loss of Teaching and Reinforcement of Values and Morals

For many years now, school staffs have assumed that teaching values is beyond their responsibility, or even forbidden. Since families differ greatly in their beliefs about this function (as well as about their own values), schools are understandably in a dilemma. Only a few decades ago, however, school texts were full of wisdom and values, and these were taught concurrently with learning to write and read. Secular and biblical proverbs were a part of many reading assignments. I firmly believe such teaching helped children connect social, academic, family, and personal issues together and apply them to life as a whole. I worry about the prevalent quality of disconnectedness of information in so many youngsters. They cannot transfer a basic value from one situation to another, and extend such information to the knowledge of how to handle life as a whole. They simply do not learn from experience.

Sex Education

This issue has resulted in raging battles for many years between parents and school administrators. Due to lack of the teaching of values and morals, parents are anxious about their children simply being given information that may stimulate sexual curiosity or acting out. Schools, on the other hand, see children at alarmingly early ages evidencing sexual attitudes and behaviors that are likely to result in personal problems.

While perfect answers to this predicament are not possible in today's imperfect world, parents, you do have the primary responsibility for your own children. Carefully check the materials your school may propose teaching. Interpret any errors you see to your children, and help them understand those errors. Reinforce the accurate information, and in discussing these issues, increase your communication with your children. Be sure you clearly teach the values and beliefs you hold dear!

Reading Materials

With some regularity, newspapers report major battles between irate parents and school staffs over the reading materials that are presented to students. Most of these struggles are concerned with teenage students, but grade-school children need some protection as well. It will take you only a short time to evaluate the textbooks and other reading materials of your children. That time could be a major investment in your child's life.

My experience shows that battles with an existing (and usually powerful) system are not only futile but also result in making concerned parents look foolish. I suggest, therefore, that you *individually* teach your children the facts involved with your concerns. Present your questions and arguments clearly and constructively, and discuss them pro and con, with each other, with your friends, and with your children. Your children will learn to read critically, think profoundly and broadly, and eventually they will know truth from error. You will have given them useful tools for the rest of their lives.

Causes of School Problems

There are some vital facts that involve you, as parents, as well as your children and their school problems.

Lack of Involvement. One of the most important issues is that of a lack of parents' interest and involvement in their children's school experience. Many times, I encounter parents who had difficulty in their own school years. They cannot bear to relive those through their child's problems, so they tend to ignore the whole thing. Other parents are simply too busy or tired and unwittingly tend to put school issues far down their list of priorities. Single parents, I find, are especially vulnerable in this matter.

Allowing Children to Manipulate. Children have a natural tendency to get by with the least work and seek the most privileges possible. They start early with their parents, and are masterful at discovering who is the easier mark. If you parents have fallen into such a trap, and have allowed your child to work one of you against the other, you can count on it—he will use exactly the same techniques with his teachers and you. He is not above an outright lie, and certainly will weight the facts in his favor. If you fail to recognize this, and allow your child to set you against the school, you can do serious damage to him.

Overprotection. Closely related to the manipulative techniques of children is their willingness to take advantage of people. If you tend to be lenient and protective, your child will be quite likely to use that in order to get out of very difficult assignments or projects. Be sure to expect the best of which he or she is capable. Children grow by stretching!

Television. Many careful studies have shown some of the damaging influences of television on children. There are other concerns that are harder to prove, but you need to consider them. Children who watch television too much can become preoccupied with programs. The rapid change of scenes and exciting themes of most programs can make school seem exceedingly dull by contrast. Children who are worried or sad are especially susceptible to television, because it offers an instantly available escape from their problems. School only adds burdens.

Failure to Build a Team. Due to the concerns just listed, misunderstandings, and poor communication, far too many times teachers and parents become adversaries. Instead, they need to become a team, united in their wishes and methods to help each child learn and grow to her maximum. Do your part to build such a team by getting to know your child's teachers, and encourage and help them in any way you can. Believe it—they will benefit from this and so will you and your child.

Helping a Troubled Schoolchild

A Good Teacher. First, let's take a look at what you may expect from a good teacher.

Reinforcement of good parenting. Until a teacher establishes good authority by consistent discipline, very little learning can take place. Let your child's teacher know the sort of discipline you have found successful, and work out an appropriate plan with her to provide consistency. If you have not been quite satisfied with your own methods, do not be afraid to admit that, and be open to learning from her or him some ideas you may not have tried. Single parents, especially, find in your child's teacher an invaluable support and help in your parenting efforts.

Consistent, caring attitude. You must remember that most public-school teachers have about twenty-five students most of the day. Some of them are a joy and some are a trial. She cannot give exactly equal time to all of them. Remember, too, that her caring may be expressed tenderly or toughly. If, however, she or he is uncaring, hostile, or indifferent, do your best to help, but if that is impossible, do your best to transfer your child. An entire school year spent under such a person can damage your child's attitude toward school for years to come.

Building confidence through success. A good teacher will find each child's area of unique skill and interest and build on that. One teacher was thoroughly frustrated by a boy who wanted to do nothing but play with Matchbox cars. She confiscated them, scolded him, and even sought the parents' help. Nevertheless, there he was, daily slipping those cars in and out of his pockets or desk. Finally, she asked him to share that consuming interest with the class. He used his collection in "show and tell" time. This ingenious teacher helped him learn to sketch new designs for cars, and finally found books about cars that captured his interest. The child became one of her star students. Each child needs that primary quality of approval in order to build success. Success generates success!

Expect only the best. Teachers become adept at evaluating a child's abilities. Work with your child's teacher to develop his abilities to their very best. A friend of mine required his son to rewrite a theme three times on a weekend, because he knew that it would not meet the approval of the teacher. He had found out from her what that boy was capable of doing, and together they challenged and required that. After he quit resisting, that child became an outstanding student.

A Poor Teacher. As well as knowing what you may expect from your child's teachers, you need to know the signs of those very few dangerously poor teachers.

Extremes or inconsistencies. Just as parents need to develop reasonable consistency in dealing with their children, so do teachers. I vividly recall a teacher from my childhood. She was a brilliant teacher and always looked attractive. There were days when she was courteous, encouraging, and fun to be around. On other days, however, she was sarcastic, rude, and generally obnoxious. Such inconsistency does not stimulate a healthy classroom atmosphere or consistent learning.

Generally indifferent or hostile attitude. Such a teacher will impart these negative attitudes to the students. You may need to visit a classroom several times to pick up this attitude, but listen carefully to your child and to other parents, and you will form a fairly accurate picture of such a teacher.

Adversary relationship with parents. Through no fault of theirs, necessarily, many teachers come to feel that the parents of their students are all against them. Parents who want their children to do well often tend to look for the causes of their falling short in the teacher. Parental criticism can be useful, but often it is painfully unfair. You see, teachers also want their students to do well. Since they try their very best to make that success come about, they are likely to resist such criticism, and instead, they feel critical of the parents. So much of this stand-off is unconscious that neither side can ever talk things over and work out that essential team approach. A good teacher will accept criticism and talk out problems with a child openly and constructively with parents.

Teacher's values. If you visit occasionally with your child's teachers and listen to the child himself, you will soon build a fairly accurate sense of that person's values. Such values are rarely taught directly, but they are infused gradually and subtly into your child's mind. The way that teacher dresses, talks, walks, and acts, all say something to your child about his or her beliefs. Be aware of these and talk about them to your child. Be careful to avoid causing a loss of respect, but keep very clear the rightness or wrongness of these influences.

Gossip sessions. Remember that teachers are human and they are teachers—not mental-health professionals. It is easy to confide some very personal issues in them, forgetting this important fact. I have known some things to be discussed with others that should not have been revealed. Be very careful, therefore, to reveal only information you would not mind anyone knowing. This is *your* responsibility, not the teacher's.

Abuse of children. When our son was in kindergarten, I learned of a seriously abusive act of his teacher. He was the youngest in his class, and still sucked his thumb when he was very tired. This teacher apparently felt it was her duty to stop his habit, so she made him stand in front of the class and suck his thumb. She then made teasing comments that caused all of the children to laugh at him. This was one of the most cruel acts, at a tender age in a shy and sensitive child, that I have ever heard! The ridicule of one's classmates is intolerable. Be aware of your children's teachers. If any of them ever actually abuses your child, take the most aggressive action possible to stop that, or remove your child from such an environment.

You, as parents, also have many opportunities to help your child who may have school problems.

Finding Opportunities to Help Your Child

Make a team. Surely you will agree, at this point, that you are the one to initiate a cooperative team with your child, his teachers, and his school administrator. Do whatever you must to get to know them, and let them know you. I hope you can do this in a friendly, warm, and constructive fashion. Remember that you all have one thing in common: the welfare and academic advancement of your child. Work at seeing each other as mutually helpful, not opponents.

Be involved. There are several existing avenues for your involvement in your child's school. Here are some common ones.

1. *Parent-teacher organizations.* These exist under varying titles in almost all schools. In some communities, these may have deteriorated to a competition for school leadership and social advancement. If so, please put your energy into restoring your groups to a constructive power for good in your school and neighborhood.

2. *Parent-school recreational programs.* Many schools have tried to organize family-fun nights wherein the whole

family comes for a gym night, a picnic, or roller skating. This is a fine chance to really get acquainted and further the functioning of that team for your child! You will also be helping the other students, their families, and your school.

3. *Student performances.* Many schools recognize the need of all children to perform—to be "stars." Whether this is dramatic, musical, physical education, or some other event, be there! Your presence is an unparalleled chance to say to your child and his school, "My child and his school are important, and I'll be there to applaud both of you!"

4. *Parent conferences and open house.* Most schools now have individual conferences for parents with their child's teachers. Missing work to be there may cost you some money, inconvenience, and time, but be there! Your child's school welfare is your responsibility. This conference can help you and that teacher to get a great start for the year or correct and improve a situation that already exists. Remember to be open and positive at these sessions.

5. *Communicate with other parents.* Make a chance to get to know the parents of your child's classmates. Parents need to know and encourage each other to establish and maintain healthy community policies for their children. Whenever a child asks for a doubtful privilege by saying, "Everybody else is doing it!" you needn't wait. Call the other parents and find out if, in fact, everybody *is* doing it. More likely than not, they are waiting to find out the same thing. You may effectively change some risky plans into good ones by such checking out!

You do, of course, have a right to say no when you feel this is best for your child, even if everybody else *is* doing it!

Volunteer! If you have time, consider offering your services as a school volunteer. Helping teachers by preparing materials, decorating the room, grading papers that can be done by a volunteer, mimeographing, and any creative project you may think of, are ways you can help all the children in your neighborhood.

Many schools also encourage or even sponsor Boy and Girl Scouting, Camp Fire, or other extracurricular groups. My involvement in such groups for nearly twenty years has taught me their value. A child may learn social and personal skills as well as lifelong values through these groups. Do consider helping.

Schools are second only to homes in the molding of children's lives. Think carefully and act responsibly in helping your child's school to be the best!

THE UNGRATEFUL CHILD

A mother of three young children recently asked me a thought-provoking question. "Why is it," she wondered, "that our children are ungrateful? We try so hard to please them, but no matter what we give them for Christmas or birthdays, they never seem excited or appreciative!"

Newspaper advice columns often publish letters from older relatives asking why they rarely receive thank-you notes for wedding or graduation gifts. Even expensive presents, they write, often go apparently unacknowledged.

Quite recently, I attended a birthday party for an early-school-aged girl. She was so busy opening her next box that it was evident she hardly noticed the contents of the gift she had just found. At no time did she turn to the giver and express any thanks.

The sad meaning of such ingratitude is not the rude thoughtlessness it conveys. It is the absence of any awareness of the love of the giver and a lack of genuine pleasure in the gift—a symbol of that person's love and caring. When a gift (whether it is a thing or a warm smile) is not acknowledged, a transaction between the giver and the receiver is left unfinished. And such uncompleted communications make fragile relationships.

The Qualities of an Ungrateful Child

Boredom. The most common characteristic of an ungrateful child is that of boredom, and even unhappiness. He is unable to enjoy the things he has because he has learned to look for excitement in anticipating the next big event. When no such event is on the horizon, he becomes unhappy. Even when his birthday is near, he may not feel really good because he fears this year won't be as good as last! Parents of such children are quickly lured into a defeating habit of trying ever harder to please their saturated children, who need more and more sophisticated things to please them.

Competition. Families within a neighborhood sometimes compete with one another for bigger and better parties and entertainment for their children. Such rivalry feeds a false value system that children are quick to imitate. Even five- and six-year-olds, I recently learned from a mother, give insults to friends who do not wear designer garments.

Too Much Money. Ungrateful children usually have too much money to spend. They either receive a large allowance or they have learned that money is available simply for the asking. If Mom or Dad object at all, the children have learned to threaten or cajole, and usually get what they want.

Greed and Selfishness. Despite their excessive quantities of things and privileges, ungrateful children are greedy and demanding. They prefer not to share, yet they may not take good care of their possessions. Nothing but the best and more of it is what they take for granted as their right.

Rudeness. Often, ungrateful children are somewhat unpleasant and even rude, because they are pampered when it comes to having good manners, as well as in other areas of life. They are usually unhappy and unloving as well as ungrateful.

Causes of Ungratefulness

Too Many Gifts. Perhaps the most common cause of ingratitude is the receiving of too many gifts, too early in life. Many parents want their children to have the things they would have liked in their early years, whether the children want them or not. So they give those items, and then are upset when a child fails to enjoy them. Since the child didn't really want them, he may not appreciate them, and may feel confused as well as angry over the parents' frustrations.

Competition Among Relatives. Relatives may compete with one another to give the biggest, most exciting gifts, hoping to win the love or loyalty of a child. This is especially true when parents have been divorced, but such rivalry is also possible among grandparents and others.

Lack of Proper Teaching. Parents who, in general, pamper their children, may fail to teach them the courtesy of expressing appreciation. It is some trouble to telephone or write letters, and spoiled children prefer not to be inconvenienced. The habit of giving in to spoiled children is one that is easy to form and difficult to recognize and break. Thus children may get by without remembering to say, "Thank you!"

Things Substitute for Love. When giving becomes a substitute for saying, "I love you!" or showing love through affection, children understandably fail to feel grateful. They are also good at recognizing such gifts. No amount of things or privileges can satisfy the profound need of all children for time and activities together, and the warmth of affection from their parents.

Child Feels Unworthy. Occasionally, I have known children who felt so chronically guilty that they could not express gratitude. One such child was extremely lazy and manipulative. He had learned to evade most of his duties, and found that his mother would eventually take care of them for him. He did, however, have enough sense of caring to feel like the little rascal he was. When his parents gave him special treats, he would hide them or give them away because he knew he didn't deserve them!

Anticipation of Child's Wishes. In anticipating a child's wishes, you may deprive him of the chance to experience a real yearning for anything. When children do not long for an item and rarely, if ever, have to earn it, they frequently fail to appreciate what they are given.

The failure to be grateful may become a habit. Children take their gifts and favors for granted and no longer are aware that they should be grateful.

Helping an Ungrateful Child

Stop Trying to Relive Your Childhood! Whatever your reasons may be for giving too much to your children, discontinue that practice. You may need to sort through your reasons. Did you feel deprived as a child? You really cannot relive your childhood anyway, so avoid the temptation to try through your children.

Are you tempted to give to your children to try to compensate for your lack of time or your excess of gruffness? Even though gifts bring some excitement at the time, they will not convince your child of your love or satisfy his need for your personal involvement in his life.

Explain to your children that you have been mistaken about your excessive giving, and let them know you will be stopping that. Do plan, however, to give them the time and loving attention they crave! Then put that plan into action.

Teach Your Child to Anticipate and Participate. Wait for your child to ask for something he wants, and then talk with him about that wish. In talking, help him discover what he finds worthwhile or interesting about that item. You may be surprised to learn that he has no real interest in it at all, and that the whole wish was just a passing fancy.

Of course, your child may seriously want a new bicycle or a pair of skates. If so, take him shopping and let him compare prices with you. Make this a lesson in economics, and then help him figure out a plan for earning a fair proportion of the cost. Even if you must help a younger child find extra jobs around your own home, do so, and pay him a fair child's wage for those jobs. Work out an agreement with him, set up books, and then follow through. Only when your child has earned the agreed-upon amount should you actually go with him and purchase that new bicycle (or whatever he wants). His pride in having some input in that big transaction will probably teach *you* an important lesson!

By waiting for your child to really yearn for a special object, you will find his excitement and enjoyment so much more real and fulfilling than when he gets it too easily. Gratitude is then a natural result of that anticipation. All that is left for you as parents, in that case, is to teach him the words to use in verbally expressing that!

A Child Owes as Well as Wishes! Teach your child that he owes something in return for favors and gifts. Every child, for example, owes his family helpfulness, courtesy, and respect. He owes others the same! Remind him of that, and teach him how to give those priceless gifts to friends, teachers, and anyone whose life he touches.

No More Travel Mementos! Stop bringing home gifts every time you must travel. Whatever your reasons for beginning this practice, I suggest you review them. Perhaps the time has come when your children have taken such remembrances for granted. When they are more interested in getting their gifts than they are in your safe return home, you are allowing them to be ungrateful as well as confused about priorities. It is wonderful to help your children know how much you missed them while you were gone, but a simple memento you find can symbolize that even more meaningfully than expensive gifts you purchase. A wild flower, a little rock, or any gift from nature is special, if you have a chance to find it. A friend of mine used to save the gum that was given out on airplanes to relieve popping ears. "Airplane gum" was the only chewing gum his children really enjoyed—because it symbolized their dad's loving thoughts of them!

Teach Your Child About Real Poverty. When children recognize the contrast between the real want of poverty and their selfish wishes, many of them will change. Such a reversal, however, requires constant reminding from you parents, as well as new techniques of your own to finish breaking those old habits. You may help your children earn some money, or give up some of their wishes in order to contribute to world relief—or to a needy family in your own town. Such giving makes ungratefulness impossible, since it is not likely that one can be generous and selfish at the same time!

Practice Gratitude Yourselves! While modeling the graciousness of appreciation is not the final answer to teaching it to children, it does help. As you eat meals, discuss the work and discomfort of the farmers and laborers who make food available. Father, remember to thank your wife for her work in fixing the meal, and teach your children to say, "Thank you!" before they are excused from the table. Be especially aware of thanking your children for their help and for the special gifts they make for you. Most very young children make pictures or give their toys (very temporarily) to adults. Take time to describe their generosity and to thank them for sharing. As tiny children grow, such efforts on your part will encourage them to be generous, and it will also be a pattern for them to use in expressing gratitude.

Real enjoyment in life demands a grateful heart. Cultivate such an attitude yourself, and teach it to your child!

Part IV

The Resource Guide for Troubled Parents

13
Warning Signs—
How to Recognize Them

In each chapter of the last section, I have tried to give you a complete listing of the symptoms of a specifically troubled child. Here I will summarize the signs of impending problems that are serious enough to demand professional consultation.

Kevin was a difficult child to raise. He was born late in his parents' lives, after his older sister was in elementary school. His parents, however, really welcomed his birth, because they had enjoyed his older sister, and were especially glad to have a son.

He was full of energy—a determined child—and his parents found their strength drained by him. It seemed so much easier to finish his jobs, and they finally refrained from asking him to do anything rather than stand over him in order to make him finish. They lectured and punished, but often failed to get him to do the job—whatever it was. Lines of worry and resentment formed on their faces, and Kevin knew he was the cause of them, yet he could not make himself give up his battles.

Despite his energy, Kevin also had a sensitive, artistic side. He wrote poetry and stories that revealed an increasing sense of confusion. Often he just wanted out of this world. If he could only live in Africa and hunt lions, how happy he would be! He rejected his parents' faith, even while still in grade school, and resisted attending Sunday school and church.

Day by day, Kevin became ruder to his parents, more withdrawn into his room and his own world. Social events didn't interest him, and his earlier friendships died of neglect. He slept poorly, and ate so much that he was quite overweight. One day, to their horror, Kevin's parents found him dead, killed by his own hand with his father's revolver.

The warning signs were evident long before, but circumstances were deceptive. Kevin's parents attributed his problems to *their age, his position in the family,* and later on to *his disposition, the preadolescent blues,* and many other factors. Their hindsight was clear—but too late.

PROBLEM AREAS TO LOOK FOR

Look for unresolved problems in the following areas in order to be forewarned of serious difficulties in your child.

Troubles With Discipline and Training

Is your child either too agreeable and adaptive, or too resistant and rebellious? Either extreme may be a signal that there is trouble ahead.

Do you, Mom and Dad, find it difficult to agree about your expectations and disciplinary methods? Are you likely to give in to your child one day but demand obedience the next? If so, your inconsistency will confuse your child.

Are you just too busy and gone so much that you cannot manage the follow-through your child needs?

Could it be that you have slipped into reacting to daily crises rather than keeping clearly focused on the goals you know to be essential to your child's healthy development?

Disobedience, disrespect, testing your limits, and manipulating for his way—these are the signs in your child that should warn you that there is weakness in the area of training and discipline. If these qualities are severe, and if you cannot shortly reverse them, seek help. A maximum of two or three months of your own efforts, without significant improvement, should tell you that you need some reinforcement or advice from a counselor. Don't wait too long!

Physical and Emotional Signs of Trouble

Has your child developed a physical habit that reflects or creates social isolation or loneliness? Tics, thumb-sucking, nail biting, picking at the skin, and many more physical habits will cry out to you (if you are listening) that something is very wrong. One child I know was so filled with anxiety that she pulled out her own hair to the point of requiring a wig. Yet her parents never admitted that she—or they—needed help.

Stomachaches, headaches, and other complaints of physical pain often are disguised expressions of anxiety or fear. Don't be misled by these into thinking your child is just "faking" or manipulating. That is possible, but it is also possible that serious mental or emotional problems are underlying such aches and pains. Get an outside opinion to help you know for sure.

Is your child accident-prone? There are, of course, periods in a child's development when he just falls over his own shadow. Those are transient, and obviously due to the awkwardness of his stage of development. But repeated accidents due to "showing off" or obvious risk taking are warning signals. Heed them!

Is your child showing signs of constant worry or anxiety? Does she cry easily or fly into a rage over minor events? Is she impudent to her friends, or rude to her teacher? There is always a reason for such behaviors. The reasons do *not* excuse the actions, but they will guide you to know how to help your child stop them! Any extended period of painful, emotional expression needs to be evaluated. Emotions that cause pain always result from unmet needs. If you and your child cannot discover those and satisfy them, find someone who can help you do just that.

Problems in Communications

Have your family communications degenerated into constant arguing and yelling? One sign of a seriously troubled child is exactly that. A child who argues with or yells at siblings or parents more than he laughs and talks in friendly ways is in trouble.

Is your household too quiet? No doubt about it: the worst communication gap of all is *silence.* If your children stay in their own rooms alone too much, listening to their music or

watching TV in private, you also have a problem. Children do
not become healthy adults by isolating themselves from the
dear ones who should be their models.

Abrupt Mood Changes. You need to be especially aware of a
child who has normally been a part of the family but who
abruptly withdraws into moody isolation. Every troubled child I
have seen tells me that he or she has just been waiting at such
times for Mom or Dad *to come to him.* He deliberately waited to
see if his parents cared enough to invade his moods. He yearned
for his parents, but all too often, neither Mom nor Dad appeared.

Have you learned to read body language? It's not really a
difficult language to master, and it can tell you so much more
than words. A child who sounds angry often looks frightened
when you see his eyes. And a weeping child may reveal more
honest anger by the set of her jaws than the sadness she
pretends.

*Are you aware that your children overhear the arguments
you have, Mom and Dad?* They may not understand the question, and often they miss the outcome, but they know more than
you think! They are aware of your angry voices and you may be
sure they miss none of your body language. One of the most
common causes for the worry of the troubled children I see, is
that of the fear that Mom and Dad may get a divorce. Even if
that is far from your minds, it is in the concerns of your child. So
keep your arguments fair enough to have them out openly in
front of your children, or keep them so remote they do not know
of them at all.

Guilt Feelings. Many parental arguments do involve concerns
about the children. Though they rarely express it, your children
may blame themselves for your arguments and develop serious
guilt feelings. Such worries, over a period of time, can take their
toll of your child's peace of mind and performance in school as
well as at home.

Is your family's communication too superficial? It is possible
to keep everything in a family so smooth and happy that no one
can be honest or real! Hiding worries or frustrations in trying to
keep things happy all the time is a great mistake. Painful events

do happen, and disagreements and irritations are bound to arise. Give your children permission to be honest, and teach them how to work out the problems. I have seen serious emotional storms erupt without warning in such families. One can keep the cap on upset feelings only so long. Be careful that you do not try to exceed that critical point!

Attitudinal Warning Signs

Cover-up or Super Ego? There is a strong likelihood that some of you parents will find you have a child who is a bully, or acts as if he or she is superior to any of his classmates. Now such an attitude is often a cover-up for feeling quite inadequate, but it may be the result of your super success at building self-esteem. It is possible for children to get the idea that they can run the world, and everyone had better get out of the way and let them do it. This superior attitude will gain for them certain followers, but it is almost sure to cost them any true friends. If your child acts as if he is better than anyone else, you had better increase your criticisms, decrease your compliments, and initiate some meaningful discipline for such attitudes.

By the way, *take a look at yourselves!* I often find that one or both parents of such children share those attitudes!

Negative Reactions. More problems are likely to come to your attention, as parents, from children who feel inferior to their friends than those who feel superior. It is not any more common, I suspect, but feeling inadequate hurts more than feeling superior. Children who feel inadequate generally develop a negative, helpless attitude. They often feel resentful, but they really don't know what to do about it all. When such negative attitudes take root, they will grow into a series of defeats and failures that can be really hard to reverse.

Children who develop a negative attitude are difficult to handle. They reject the very compliments that could change their attitude because they don't want to get their hopes up about themselves, only to have them dashed again. If you cannot help your negative child to gain a more positive attitude, *get professional help,* because this issue can worsen to the despair that prompts suicide.

Generalized Pessimism. This is the worst of all attitudes. Even the child with an inferiority complex admits there are better people and a better way in life, though he has little hope of finding it. The totally negative attitude believes that everything and everyone is bad, including himself. He sees no hope and, therefore, no use to try at anything. Such children are fairly rare, but I am seeing some of them. Usually their parents have had a very hard struggle in life due to handicaps, drug or alcohol addiction, and steady "bad luck." The life experiences of such completely negative people seem to prove their attitude to be correct. Life is, for them, a mess!

If I could summarize all of these warning signs simply, I would say: *Be aware of pain—your own and your child's.* Respond to that pain with loving concern, and find out its cause. Remove that cause and build more confidence, positive attitudes, and strength into and about that child. You can help your troubled child!

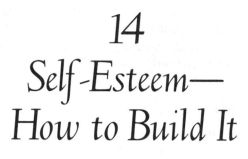

14
Self-Esteem—
How to Build It

A major factor in childhood's heartaches, large or small, is often the loss of self-esteem. Babies are born with a clean slate—no guilt, no wrongdoings, no successes—only the potential for both good and bad. Perhaps, as parents, you have blown it a bit—or even a lot! I know that makes you sad and worried, but you can work at helping your child recover that potential, and build better from now on. So don't give in to your own negative feelings and let your child go from bad to even worse problems! Here are some ideas to help you recover your losses as well as those of your child.

RESTORING THE FOUNDATION

Is Your Love Unconditional?

Think back over your child's earliest months and redefine his needs and feelings. *Have you given him enough loving attention, and has your love been unconditional?* Your child must have that as the cornerstone of the very foundation of his self-esteem.

Is Your Approval Clear?

Another essential part of that foundation is your child's craving for approval. *Have you remembered to praise your growing child's little achievements?* It's easy to get excited about his first teeth, first steps, and first words, but later, as you battle those Terrible Twos, you may lose that earlier excitement, and show more disapproval than pride. It's natural to take things for granted, but your child's self-esteem will continue to suffer if you don't correct that tendency.

Are You Consistent?

Have you remembered to be consistent? In similar situations, do you react reasonably the same, day after day? When your child doesn't know what to expect, he is likely to become nervous and afraid. It will be hard for a frightened child to find the security for this third foundational corner.

Enjoyment

How long has it been since you and your family laughed together? Without healthy merriment, life can become so grim that one may not want to stay alive. I never knew a seriously depressed child who could laugh spontaneously and frequently. Enjoyment and laughter become, then, the fourth corner in building your child's self-esteem.

SHARPENING YOUR "TOOLS"

In rebuilding self-esteem, you need certain basic tools. Without them, I doubt you will be successful.

Sound Discipline and Training

Sound discipline is a bit like a carpenter's hammer, and that is one tool that is essential in building. If its handle is crooked, it will be off balance and will fail to drive nails accurately. Be sure the hammer of your discipline is strong and true. See if you have fallen into the use of name-calling, yelling, or explosive episodes, letting off your frustration, but failing to teach your child the very basic lessons you wanted him to learn. Does your child know what you expect or does that change too frequently? Are you and your child clear about the consequences for his irresponsibilities? Do you enforce those consistently and firmly, yet lovingly?

Honest Acceptance of Your Child's Limitations and Gifts

In pouring the foundation of a building, there are strong forms that mold the shape and determine the strength of the walls. Parental attitudes of unconditional love and acceptance are somewhat like those forms. A parent's failure to accept that child as he or she is will result in a faulty foundation. An unconscious or expressed wish that your child were inherently different (in any way that cannot be changed, of course) makes that basic need of approval simply impossible to fulfill. If your child was born with a major handicap, suffers a crippling accident or illness, or develops serious mental or emotional problems, your acceptance may seem nearly impossible. If, however, you are willing to face such disappointments, and go through the grief process, you can bring yourselves to genuinely find that essential acceptance!

Clear Communication

A carpenter's saw is absolutely necessary to cut the building materials into the required sizes. A great destroyer of self-esteem is misunderstanding. Clear communications, like a saw, cut through complex problems, reducing them to sizes that can be handled. Serious misunderstandings usually are built into a family by a husband and wife who are not clear in their communications. A friend of mine, a new husband, wrote down a problem that happened between him and his bride in the morning. He intended to write it down simply, so he would not forget to talk it over with her in the evening, when they both had more time. Even by writing it, however, he gained a deeper understanding about the feelings his wife was really trying to share. He was able, then, to feel loving toward her because he recognized her needs rather than hearing the accusation he had at first inferred. There are few spouses who take the time to think through the deeper levels of communication as this man did, but failure to do so, in one way or another, results in unnecessary hurts, mounting resentments, and retaliation. Eventually, these habits of poor communication hurt children as well, and are a painful part of their loss of self-esteem.

Are Your Attitudes Positive?

Attitudes are so pervasive in building self-esteem that they can be compared with the nails that hold a building together. When your child has a problem, it can be difficult to maintain a loving, positive attitude. A troubled child is certain to create anxiety in parents, so you may have lost your calmness and your sense of humor. Try to think, for just a moment, about your child as one who is perfectly normal, except for one or two limited areas. Doesn't that help you to form a better attitude than seeing him as a totally troubled child? Your attitude is extremely important in building your child's self-esteem.

Once you have reviewed these basic building plans and your tools for working, you are ready to fill in the rest:

STRENGTHENING THE WEAKNESSES

A Fresh Inventory

In order to change any negative attitudes you may have, try to take a fresh inventory of your child. You no doubt know those problems and weaknesses all too well, but *list them anyway*. Try to group them together in general categories, so they won't seem so monumental!

For example, Jimmy is late getting up and must be called ten times. He is slow in dressing, and is often late to school. It is hard to get him to meals on time; he hates to stop playing to get at his homework, and he always resists going to bed. More often than not, he forgets to feed his dog and leaves her water dish nearly empty.

Jimmy's mother reminds him, scolds, and lectures him, and then feels remorseful for being too tough on such a little boy, so she rescues him. When he is likely to be late for school, she takes him, so he won't have to stay late to make up his work. His father punishes him now and then for always being late, but he is too busy to do so very consistently.

You can see that this vicious cycle of tension, scolding, rescuing, loving—yet disapproving—will result in Jimmy's losing any good feelings about himself, because he is confused, anxious, and resentful. All he can do is try harder and harder to resist what he feels as crushing pressure.

A Fresh Start

Jimmy is a real person, and his story is true. What actually helped him was his mother's awareness that she was focusing almost entirely on his *problems.* He also had many *strengths,* but they were not causing any pain, so she seldom mentioned them. One day this mother sat down with Jimmy and ceremoniously explained her mistakes to him. She listed a number of his good qualities and then told him how sorry she was for the fact that she so rarely complimented him on these, and so often lectured him on his few basic faults. She promised to change and together they made a plan to ensure that change would last.

The Happy Rescue

To be certain, Mother sometimes forgot her new resolve to stop nagging, but according to their plan, Jimmy reminded her, and she tried harder. On his side, Jimmy tried to do things at once before he forgot, and accepted Mother's needed reminders with good grace. It was a turning point in Jimmy's life, and certainly in his relationship with his mother.

Whether your child's weakness is that of passive resistance to your authority, angry explosions, or selfish greediness, you can spot that problem area. Recognizing the issue and admitting your responsibility for it (as well as your child's) will guide you to finding solutions and working them out.

Ask for Help!

It is possible that your problems seem too complex for you to solve alone. Please do not be reluctant to ask for help. There are many people who can see your problems from an angle just different enough from your own to give you a fresh point of view. A trusted friend, relative, clergyman, or a professional counselor will be invaluable to you.

Be careful to listen with an open mind to hear your own mistakes and avoid arguing or defending yourself. Seeing your own goofs is painful, but you can't begin to improve until you recognize and admit them.

DEVELOPING THE STRENGTHS

Find Your Child's Special Talents

After your problem or weakness inventory is complete, and your plans to reinforce them are in effect, you are ready for the exciting part of building self-confidence. That involves the discovery of your child's special talents. If you will explore with open minds, Mom and Dad, you will find certain special abilities and interests in each child.

Special gifts may be academic, and the school your child attends will help you define and develop those abilities. Many times, however, a child's special skills are overlooked, or may even be devalued by a school system.

Unusual Ability. I know a young man who did not make outstanding grades. He was never chosen for a school sports team, and everyone overlooked him as an average person—not likely to be a great success. After high school he found a job with a paint company, and his supervisor discovered that he had an unusual eye for matching or differentiating colors. He was given some training, and became an invaluable employee in that large company.

Skilled Craftsmen and Technicians. In recent months, several large department stores have searched for tailors or seamstresses who could mend or alter garments in their ready-to-wear divisions. They found no young people who had the skills, or even the interest, to do this tedious but needed job.

This is an age of machines and scientific development is accelerating. Skilled mechanics and technicians are just as essential in keeping the equipment operating as are the people to invent it.

The Arts. The best music and literature have not been written, and the best paintings have not yet been created. Your child may be the one who will give a special gift to the world. *But*

*even if he or she gives nothing but warm, encouraging words
and smiles to her private world, be sure that will make the
world a significantly better place!*

Develop this exploring attitude. Keep your own words and
smiles positive and encouraging at home. Set an example of excellence. You will be giving your child a big boost toward perfecting self-confidence.

Develop That Talent

Once you have discovered your child's special talent, you will
need to help him value it and develop it. Usually special skills
demand time, energy, and discipline in order to make the very
most of them. Lessons, practice, risks—all of these are common
cost factors in building your child's self-esteem through promoting his or her ability.

Importance of Practice. A very dear friend of ours recently was
elected a dean of the American Guild of Organists. She teaches
organ in a well-known college, but she recalls the years when
she was just learning to play the piano. Being an energetic little
girl, she much preferred to run and play out-of-doors, but her
mother recognized her special ability. This faithful woman demanded a fairly difficult practice schedule of her daughter.
When the girl wearied of practice, she would slip outside for
playtime. Her mother called her back, and actually cared
enough to sit near the piano with a ruler in her lap. If the music
stopped for very long, the ruler went into action in the firm
grasp of Mother!

In today's era of children's rights, we may all feel sad for that
child and angry with her exacting mother. But my friend is
grateful for the discipline that helped her achieve excellence in
a skill that is rewarding to her and enriching to those who hear
her play and benefit from her teaching.

You parents will need to be ready to establish priorities and
set up the rules that will be needed by your children, until they
are mature enough to discipline themselves.

Sharing the Cost

The development of some gifts may demand extra costs. Providing materials, lessons, and transportation may be quite ex-

pensive. You may well need to sacrifice in order to provide such opportunities. Whether your sacrifice is money, energy, time, or all of these, be sure it will be worthwhile.

I strongly believe in children's earning some of the costs of their special privileges. A few opportunities remain available to motivated children for earning money. Errands, baby-sitting, lawn care, and other chores for neighbors or relatives can collect surprising wages. Even paying your own child some money for extra jobs done for you can help him have more self-respect and more motivation toward achieving a special goal.

Of course, a child's willingness to work for the extra expense involved in taking lessons or buying equipment depends on his own feelings about those goals. If this is an objective you have for your child, and he does not share that, he is not likely to want to work to support more efforts and expectations from him! So use your common sense, and wait until he becomes really excited about the idea before insisting on such involvement.

Phases in Developing a Talent

Let me forewarn you. In developing any interest or skill, most children go through *three distinct phases*. First, they are *excited* and *eager* to learn this new skill. The excitement lasts for varying periods of time, but sooner or later it will be followed by a time of *defeat* and *failure*. Learning and practicing are often tedious and boring. A child feels he would give anything to quit, and he will try almost anything in order to do so!

Hang in There. It is in this second period of tediousness that many parents give up and allow a child to quit. *Do not give in to the temptation to quit at this point, no matter what happens!* Encourage, discipline, plead, or find whatever method you can effectively use to keep him at the job until he is well into the next phase, because quitting when the going gets rough is a character-weakening habit that will be hard to break.

The Thrill of Success. Once a child works through the tedious period of learning, where he finds no successes and only more hard effort, *he will experience the thrill of success.* This third phase may vary in its degrees of success, but even a taste of it will motivate a child to do more. Such experiences of success, valued and reflected by you as parents, will do more tangible building of self-esteem than any other factor I know about. You can count on this! Success breeds success, and success builds self-esteem.

THE FINISHING TOUCHES

Each child's life is part of the structure of the whole family, so building self-esteem with your child demands building the self-worth of the family as well.

Working parents, *be proud of your job or profession.* If you are giving it the very best you have, it needn't matter what kind of job it is. Share it with your children and with each other with pride.

Respect each other as husband and wife, and build up one another, honestly, for your children. They will be the most secure when they know your relationship is safe and loving.

Keep yourselves and your household and clothing neat and as attractive as possible. Looking well does not prove your worth, but it does show external evidence of *your* internal sense of self-esteem. As in all other areas of life, you parents must model the esteem you want your children to develop.

YOUR CHILD'S FRIENDS

One of the evidences of your child's self-evaluation is his choice of friends. If you are worried about the poor quality of those friends, you will solve that problem best by rebuilding your child's self-esteem, *not* by condemning those friends. Even in your condemnation, you further tear down your child by finding fault with his judgment.

Work hard at loving and helping your child's friends (even those who worry you) as you help him. As he outgrows them, they will drift apart, or you can help your child recognize the danger they represent to his continued development.

Create a warm and congenial atmosphere in your family. Keep a sense of openness and frankness within your home. I have known such an attitude on the part of parents to make a major difference in the friends of a child as well as the child herself.

HONEST COMPLIMENTS

Working on weaknesses is very important in rebuilding self-esteem. *One of the best of materials to use in that work is the paying of honest compliments.* Instead of nagging your child's habit of forgetting, wait until you find even one occasion of remembering and comment simply, positively, and sincerely about it. Be very watchful lest you insert that habitual *but* after it. Don't spoil the compliment by asking, "But why don't you do that all the time?"

Pass on to someone else your compliments of your child. He is likely to have heard your worries about him if he has low self-esteem, so be even more certain that he overhears your compliments. Tell your spouse or telephone a grandparent, but try to let your child overhear your comments as simply stated and sincerely as you express them to her. Being too excited can seem put on or dishonest.

Surprise Rewards

As your child's efforts to improve grow, you will find a surprise reward now and then very useful. A flower from your own yard, or even a wild flower carefully placed in a neat room that has usually been messy, is a magnificent way of saying, "I noticed your efforts, and I appreciate them!" A family outing, if that can be a special treat, or any appropriate extra for that troubled child, will often tide him over a rough spot and encourage him to keep building.

YOUR INVOLVEMENT

You must, of course, notice what he does in improving! Be involved in his life, and evidence the caring that you feel. Go to her school events, or the sports in which he participates. Applaud and express your pride in those efforts. Leave the criticism to the teachers and coaches. If you are in the process of rebuilding your child's self-esteem, he needs to hear your *positive* regard, not your disapproval.

When your child's self-esteem is quite well rebuilt and sound, there will come a time for positive criticism. You can give that by keeping your own positive attitude and adapting it to a constructive critique of the areas that can help your child's esteem to continue to grow stronger.

Self-esteem is hard to find in today's world, but it can still be built, *if* you are willing to put the effort into doing so.

15
Information—How to Research the Data

Once you face the pain of your child's problem, whatever that may be, you will encounter the need for accurate information. There are many resources from which to gather the facts you must have to cope successfully with that problem.

YOUR FAMILY DOCTOR

To begin collecting data, I suggest you ask your family doctor or pediatrician. Doctors' offices are often equipped with pamphlets or books that will focus exactly on your child's individual predicament. It will usually cover only the major topics involved, however, so you will find yourself asking specific questions about certain areas.

Finding the Areas of Specialization

Included in the general discussions of the pamphlets from your doctor, there will be a bibliography or a listing of some organization or foundation that specializes in the very area you are wondering about. I suggest you write and ask for more literature from those groups. You will probably be surprised to find that the cost of such literature is most reasonable, barely enough to cover the costs of printing and mailing. And each new

331

information packet will lead you to other sources, until you collect all that is available.

YOUR SCHOOL STAFF

School Nurse

An often overlooked resource for parents in need is the school nurse. She will know about a wide variety of information sources for you and your child. Furthermore, since she may be able to help him at school, she will want to know about his problems, too. Her help extends to emotional and psychological problems as well as physical ones.

Counselor

Many schools now have a children's counselor on staff. Such a person, with little or no cost to you, can be of invaluable assistance to you. Do not be afraid to contact him or her, and visit on as regular a basis as you can. The ideas you share can help form a pattern of consistency and care that is conducive to the best possible growth of your child.

Teacher

Your child's teacher will spend almost as many waking hours with your child as you do. Be sure to spend some time with that teacher. Try to find out how your child relates to him or her, and look for special skills she probably has in dealing with problem children. You can adapt those ideas to your own personality and further enhance that essential of consistency in your child's life.

If you do not act angry or superior, you may well find that teacher anxious to learn from you as well as to teach you. Appropriate disciplinary measures at home can't always be applied at school, but many times your ideas can be adapted to the school situation. Many schools, for example, have small time-out areas where aggressive or nervous children can go apart from the class and calm down. Watch how such procedures are used in your school, and be sure they do not shame or anger your child even more than he already is. When you and your child's teacher use similar methods of discipline it increases the consistency that will help all of you.

PUBLIC LIBRARIES

Almost every community in the United States is served by an excellent library, so I suggest you find time to spend there. Since libraries may be quite confusing, ask your librarian to help you find books or articles on the problem you and your child are facing. If they do not have such books on hand, ask them to order or borrow them for you. Most public libraries have a network of resources for finding books on almost any topic. Don't be afraid to ask, and *do* be persistent if you must. Do not, by the way, be embarrassed to ask for materials that are understandable for your own reading level. There are technical books that could confuse or worry you, instead of helping you.

MENTAL HEALTH CENTERS

If your child suffers an emotional or psychological problem, a mental health center may be most helpful. Look in your telephone directory for such an institution, and call for information about their published materials. Just as your doctor's office is usually stocked with useful leaflets, so are most mental health clinics.

In many communities, every place you call will give you another person or a different phone number. Sometimes, in fact, it is absolutely infuriating to try to get through this maze, but be patient and persistent. It's you and your child who will suffer if you fail to hold on for that just-right information you need.

PUBLIC RESOURCES

Visit a bookstore as often as you can afford to, and research its materials. Most stores are organized according to subject, so you may need to ask for the child psychology section, or a special area dealing with a particular physical handicap your child may have. Most stores will order books for you if they do not have them in stock.

Many communities have *special lectures, TV programs, or newspaper articles* on a variety of children's problems. Be sure to listen and read as much as you can in order to learn the most possible. It is always wise, I warn you, to double-check information from *any* source. There are many new philosophies in the world today. Some are wise, but many are risky or dangerous. Be sure your mind is as clear and open to discern and discard falsehoods as to receive and retain truth.

Your church may be another excellent resource for you. Many people do not have a church of their own, but ask your friends or neighbors, or try visiting about. There are some remarkably supportive groups in various churches in my community. These range from day-care centers, lovingly geared to the needs of severely handicapped children, to parents-helping-parents support groups.

If you can find no support groups in your community, become a leader and *form one*. Once you have collected information you will become a resource yourself, and can organize a group around that fact. As other parents, sharing your concern, are added, you will be surprised how much good can be accumulated and dispersed.

MENTAL HEALTH SPECIALISTS

There are four major categories of counselors available in many communities for parents and families with serious problems. Any one of them may offer some help for almost all families, but each is more useful than others for certain problems.

Counselors

These are people who have a college degree and usually a postgraduate degree in the broad field of guiding and counseling people. They are trained in good communications skills and in helping people separate facts from feelings. They are familiar with various resources in the community, and can offer guidance regarding individual needs and matching those with the resources available. Within this group, there are various specialties, for example, family or vocational guidance.

Depending upon the individual experience and type of person, those who are trained in this field offer great practical help to those who need outside wisdom, a "sounding board," or advice.

Social Workers

People trained in this field have spent four years in college, and to be in the practice of therapy must have a master's degree as well. That represents two additional years of training and experience.

Social workers are especially trained in the area of interpersonal relationships and their problems. They usually are skilled in family dynamics and how to make those positive rather than destructive. They also are trained in interviewing and motivating people with problems. They are knowledgeable about group therapy, and capable of helping individuals develop support for one another in such groups.

Social workers are also helpful through their awareness of community and national resources to help individuals with a variety of problems. They can direct individuals to appropriate agencies for such needs as training or job placement, as well as counseling regarding personal problems.

Psychologists

This field of study relates to the workings of the mind and the behavior of human beings. Information that has come from the research of many years has made this field so vast that it is subdivided into the following areas:

Clinical Psychology. This deals with the mental and emotional problems of individuals, and how to help them.

Educational Psychology. How people learn, and the forces that hinder such intellectual pursuits, is the aim of this field. There are many tests and measurements that psychologists have developed to diagnose learning disabilities and to measure improvement.

Psychometrics. This is the specialty of testing the inner workings and feelings of people who have problems. Tests have been devised to help evaluate the severity of depression, for example, and the possibility of suicide.

Behavioral Psychology. This specialty focuses on the actions of a person and how such behaviors can be encouraged or discouraged, depending on rewards and punishments. It deals relatively little with the deeper needs or feelings that may prompt a given behavior.

Developmental Psychology. This specialty outlines the various stages of a child's and adult's personal development and growth. It defines the needs, dangers, and desirable outcome of each stage. It has given us increased understanding of how and why people react as they do in various periods of life. This, in turn, helps us define the habit patterns that are usually unconscious, yet can cause some of the serious problems that we have been discussing in this book.

Most practicing psychologists have master's degrees and many have doctor of philosophy degrees that will consume two to four years of study and experience under careful supervision, after their four years of college.

Psychiatrists

These are people who have completed three or four years of college, four years of medical school, and three or four years of specialty training after that. The last years are spent in specifically studying how to diagnose and treat mental and emotional illnesses of all kinds. They are, therefore, qualified to identify and treat the various physical problems that almost always interact in some way with emotional and psychological symptoms.

Help From Medications. Currently a wealth of research is being done to evaluate physical, neurological, or biochemical factors in psychological illnesses. Many medicines have been discovered or developed that will remarkably relieve anxiety and depression, or even schizophrenia or manic-depressive illness. The medicines, unfortunately, do not *cure* these problems, but they relieve their symptoms well enough so that most patients can function quite successfully in the community. Doctors need to regulate the kinds and doses of medication in order to maintain their effectiveness and safety.

Teamwork. Most psychiatrists work with a team of people. A social worker interviews and helps the family as a group. The psychologist does many tests and interviews to help make the diagnosis, and the psychiatrist evaluates the physical aspects as well as his or her own psychiatric assessment. You can see that such an in-depth study, with the available combination of group and individual treatment, is the most thorough.

Public Agencies. Unfortunately, such an intensive study and treatment is very expensive and many people cannot afford this cost. For this reason, most communities have established public agencies to help provide these services at more reasonable costs. A public agency is usually funded in some degree by taxes. People are asked to pay what they can afford, and staff people are usually not paid quite as well as are those in their own private or group practices.

Unfortunately, in a public agency, patients do not have the privilege of choosing their own therapists, and must accept the services of whoever is available. My deepest respect goes to these devoted counselors. Overworked and often underpaid, they are, in my experience, dedicated folks who try, under difficult circumstances, to help patients with troubles.

WHAT TO EXPECT IN MENTAL HEALTH TREATMENT

People often think of the mental health field as one that is magical, and a bit frightening. I find children commonly fear that they are "crazy," and worry about being locked away someplace. Even adults are very nervous and unsure of themselves for the first visit or two. Actually, counseling and psychotherapy are very ordinary skills that include the arts of careful observation, awareness of the therapist's feelings and reactions as well as the patient's, and the extreme care to avoid letting a single clue go unnoticed. Every bit of body language as well as verbal communication is important. So is a detailed family history, because it is from the family's habits and beliefs that the patient and his problems are formed, and they influence his problems as he reacts to theirs.

Evaluation

The first several visits to a therapist will include this close scrutiny of the patient's symptoms and the personal pain they cause. A careful tabulation of family and medical history, developmental milestones, and educational and social experiences, will be done. Psychological tests of selected types will probably be done, and there may be a need for special neurological and other medical and laboratory tests.

At the end of such a careful evaluation, you and your child should sit together with your therapist and hear an explanation of those tedious tests and what they reveal. Do not feel that reports telling you that everything turned out fine means they were a useless expense. Sometimes these tests fail to reveal any serious problems, and you may resent their cost in time and money. A report being normal, however, helps your therapist just as much as one that reveals serious pathology. Just be grateful, and trust your counselor.

You deserve an interpretation of those studies in terms you can understand. Every specialty area has its own vocabulary, and those who are not initiated into such a field may well feel very ignorant. Do not allow such feelings to make you feel ashamed to ask questions. Just ask—and keep on asking—until you truly understand all the information about your child's problem and what caused it.

Recommendations for Treatment

Next, your therapist should outline for you his recommendations for treatment. Again, ask until you clearly understand what he feels needs to be done and why. If you have serious doubts, you have every right to ask for consultation for another opinion. If this is available and you can afford it, it may increase your confidence in this entire process.

The recommendations once established and agreed upon deserve the same conscientious follow-through as your discipline does with you and your child. The more honestly you cooperate, the more rapidly those painful problems should be resolved. Don't waste time and money by quitting too soon, or by hanging on too long.

The Follow-Through

Be sure to practice the new ideas and plans your therapist will work out with you. You will find it hard to change old ways, attitudes, and feelings, but do it. When you fail and slide back into the old habits, do not give in to the discouragement you will feel. Just return to the new ways, and work with redoubled determination. In making certain changes in my own life, I found it took several years before the new habits became automatic.

WHEN DO YOU NEED TO SEEK PROFESSIONAL HELP?

A question I am often asked is this very one. Most children go through stages as they grow up, and it may indeed be difficult to know whether Susie or Jimmy is in just another phase, or experiencing serious problems.

Guidelines

Here are some guidelines that should help you.

Physical Changes. Any unexplained and sustained changes in eating or sleeping habits, or any other noticeable physical change, should make you parents at least seek an evaluation. Growth spurts can increase a child's appetite and cause a need for more sleep. Apart from such a physiological process, however, increased or decreased food intake and excessive sleep or inability to sleep are serious signs of emotional distress.

Gini was eleven when I first saw her. She was so obese that she could not enter into the games of her classmates. Despite lovely hair and expressive eyes, her weight made her feel ugly and awkward. She related to me the origin and reason for her habit of overeating. She recalled, at the age of four, hearing her parents argue intensely. She found that she could feel a bit safer by going to the refrigerator and eating until either they stopped arguing or she could eat no more. This habit became so ingrained that she continued to eat every time she felt upset or worried.

Emotional Changes. Again, it is any dramatic change from your child's normal attitudes and behaviors that is significant. Such a change needs to last several weeks before one should be alarmed. Even the normal mood swings, however, can become intensified so much that on a daily basis you should take note. Major loss of control over one's feelings or behaviors may be a warning sign.

Amy had been a happy-go-lucky girl until she suffered the loss of her grandmother through a stroke. Her parents did not get along well, and she found her childish tricks less and less effective in stopping their fights. Amy began to worry, and couldn't wait to get home from school to see if they would both be there. Her schoolwork suffered and her happiness was gone—replaced with worry and sadness. She eventually needed extended counseling to set her emotions right.

Changes in School and Work Habits. Since school is to a child what a job is to an adult, we examine the school performance closely to determine the state of a child's personal health. Again, it is the degree of change or severity of trouble that is a clue. A child who has done average work or better, then goes into a prolonged slump, is certainly deserving of an evaluation by a therapist. More rarely, a child who has been a poor student may suddenly work very hard to do better. Such improvement may have a healthy basis, but it may come from a last, desperate attempt to please the teacher or prove himself to his parents. If such efforts demand too much, the child may burn out and sink into despair.

Social Changes. A child who has been a bit shy may become the class clown or take needless risks, becoming accident-prone. A child with many friends may suddenly withdraw from the warmth of those relationships into isolation. If this is prolonged over several days or weeks, you need to find out what is wrong.

Inside Changes. A child's attitudes and self-image may slowly change over a period of time. When these steadily deteriorate without returning to a positive level over some days or weeks, you must find out what is wrong. Losing self-esteem, becoming angry or pessimistic, are signs that something is wrong within your child's very core. Don't take a chance.

When you, your spouse, friends, and your child's teacher all agree on some concerns over your child, a visit to a professional therapist may be lifesaving. Certainly it can restore the joy and peace of mind every child and parent deserve!

16
Sudden Crisis—
How to Respond

When you hear the word *crisis,* most of you probably think, as I do, of a life-threatening emergency. But there are many small crises that occur nearly every day. How well you recognize those and respond to them will largely determine how you handle the more serious situations.

MINOR CRISES

In some families, spilling a glass of milk on the dinner table will cause a parent to become irate. There will be some yelling, threatening, and perhaps banishment of a child to her room. Usually, children do not spill milk on purpose but because their coordination is poor, or the glass is slippery, or too easily tipped. Being treated in this fashion, therefore, is certain to add to her nervousness, making her even more clumsy.

Furthermore, if she should ever suffer a true crisis, such as being lacerated by a broken glass, she would very likely react in exaggerated anxiety and shame.

When parents overreact to such small daily events, they add to the atmosphere of all crises a tone of intensity that complicates or defeats good solutions.

Managing Those Troublesome Events

There are many troublesome events that could be considered crises that occur in many families with regularity. Temper tantrums, fits of anger, fights with friends or siblings, broken treasures, accidents, and illnesses—all are part of the growing-up experiences of childhood. At the time they take place, their very intensity may crowd out the rest of your interests or responsibilities, and demand your sole attention. How do you manage such events?

When our son was three years old, I found myself in a predicament that taught me how important it is to handle emergencies wisely. Our family had been working in the yard on a weekend afternoon. Lyndon had been busily engaged in fighting off imaginary bandits while we worked, but suddenly I became aware of the unusual calm of his absence. I called his name, but he did not come running as usual. I looked carefully under bushes and in the crannies where he may have been hiding out from his foes. But no charming, disheveled boy with his sheriff's gun belt could I find. I searched the house with increasing panic welling up. Still no sign of my son! I could not get anyone to panic with me, though I even asked my husband to call the police to help us search for our lost boy. Since he did not share my panic, he refused to bother the police!

Finally, I went through the house once more, methodically, carefully, with the proverbial fine-toothed-comb approach. At last, in the closet where his toys were stored (or strewn), I found him. He was sound asleep, still clutching his toy guns and utterly exhausted. My fear and overreaction could have created a needless neighborhood panic.

Now, if I had not found that tired lad with a careful, methodical search, it would have been even more foolish to neglect reporting the loss of such a priceless person. Keeping the balances in life is not an easy endeavor, but it is very important in dealing with a crisis!

MAJOR CRISES

When small crises are compared with big ones, it often helps us to cope more effectively with them. Major disasters are actually quite common in today's family life!

Divorce

From a child's view, perhaps one of the saddest, most threatening tragedies is that of divorce. In the troubled children with whom I work daily, the fear or heartbreak of parental fighting and separation is one of the most common problems. In spite of disagreements and problems in all but the most severely embattled marriages, children prefer their parents to stay together. They, in fact, add to the crisis of an endangered relationship many of their own clever crises, hoping to avert that major one.

Running Away

Running away from home is still a common occurrence. In fact, in all too many families, such an event no longer is cause for much alarm. And getting assistance from public agencies to find such runaway children is becoming harder. Young people band together to support one another in such rebellion, making lengthy times away from families possible.

Tragically, as families deteriorate, more and more runaways are related to neglect and serious abuse by parents. Only recently a depressed young adolescent told me the sordid story of her alcoholic parents, and the unbearable life she endured with them until she finally ran away.

The story of runaways is ludicrously expanding to the parents themselves. It is not uncommon for a father to leave his wife and children, but in recent years we are seeing mothers, as well, abandon their families. Even the instinctive parenting habits seem to be weakening.

Suicide

Suicide, either successful or attempted, is another major crisis faced by many families in our world. The most common cause of death in adolescence is accidents. Second to that is death by suicide. Studies of suicide in children prior to adolescence are not available in this country, but we do know that in 1977, 188 deaths by suicide were reported in ten- to fourteen-year-olds, and 1,871 suicides were committed by fifteen- to nineteen-year-olds.

Certainly death, serious illnesses, and accidents hit every family sooner or later, and children are impacted by that crisis, too. Be sure to review the section in chapter 9 "Emotional Problems" on children troubled by grief if you and your child must face this type of crisis.

Natural and Other Disasters

Storms, earthquakes, or other natural disasters, fire, robberies, and catastrophes that are predicted if war should be de-
clared in our world—all affect children. In fact, children in
grade schools are reported to show immense anxiety about the
possibility of war.

With economic stress, there may well be the threat of job loss,
deprivation of the necessities of life, and even hunger.

CAUSES OF CRISES

While no one wants to contemplate such grim but often unavoidable catastrophes, I hope you are mature and wise enough
to do so. The more you understand of any serious situation, or
even threatening crises, the more effectively you can handle
them.

Factors Within Parental Control

Crisis Related to Disciplinary Failures. The temper fits, fights,
or other behavioral crises of children are often due to inconsistencies in discipline. The failure to make your rules and expectations clear is a sure setup for your child to create havoc in
testing them out. If you are not strong and firm in your authority as parents, you will leave too much power in the reach of
your child, and he or she is likely to divert that power into
creating trouble. And if you do not follow through with the consequences you have set up for disobedience, your child will
again need to test those out with increasingly troublesome
behaviors.

Crisis Related to Marital Distress. If you are facing estrangement from each other as husband and wife due to misunderstandings, get those problems resolved. Find out how to
communicate clearly and lovingly—either by your own efforts
or with the help of a counselor. Failure to provide a secure family structure for the protection and nurturing of your child con-
stitutes serious child abuse. Do not deceive yourselves—the
strength of your marital relationship (or its weakness) can prevent or create serious crises for your children.

Crisis in the Community. Problems in school or in the neighborhood can create crises that are at least partially controllable by you, the parents. Many schools face almost insurmountable difficulties with basically uncontrollable children. I have known of schools in which even a small group of violent children have terrorized the others by their attacks or threats. In some areas, families become caught up into animosity that creates a crisis-laden atmosphere. Even one thoughtful, open-minded family can sometimes defuse such a time bomb in a neighborhood. Good judgment and wisdom, however, are absolutely essential if you are to be successful in such an admittedly risky enterprise!

Factors Beyond Parental Control

Crisis Due to Physical Causes. Staying calm and in control when a physical crisis of any sort strikes is not easy, but it is often lifesaving. Physical disasters may be due to carelessness, disobedience, or an act of God, but they must be dealt with carefully before assessing blame or levying punishment.

A friend of mine climbed a tree when he was a child, against his mother's strict orders. He fell from that tree and broke his arm. Before she even looked at his painful arm, that mother scolded and spanked him. He was left with a lifelong fear of heights that took a great deal of work to overcome. In many cases, the crisis of an accident itself becomes punishment enough to teach a needed lesson.

Crisis Caused by One Spouse. In today's mixed-up world, the best of marriages and families suffer, but the weaker marriages often result in disaster. Addictive problems of one spouse are certainly beyond the control of the other. True enough, such a person may be influenced by a "tough love" approach, but occasionally, a divorce may even be necessary to protect the children. Certainly, an addictive parent (drug- or alcohol-dependent) can create heartbreaking crises.

An abusive parent or spouse also creates a series of crises. A woman came to me after a workshop on parenting with a sordid tale of severe sexual abuse her husband committed upon their children. She felt trapped by trying to keep her family together and to avoid divorce, and yet protect her children. The husband refused to change or get help. I strongly feel that in such a situation the father causes serious crises, resulting in lifelong damage to the defenseless children. In her case, divorce was necessary to resolve this problem.

The abandonment of children by one or, rarely, both parents is almost always due to their immaturity or mental or emotional illness. Unfortunately, this is all too common. Such a crisis is one that usually has some forewarning, if the healthier spouse is alert and able to face the situation. As stress builds within the weaker person, he or she will evidence symptoms of irritability, withdrawal and isolation, moodiness, or increasing failure to fulfill responsibilities. Recognizing impending trouble can enable one parent to avoid some of the problems that unexpected abandonment creates.

COPING WITH CRISIS

Whatever the cause of a crisis in your family, the important thing is to deal with it as quickly, effectively, and lovingly as possible.

Face the Facts

A young woman once called me in desperation. She was unmarried and pregnant. In fact, she was at that very moment in labor and about to deliver the baby at home. Though her father was at home, she refused to seek his help, because she was afraid of his anger. At her urgent request, I telephoned him, explained his daughter's predicament, and told him how much she needed his help!

The man was irate with me—a stranger—and assured me that such a thing could never happen in his fine family. He finally did believe me, but I was horrified and saddened to realize how much time had passed for this frightened, teenage mother to endure such a burden alone. Her parents had denied a crisis until it became a potentially grave danger to their daughter.

Whatever your crisis, major or minor, be sure that you admit it. Discuss it with a trustworthy, objective friend until you resolve it. Let me recommend the following steps in such a discussion.

Steps to Take in Discussing Crisis

1. *If the crisis demands immediate action, take that action!* Be careful and wise, but get the emergency under control. We will discuss such events in the next section.

2. *When time permits, let yourself recognize and talk about your feelings.* If you are afraid, angry, worried, or confused, putting that feeling into words will help you to gain control over it. And when you are in charge of your emotions, you will think and plan with much greater wisdom.

3. *After you gain mastery over your emotions, discuss the facts involved in the situation.* As you outline the information you have, you will become increasingly clear about additional questions to be asked or solutions that are possible. Your listener will be able to help you to further clarify the crisis.

4. *When all the facts are as clear as possible, formulate a good solution.* In my experience, an ideal solution is rarely possible, so you need to have alternate plans available. Again, thinking aloud and discussing a solution with a friend can be amazingly helpful. If no friend is available, write down some of these feelings and thoughts—writing and reading those reactions will clarify them remarkably.

Take Action

Many solutions generated out of sheer genius lie unused for lack of follow-through. Do not let that happen to you. One of the benefits of a crisis is the strong motivation to resolve a problem that may have been building for some time. Here are some examples of energetic action that you may need to take in carrying out the solution to your crisis.

1. *You may need to change your job, your hours of work, or your living standards, in order to provide the care and protection your children need to cure or prevent a crisis.*

2. *If your parenting skills are lacking, you will need to read, learn, or seek counsel to guide or teach you more effective methods.*

3. *If your family is endangered by your neighborhood or*

*an emotionally ill spouse, you may need to seek a move
or a separation in order to protect them.*

Emergency Crises

In a life- or safety-threatening situation, you may well need to
seek dramatic means of help. Do not hesitate to do so if your
judgment suggests real danger. Hesitation could delay a phone
call a few seconds too long!

Police Help. Out of embarrassment or shame, I have seen some
parents refuse to seek the help of police in threatening situations. Your safety and that of your child is far more important
than any possible criticism by neighbors! Have the telephone
number of your nearest police station posted by your phone.
Call it and ask for help, clearly giving your location, if:

1. *There is actual or honestly threatened violence.* Intox-
ication or drug "highs" may quickly turn into violence, so do
not wait too long. Avoid, of course, unnecessary calls based on
faulty judgment, retaliation, or attention getting.
2. *There is a runaway child or serious threat of running.*
Some police stations have had so many calls regarding runaways that they simply cannot respond to these calls. Sometimes they *can* come and may help you and your child
through a crisis and back to a constructive relationship. A report will at least send out over a wide area your missing
child's description, and the assurance that someone wants
him back.
3. *There is evidence of drug abuse and possible overdosing.* Drug abuse is illegal and a report to the police has, in my
experience, often helped a wayward child to face that fact. It
will be a sure way of letting him know that you take it
seriously, and will call on any resource to stop him.

Juvenile Court. Some parents are reluctant to seek the help of
our judicial system for fear their child may be taken away from
them. And that is possible, so if you parents have any other effective resource for helping a rebellious child in a crisis, by all
means use it! If you have, however, used up all other resources,

please consider giving the court, and the authority it represents, a chance to help.

Emergency Medical Help. Beside the phone number of your police station, please post the number of your nearest ambulance and emergency resources. If your child has suffered an accident, or is suddenly and seriously ill, as in a convulsion, call at once. They can tell you what to do until an ambulance arrives, or may inform you that you can safely transport your child in a car if one is available.

Rarely, I *have* known of a child to die from severe abuse, because one or both parents are afraid or ashamed to have that fact known. If you are honest with the physicians, they can often help you to avoid needless publicity. They are, however, required by law to report any suspected abuse to qualified and trained people in agencies who can help you to get protection for your child, as well as help for the abusive person.

Psychiatric Emergencies. Any hospital can give you some help for a psychiatric emergency, but if you have access to a special psychiatric hospital or unit, it is bound to be more effective. Psychiatric emergencies include any person who is out of control and trying (or threatening) to destroy property or hurt himself or others. Psychotic children or adults may become violent with little warning. Take such a person to a hospital for help. Call for police help if you must, but do not risk the tragedy of allowing that person to do damage to himself or others.

It has become very difficult to confine a dangerously disturbed patient in a safe environment, due to laws that intend to protect the freedoms of individuals. You can, however, gain up to three days of such care for disturbed persons. Within that time, perhaps, a physician and attorney can gain additional information that will justify longer confinement if that is needed. It is my experience that, once through the crisis, most emotionally disturbed persons will improve enough to be rational and to cooperate voluntarily with more care.

Church or Synagogue. Many churches have caring people on their staff or in their congregation who have special skills. Do not hesitate to call your church, or that of a friend, for help in a crisis.

Friends, Relatives, and Neighbors. These can be of immense
help in a crisis. Be certain that you never abuse their caring by
needlessly crying, "Wolf!" as the boy did in the old story. And
be careful to return the favor and express your gratitude. The
mutual caring and sharing of one another's problems and burdens is a part of the warm intimacy of healthy living.

Coping with any crisis demands both inner and external resources. Courage, wisdom, good judgment, and a caring heart
are qualities from within us that enable us to cope. Having
knowledge of available resources, a workable plan, and the help
of appropriate people are the external components of successfully getting through a crisis. Patience to follow through with a
plan can help prevent many of the possible recurrences of crisis
situations.

17
Child Abuse—
How to Understand
and Overcome It

With almost daily news articles revealing the tragedy of child abuse, we think it is a new phenomenon. It has, however, always existed, and seems to be a part of the condition of mankind. It is not easy to define child abuse because a practice some people believe to be good discipline is the very thing others see as abuse. Child abuse is much more widespread than many people could believe. It is estimated that in one year, in the U.S.A., there are thirty to forty thousand battered children, one hundred thousand sexually abused youngsters, and nearly three hundred thousand psychologically abused children!

DEFINITION OF CHILD ABUSE

A definition I personally find helpful is this: "Child abuse is any treatment of a child that threatens his safety or leaves in his life physical or emotional scars." If your methods of training and discipline leave such marks on your child, please commit yourself to changing.

DESCRIPTION OF CHILD ABUSER

Typical Example

Susan was a blond, blue-eyed six-year-old when I met her. She was a model student, quiet, hardworking, and courteous. In fact, she was too good, and her face often looked so sad that I felt troubled about her. Furthermore, she evidenced unusual bruises, and evidence of burns became so clear that her case had to be reported to the authorities. Susan was obviously terrified of the questions that had to be asked, but finally she revealed the fact that her father burned her with a glowing cigarette to teach her to stop playing with his lighter. This father hit her face to teach her to stop pinching her annoying baby brother.

Certainly Susan needed to learn to stop playing with fire and pinching her brother; but she evidenced the ability to learn without such damaging forms of discipline. In fact, no child needs such ferocious methods in order to learn life's lessons.

There are several *common denominators of parents who abuse their children:*

1. *They are lonely* and usually emotionally or physically far from their families. They are often so afraid or suspicious of people that they become "stuck" in their isolation.
2. *There often is conflict* in their marriages, or they are divorced. This increases the loneliness and allows for the displacement of their hurts and anger at the spouse upon the children.
3. *They are people who live under great stress.* This may be financial, job-related pressure, trouble with neighbors, or housing. The stress seems to become focused on the child—a safe target.
4. They usually are *parents who were abused* by their own parents in childhood.

One abusive mother recently told me about the cruelty of her own mother. She said, "But you know, I wish I could go back to her, even now; I miss her so much!" She was explaining, a little bit, how it is that being abused creates habits of abusing. When this mother abuses her children, she is unconsciously being like her mother, and can feel the old closeness. Pain, bad as it is, is better than the numbness of indifference.

Strangely enough, the abusive parent really loves his child. More often than not, I have seen abused children prefer their own parents to the safest of foster care. Partly this is due to the love—strangely as it is expressed—of those parents. Abusive parents also generally are energetic people, and children tend to be attracted to people of high energy.

QUALITIES OF THE ABUSIVE PARENT

On a personal level, there are several qualities of the abusive parent that I feel need to be understood.

1. *Lack of self-control.* Abusive adults often act like spoiled children. Their abusive actions are like temper tantrums and at those moments, the intensity of their anger makes them feel powerful rather than weak, as they usually feel.

2. *Lack of self-confidence.* Parents who do not know their true wisdom and actual strength go to great lengths to try to prove themselves. Such people overreact to fairly normal situations with extreme rage in the attempt to prove a power they fear is lacking. Just like children, they unconsciously cover up their fear and weakness with anger.

3. *Lack of trust in their parents.* While they usually loved their parents, they were also commonly insulted by those parents. They usually felt either excessively intimidated by, or extremely powerful over, their parents. Strength, in the entire life history of a child abuser, is represented by anger and power struggles.

4. *Failure to see child for himself.* They see in their child some negative quality that was present in their parents, in each other, or themselves. Unconsciously, such parents take out on the helpless child vengeful feelings that really belong elsewhere.

5. *Lack of sense of self-worth.* Because they basically feel so unworthy, abusive parents find it impossible to ask for help. They don't want anyone to know how bad or inadequate they feel, and they believe if anyone knew, they would be even more rejected. They simply try harder and harder to win through rage.

6. *Child learns to fit into the pattern.* Children quickly learn how to get a parent's attention. They may even sense that they are meeting some need in the parent by evoking the anger and abuse. So the child forms the exact habits that fit with the parent's vicious treatment.

TREATMENT OF CHILD ABUSE

Obviously the best treatment of child abuse is the prevention of it. The following ideas will help in that prevention as well as contributing to a cure:

First of all, if you even suspect that you are an abusive parent, do something at once! Do not wait for the next explosive episode to happen. It could be the time when you lose control and seriously hurt your child. No abusive parent intends to break his or her child's bones, or rupture a spleen or kidney. They simply have allowed their anger to gain control of them rather than staying in control of it!

Talk with your minister, some trusted friend, or a professional counselor. Explain your short fuse, and what happens when you become angry. Even describing this process will help you understand yourself and establish better controls.

If you can't bring yourself to talk to someone you know, call your local child-welfare agency. You need not identify yourself until you feel more comfortable, but ask them for any help you need. They are well trained in exactly this sort of situation, and they can be of inestimable value in getting your habits of abuse stopped.

Find a "Parents Anonymous" group. They are parents who are or have been abusive themselves, and they will fully understand your feelings and habits. The national headquarters are:

> Parents Anonymous
> 2930 West Imperial Highway
> Suite 332
> Inglewood, California 90303

> *or*

> Parents Anonymous
> 250 West 57th Street, Room 1901
> New York, NY 10019

They will help you find or organize a group in your own vicinity.

Reread the above paragraphs and try to identify your deep needs and feelings. By knowing them and admitting them, you are well on your way to finding real solutions. Do not, however, be misled by your new insights into believing you can change this habit all by yourself. You will certainly benefit from the support and understanding of an objective, trained counselor.

DEALING WITH POTENTIALLY ABUSIVE SITUATIONS

In dealing with such situations, try one or more of these suggestions:

1. *Get in touch with your feelings of desperation and rage as soon as they begin, and before they explode into an intensity that is beyond your control. Put those emotions into words. Make yourself think about why you feel them, and clarify the positive choices you can make about them.*

2. *Remove yourself from your child and that explosive situation at once! Do not stay in the vicinity that can tempt you to spill out your rage on a child. Getting out of range will protect both you and your child from that danger.*

3. *If you believe in God, talk with Him. Imagine His presence in any form that is meaningful to you, and tell Him how you feel. Ask Him for whatever you need: love, guidance, strength, or tenderness. Many people who have learned to practice this have found remarkable help.*

4. *Call a friend, if you can. Talk over your problem and ask specifically for what you need. A person who will listen can help you to organize your thoughts and control your feelings and behavior. With the help of this friend, plan how you can discipline your child successfully or handle a touchy situation without losing control.*

5. *With courage and caution, go to the waiting child and put your disciplinary plan into effect. Explain your new*

*way of handling necessary punishments, and seek the
child's cooperation and obedience to help you. It is a
high compliment to a child to need his help and does
not, as you may fear, make him lose respect for you.*

6. *Remember your childhood. By recapturing your own
    fear and anger, you may understand your child more
    accurately and learn to treat him better.*

7. *Learn to love and treat yourself kindly in your deepest
    emotional being. When you can truly love and accept
    yourself, it becomes much easier to accept and love
    your child.*

If you have ever been an abusive parent, you probably should
religiously avoid all physical punishment of a child. Just as one
drink can revive an alcoholic's old habits, one such punishment
can trigger a chain reaction of abuse. Avoid it like the plague!
Master a nonviolent mode of discipline that is consistent and
meaningful to your child and stick with it.

Counseling

For most people, the best answer to child abuse is professional counseling. Swallow your pride, and go for it! It may save
your child's life. It will certainly improve yours. You may learn
how to understand and accept yourself as a whole person, as
well as learning how to deal with your child. As you discover
your strengths and weaknesses, you may find they balance out
better than you feared. Learning to truly love yourself will inevitably teach you how to love others—including your child.

(Portions of this chapter have been adapted from chapter 16,
"Handling Difficulties and Suffering," in *The Complete Book of
Baby and Child Care for Christian Parents* by Grace H. Ketterman, M.D. and Herbert L. Ketterman, M.D., Copyright ©
1982, published by Fleming H. Revell Company.)

18
Family Priorities—
How to Reorder Them

When I look back and survey the basically warm, loving environment in which I grew up, I can identify four fundamentals which composed that. I see these repeated in successful families that I touch in today's world, as well. You may rearrange the order of these four qualities, but if each of them is present in your family, I believe it can make your family healthy.

FOUR FUNDAMENTALS FOR A LOVING ENVIRONMENT

Caring

In today's world, people who have lost the vitality of a healthy faith and a personal sense of safety often develop an attitude of indifference. They learn to stop caring. In reordering your priorities, then, you will need to take a look at your family. *Do all of you care about each other, and do you communicate that concern?*

Caring About Yourself. At the risk of sounding selfish, you must love *yourself* if you are to be able to love others. This wholesome self-love makes us take care of our health—mental, physical, and spiritual. It makes us take care of our appearance, and the way we act. Healthy self-love results in strong character, a positive self-image, and a natural outflow of loving concern for others, as well.

Caring About Others. It is as natural for a person who loves himself to care for the people who surround him, as it is to breathe. The biblical command to love one's neighbor as one's self was my original lesson about this principle, and it works. When you develop the habit of loving and caring about yourself, you will be able to extend that. Fortunately, the more you care about others, and show them, the more they will learn to care about themselves and you. Caring generates caring.

Caring About Your Environment. Many times I am physically fatigued, and when I reach home, I'd like only to fall in a heap—but because I care about myself and my family, I muster the strength to make our environment pleasant. I am not an immaculate housekeeper, but I do pick up the clutter, prepare appealing foods, and work for a warm, loving climate in our home. I try to extend this to my office, and wherever it may be that I serve.

Sharing

If caring is genuine, it must create sharing. Sharing ideas, feelings, and needs is the essence of good communication. Sharing activities, in both work and play, is the bond of a family.

It takes time. The old cliché about the quality of one's time being more important than the quantity may be true. In many families, however, the amount of time spent together is in such short supply that the quality is difficult to define or even find! So you must ration out your minutes, and keep at the top of your list of time priorities the needs of you and your children to be together. Discipline yourselves, parents, to be at home for at least two meals daily. Limit your social and volunteer activities, so as to be at home most evenings and weekends. Be available for the occasional crises of your children as well as providing, through your presence, the security they need daily.

It takes work. Working together as a family was the rule of my childhood. Cleaning house, planting a garden, doing laundry, involved the efforts of all of us. Learning how to plan and finish a job became automatic, as I shared in the sometimes-hated work on a farm.

One day I was trying to get my children to clean our basement, and I suddenly realized a simple fact. They didn't know how to go about that job, so they put it off, argued, and in general made a mess of it. I put aside some other work I was doing and began to work with them. The old habits from my childhood returned automatically, and we were soon laughing together as we applied the brooms, mops, and dusters to that part of our home.

Sharing work can take many forms, but the warmth it includes makes hard tasks bearable, and strengthens the bonds of intimacy in any family.

It takes feelings. Working together and spending time together can be boring, or even frightening, if the feelings are not positive. Had I worked angrily with our children, or criticized their efforts, our project would have ended quite differently. Sharing laughter—as well as concerns, tenderness, and occasional frustration—are essential for a healthy set of family priorities.

It takes fun. Sharing would become heavy indeed if it did not include playing together. I can almost hear you moaning about not having time to finish the work, let alone find time to play, but *that's exactly what reordering priorities is all about!* So carefully sift through all the things you *must* do, and realize that one of those is *playing.* Each family plays in its own unique way, and that is right. So whether you go to the beach, the mountains, or the local swimming pool—in fact, whether you go anywhere at all—is not important. That you learn to laugh, play, and enjoy some congenial activities together is the essence of sharing fun.

Growth

Physical Growth. Providing good nutrition, exercise, and good medical care is a high priority of healthy families. Setting the example, seeing to the immunizations and physical checkups, and teaching good overall nutrition and health habits, are the responsibility of parents.

Mental Growth. The climate of mental stimulation and growth, I am convinced, is set by parents. My parents were unable to attend formal schooling beyond the eighth grade, but they read widely, discussed issues of all sorts profoundly, and wheedled and nudged all of us children to gain as much education as possible. Intellectual growth, for a child, occurs best in the exciting discoveries of parents who continue to explore learning.

Social Growth. Self-confidence is created in children who grow up in a warm social environment. It was through Sunday-dinner guests that I observed the grace of hospitality. The entertainment of visiting clergymen, relatives, or anyone needing a home away from home, enriched my childhood infinitely. It taught me courtesy, sensitivity to others' needs, and made it easier for me to welcome guests into our own home years later.

Spiritual Growth. In a world that is increasingly mechanical and impersonal, spiritual values are often lost to children. Parents' honest regard for spiritual growth sets the tone for their children. The practical application of their religious beliefs is an example few children can ignore. Some of my most tender memories are those of my parents, privately, and my family, united, sharing God's love and care with one another.

Recently, a colleague reported a study of a large number of young psychiatric patients he had personally treated. He found that those whose families regularly practiced their own religious beliefs were more than twice as likely to recover from their psychiatric illness, as compared with those whose families discouraged religious involvement.

Competition

Currently, I hear from some professionals who work with children that we need to remove competitiveness from the experiences of childhood. Their theory is based on the fact that competition, by its very definition, demands losing, and they believe that everyone should win and never lose. Certainly I like to win, and I promote the positive attitude of the winner as much as I can.

The Reality of Life. Nevertheless, life in reality has its failures and losses. Discovering how to lose and grow by losing, then, becomes a high value in my priorities. Furthermore, healthy competition stimulates a child's energy and magnifies his efforts, promoting great personal motivation and team spirit when a group is involved. Stopping competition can cause peo-

ple to become lethargic, deceptively convinced that a struggle in
life is never required.

Competition *can* reinforce a sense of honesty, fairness, and
compassion for others, or it can become an avenue for ruthless
aggression and destruction of the loser. Parents, you can readily
see which possibility exists in your children early, if you are
looking at them and are aware of such a possibility. See to it,
then, that you prioritize a wholesome spirit of competition in
your family—one that stimulates your children to excellence!

HOW PRIORITIES BECOME DISORDERED

Typical Example

The Jones family is a living example of the loss of good
prioritizing of values. At one time, they shared activities with
one another and with friends and neighbors. They enjoyed pic-
nics, evening excursions to the ice-cream parlor, and family-
game and TV nights.

Ever so insidiously, Mr. Jones became caught up in the competition in the large corporation for which he worked. His time
became the property of the company, and ever so slowly, so
did his values. His interest in the church declined, and his involvement with his family nearly disappeared. Social drinking
became more and more a problem until Mr. Jones became an alcoholic. The children managed to stay out of serious trouble,
but they felt estranged from their father. Their mother sought
refuge from her loneliness in the children's lives, and at times
they felt burdened with her needs. This family's priorities had
become sadly disarranged.

As I studied the Jones family and several others quite similar,
I discovered some of the factors that entered into their disor-
dered values.

Background of Poverty

Mr. Jones grew up in a family that knew the pain of poverty.
He vowed his children would never know the deprivations he
had lived with so intimately. When the opportunity came,

therefore, for him to climb the corporate ladder, he did not even hesitate. It offered material security for the family he loved—and for the basic fears that were left in him from childhood.

Self-pity

As he saw the hurt in the eyes of his wife and children at his increasing withdrawal, he covered his vague uneasiness and guilt with the private conviction that someday they would thank him for his sacrifices—for them. When the children and his wife no longer seemed to miss or need him, he allowed himself a bit of self-pity, and even felt irritated at their lack of appreciation. These feelings soon allowed him to pamper himself with an extra drink, just to numb the pain of it all.

Negative Feelings

The family of Mr. Jones felt hurt, rejected, and then angry at him. They could see, as he could not, that much of his work was an attempt to feel good about himself. They were not at all convinced that his work was even remotely for *their* good, so they covered their pain over his selfishness with indifference. His daughter summed up their relationship, as she saw it, in these words: "You don't care about me, so I won't care about you!"

It is, sadly, our vulnerable, tender feelings, then, that usually begin the confusion of a family's priorities. Mr. Jones's early poverty and his lack of healthy self-confidence drove him mercilessly in his quest for proof of his self-worth.

In his drivenness, this father lost sight of the real needs of his family. He wrongly assumed their needs and values were identical with his own, and justified his neglect of them by a mental mechanism similar to wishful thinking. By convincing himself that he was serving *their* needs, he came to believe, in fact, that was true. It was not so.

From the tender feelings of sadness over the loss of warmth, joy, and sharing, the Jones family became increasingly protected by anger. They retaliated and the mutual rejection widened still further the distance between them.

Out of the pain of their vulnerability and their angry exchanges came the excuse for the father's escape into alcohol, the mother's escape into the lives of her children, and the children's callousness and withdrawal into their own private worlds.

By denying your own needs and feelings, you may lose sight of those of the people who are dearest to you. It was not an accident that we are all commanded to love our neighbors *as* ourselves. Until you learn to love yourself in a balanced, wholesome fashion, you cannot love others—even your own family members.

FINDING THE BALANCE

Another cause of disarray in values is the loss of harmony and completeness in life. Love, for example, can be so protective that it pampers a child and drains the parent. When children become the only focus of parental time and attention, they get an unrealistic concept of themselves. In the world outside of the family, such attention will certainly not be duplicated and the children will be at a loss to cope in that world. Overly protective love is just as damaging as neglect.

Being too critical, too intellectual, too moody, too *anything* carries with it certain risks and problems. Now don't let this discourage you or drive you to seek the illusion of perfection! But do be aware of the requirement of staying open to the signs of imbalance. A sense of uneasiness within your own mind that all is not well must be heeded. Increasing estrangement from one another in a family is another sign of trouble. Increasing evidence of distress in the life of even one family member is certain proof that the entire family needs to be evaluated, including you parents. A family is a unit, a system, and not one member of it can suffer without input and repercussions involving everyone!

REMEMBER THOSE BASIC NEEDS!

If you will look at your own lives as parents as well as those of your children, you can easily see what need is least well met. And becoming *aware* will give you a fresh chance to effectively saturate the dry areas of your child's developing personality.

Affection

If your child is buying friends with favors, or your spouse is vulnerable to an affair, it may have something to do with your withdrawing too much. Facing the family's need for warmth and intimacy, and working for those qualities, can not only satisfy your child's needs for love but will also enrich your own life in a beautiful way. The time, energy, and channels for the exchange of that loving must be your top priority.

Approval

Failure to give to one another enough of a sense of pride and approval in your daily activities and accomplishments will quickly disarrange priorities. Unfair expectations will promptly result in discouragement, anger, and revenge. Too few expectations will usually cause laziness and carelessness with their loss of self-esteem, and further resentments are likely to follow.

Consistency

Without a sense of order and predictability in life, a child's world becomes frightening. He is likely to take authority into his own hands, desperately striving for some security; or he may test out the parents' rules until he does find the limits. Such premature responsibility and testing-out behaviors are equally destructive. *Setting up some regularity in a family is an absolute essential.*

Enjoyment

Without laughter, the most perfect of families sounds drab and uninteresting. When joy is lacking, people rather desperately seek for wild excitement as a phony substitute. While I have not found it to be studied formally, I am convinced after years of experience that naughty, "hyper" children are often those who fail to experience the seasoning of merriment in their homes. Try creating a reason for healthy, free laughter in your family and see what a wonderful medicine a merry heart can be!

THE STEPS IN REORDERING PRIORITIES

Just as in understanding what it is that causes problems for you and your child, so the reordering process is based on four issues.

Attitudes

Negative, critical attitudes cause many family problems. Developing positive attitudes and using them realistically will begin to solve those problems and restore health and vitality to you and your children.

Explore more than you expect! Avoid hasty judgments, and patiently garner all the information you can. Use it constructively to define all problems and resolve them quickly. Exploring for fun and curiosity, as well as for problem solving, is a wonderful way of life!

Expect only the best. Keep your expectations clear and simple, and always positive. Once a relative of mine described her favorite teacher. It was a man known throughout the school for an exceptionally positive classroom attitude, with remarkable success from even problem students. My relative believes that this unusual class was made possible because that man energetically expected only the best from each student.

I have repeatedly seen children respond to the unspoken as well as the verbal expectations of adults. It's largely up to you, parents. What do you expect? If it has been something negative, work hard to turn that around!

Keep your own emotional needs fulfilled. You cannot give what you do not possess, yet many parents vainly try. Find your own areas of creativity and fulfillment so you will have something worthwhile to share. Be careful to keep your marriage romantic and satisfying. Certainly, the best gift you will ever give your child is a mother and father who sincerely love each other.

Accept yourself as you are. You cannot honestly love and accept anyone else more than you do yourself, so love the person God made you to be, and develop every bit of yourself to the maximum. Then enjoy and feel good about that! This practice is a model for your child and keeps your attitude and his as positive as it can be!

Look for humor. In even the grimmest of catastrophes, there is usually some funny angle that may tide you through! Children are often natural humorists. Let yourself go, and enjoy their silly jokes. As you watch their free laughter, you may recapture the simple, wholesome mirth of your own childhood.

Take charge of your life. If you must work for someone else, you may lose too much of your own identity and personal power. I know you must please your boss but on your own, at least, remember that you can be in charge. One mother began to schedule her own time. She organized her work, the family's needs, and even found some time for her own rest and relaxation, simply by planning. You can take control of your time, activities, and priorities more than you may have realized.

Arrange your life, then, to be consistent, creative, and free enough to stay loving and sharing.

Communication

In the heaviness of life's stress, you may unknowingly have lost the skills of listening to and communicating clearly with your family. You can recapture or develop those skills. Think about the various disciplines of your job or profession, and see how you may apply those in improving communication within your family.

A friend of mine is an executive in the insurance field. He often sat about tables in conference rooms, thinking out with his staff the knotty problems of his business. One day he was worrying about a concern of one of his children when it occurred to him that the practices he had developed to talk through problems at work just might be useful at home.

Family Conferences. He chose the dinner hour, and approached his entire family with his ideas. They felt it might be a little bit artificial, but they agreed to try. They talked through some rules and risks, and the very first session turned into a smashing success. A fair decision regarding some really touchy issues with their adolescent son was worked out. As it happened, it was information from his younger sister that helped the family understand the problem and decide wisely. The family scheduled regular meetings, planned the agenda, and talked through the pros and cons openly together. When an ultimate decision was needed, the father was the final authority, but he never forgot to consider the needs and feelings of everyone involved.

In this unusual family, they agreed that anyone could call a special conference. One day their nine-year-old daughter asked for a meeting. Her brother and sister were then in their late teens, and the meetings had become unnecessary, except at rare intervals. Anne announced quietly at the meeting that she simply was lonely, and needed the family to gather together now and then and talk. Every family needs such reasons to gather!

(If you need to, reread the Introduction and chapter 2 of this book for a refresher on sharpening your own communication skills.)

Discipline

This was discussed as *vitally important in the lives of your children*. Good discipline can resolve many of their problems and yours. Self-discipline is equally important in rearranging your family priorities.

No matter how clear your ideas and how positive your attitudes, you must have willpower and self-control in order to follow through. Taking control of your life sounds powerful and appealing. It is, however, difficult, monotonous work. Many times you will find it easier to fall into old habits of blaming someone else for your child's problems—and yours. Do not give in to such temptations. You together, Mom and Dad, can be strong, consistent, and in charge. Practice daily by making yourselves do at least one thing that is hard—that you would rather not do. As you become consistent at this, you will find your strength growing, your children feeling safer, and your family more harmonious.

Habit Changing. Giving up old habits is extremely difficult! And forming new ones is equally hard. There will be times when you feel sure it isn't working, or that you will never be able to change permanently. Even if the change takes place, you'll feel that it's only temporary. It can't last. When such fears assail you, call a friend; talk with one another; or call a counselor. Whatever you do, do not give up! I have seen many people who gave up just at a crucial point, when only a little more effort could have won!

Acceptance of Limitations

There are some absolute limits that all of us must face. We don't like these, and most people deny them or fight against them. Just as important as hanging in to make your priorities right is the ability to face events we can do nothing to change.

These inevitables may be a handicapped child, an illness of your spouse, a frustrating job, or no job! Facing one's own personal limitations can be the most difficult task there is.

Recognizing the inevitable, accepting it, with all of its pain and grief, and transcending it, is perhaps the highest test and function of a human being. As you set the example of this for your children, you will find yourself growing in stability, character, and faith.

The right priorities can revolutionize your family life. You and your child's problems can end in the transforming of sadness and pain into wonder and joy, as you reorder your priorities.

Conclusion

One of the very common complicating factors in the problems of troubled youngsters is the failure of their parents to recognize the existence of those problems. In fact, I have known parents to deny those issues to the very point of disaster. Sometimes that denial is based on the sincere misunderstanding of the symptoms. "Perhaps," parents often say, "this problem is just a phase that Peggy or Paul is going through."

Nevertheless, they try harder and harder to correct the habits that are the manifestations of the problems. Through such interventions, tried sincerely, parents often complicate the problems and confuse the issues. By facing the issues more squarely, seeking help to evaluate their seriousness, and planning (sometimes with help) a logical course of action, the solutions are much more quickly and effectively worked out.

So do not be afraid to face yourselves or your children, even with your problems. You can understand them and come through the struggles with even greater love and joy than you thought possible.

It takes strength and courage, but seek advice and help for your specific problems. I find many people are ashamed that they cannot resolve all their problems alone. People are especially reluctant to admit they face emotional or mental illnesses and they face some judgment and embarrassment from acquaintances who still do not understand these frustrating issues. It is through the determination, however, of the families of such troubled children, that our society has some hope of overcoming such ignorance and prejudice. You certainly need not flaunt such struggles, but neither do you need to hide them.

Keep your attitudes positive, warm, and encouraging. Maintain a balanced love for your own selves and your child. Accept one another unconditionally—as you are. Find areas in one another's lives of which to be truly proud. And learn how to express that pride (as well as all real feelings) clearly and honestly. Strive for consistency in your actions and reactions to life's situations.

As you learn to face your problems with courage and overcome them, reach out to others who need your understanding and guidance.

Problems, yours and your child's, can indeed become building blocks—to be used in creating prisons or palaces. You are the architect. What will you build?

Index

Index